365 FAMILY
DINNERS &
Devotions
COOKBOOK
A Celebration of Food, Family, and Faith

Published by Barbour Books, an imprint of Barbour Publishing, Inc., P.O. Box 719, Uhrichsville, Ohio 44683, www.barbourbooks.com

Our mission is to publish and distribute inspirational products offering exceptional value and biblical encouragement to the masses.

ecpa Member of the
Evangelical Christian
Publishers Association

Printed in the United States of America.

KATHLEEN Y'BARBO

365 FAMILY
DINNERS &
Devotions
COOKBOOK

A Celebration of Food, Family, and Faith

BARBOUR BOOKS
An Imprint of Barbour Publishing, Inc.

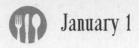
Sunday Brunch Casserole

½ pound sliced bacon
½ cup onion, chopped
½ cup green pepper, chopped
1 dozen eggs
1 cup milk

16 ounces frozen hash browns, thawed
1 cup cheddar cheese, shredded
1 teaspoon salt
½ teaspoon pepper

Cook bacon in skillet until crisp. Remove bacon from pan with slotted spoon. Crumble bacon and set aside. In bacon drippings, sauté onion and green pepper until tender; remove with slotted spoon. Beat eggs and milk in large bowl; stir in hash browns, cheese, salt and pepper, onion, green pepper, and bacon. Place in greased baking pan. Bake uncovered at 350 degrees for 35 to 45 minutes.

Yield: 6 servings

Defining Family

Every good gift and every perfect gift is from above.
JAMES 1:17 KJV

Family is a big word and difficult to define. Some would say family consists exclusively of those who are biologically connected. Others say it includes all those we call our loved ones, regardless of blood bond. We call those who live by faith in God "the family of God." However we define family, we should cherish those God has placed in our lives. They are among His greatest gifts.

Family Dinnertime Tip

"Disconnect" from the world during dinnertime.
Turn off all cell phones, tablets, TVs, and other electronics,
and savor the quiet while spending quality time together.

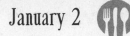

Beef Burgundy

2 tablespoons olive oil
1½ to 2 pounds cubed stew meat
½ cup chopped onion
1 (10¾ ounce) can condensed
   cream of mushroom soup

¼ cup red wine vinegar
¼ cup reduced-salt beef broth
¼ teaspoon garlic powder
1 cup sliced fresh mushrooms
Egg noodles or rice, prepared

Heat oil in skillet. Add stew meat and brown. Remove meat from skillet. Add onions to skillet and sauté until tender. In ovenproof casserole, mix meat, onion, soup, vinegar, broth, and garlic powder. Bake, covered, at 325 degrees for 3 hours. The last 20 minutes, add mushrooms and return casserole to oven. Serve over egg noodles or rice.

Yield: 4 to 6 servings

To Whom Do We Listen?

Whoever gives heed to instruction prospers,
and blessed is the one who trusts in the LORD.
PROVERBS 16:20 NIV

Our modern world consists of so many voices speaking to us throughout our day. From the morning radio show hosts on our way to work to the telephone that rings and the texts and e-mails that bombard us, there is no end to the input we get. But from dawn to dark, from our first moment awake until our last moment before sleep, whose voice speaks the loudest? In a big family, there can be many voices all vying for your attention. Above all, listen for the sound of God's voice.

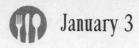

Bacon and Tomato Dip

½ pound bacon
3 small tomatoes,
    quartered and seeded
1 (8 ounce) package cream
    cheese, softened

3 teaspoons mustard
¼ teaspoon hot sauce
1½ cups almonds
3 tablespoons minced
    green onions

In large skillet, fry bacon until crisp. Drain, crumble, and set aside. In food processor basket, combine tomatoes, cream cheese, mustard, and hot sauce. Add almonds, onions, and bacon. Blend until almonds are chopped. Refrigerate at least 2 hours to blend flavors. Serve with crackers or vegetables.

Yield: 10 to 12 servings

Are You Interruptible?

As Jesus was walking beside the Sea of Galilee, he saw two brothers,
Simon called Peter and his brother Andrew. They were casting
a net into the lake, for they were fishermen. "Come, follow me,"
Jesus said, "and I will send you out to fish for people."
At once they left their nets and followed him.
MATTHEW 4:18–20 NIV

How many interruptions do you have in your daily life? If you have a family, the answer is probably plenty! How many times do you think you will complete a task only to find you're being asked to do something else? That can be frustrating, can't it? What would you do if Jesus turned your entire world upside down and changed every plan you've made? That's what Jesus did with Simon Peter and Andrew. Do you think these brothers were interruptible? Of course they were, and look what happened! Consider this: Are you?

Orange Sherbet Salad

2 (3 ounce) packages orange
    gelatin
1 cup boiling water
1 cup orange juice
1 pint orange sherbet
2 bananas, peeled and sliced

1 (11 ounce) can mandarin
    oranges, drained and cut up
1 (8 ounce) can crushed
    pineapple, drained
1 cup sour cream
1 cup miniature marshmallows

Dissolve gelatin in boiling water; add orange juice and sherbet. Stir until sherbet is melted. Add fruit; chill until firm. In small bowl, combine sour cream and marshmallows; spread over top of salad just before serving.

Yield: 10 servings

Gone Fishing

And let us not be weary in well doing:
for in due season we shall reap, if we faint not.
GALATIANS 6:9 KJV

Have you ever gone fishing? First you find just the right spot, and then you have to bait the hook. Then what happens? You wait. And wait. Then when the time is right, you catch a fish. Or perhaps you catch lots of fish. Or maybe you just keep waiting. Waiting is hard. We want to catch fish, not just sit on the bank. Does God have you waiting for something right now? Don't give up. When the time is right, He will act. And just maybe you will catch that fish!

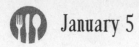 **January 5**

Quick Club Quesadillas

8 slices bacon, cooked
8 slices deli turkey breast
4 large flour tortillas
2 tomatoes, chopped

1 cup shredded lettuce
½ cup Monterey Jack cheese,
  shredded
¼ cup ranch dressing

Place 2 bacon slices and 2 turkey slices in center of each tortilla. Top with tomatoes, lettuce, and cheese. Fold in half. Cook each tortilla in skillet on medium heat for 3 minutes on each side or until crispy and golden brown. Cut tortilla into wedges. Serve each quesadilla with 1 tablespoon ranch dressing.

Yield: 4 servings

Meant for You

"I baptize with water those who repent of their sins and turn to God. But someone is coming soon who is greater than I am—so much greater that I'm not worthy even to be his slave and carry his sandals. He will baptize you with the Holy Spirit and with fire."
MATTHEW 3:11 NLT

You love your family, don't you? Well, of course! John the Baptist tells us that Jesus is greater than anyone who ever lived. God sent us Jesus to teach us about God and to pay for our sins, and He gave us the Holy Spirit to speak to our hearts. Read the words John said and know God meant them just for you and your family. Listen to that still, small voice of God speaking through the Holy Spirit. Those words, too, are meant for you and the ones you love.

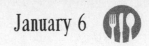

Fireside Mocha Mix

2 cups nondairy coffee creamer
1½ cups instant coffee mix
1½ cups hot cocoa mix

1½ cups sugar
1 teaspoon cinnamon
¼ teaspoon nutmeg

In large bowl, combine all ingredients. Store mixture in airtight container. To prepare one serving, stir 2 heaping tablespoons of mix into 1 cup boiling water.

Yield: 40 prepared cups

Keep Going!

Rejoicing in hope; patient in tribulation;
continuing instant in prayer.
ROMANS 12:12 KJV

Don't you love it when someone you know gets good news? Isn't it easy to celebrate, especially when the happy person is a family member? What about when that same family member gets bad news? You're there to help, right? That's what families do. In the same way, God wants you to celebrate with Him when good things happen and to be patient when things don't go your way. In all things, whether good or bad, whether happening to you or someone you love, keep praying. Prayer is how we keep going no matter what!

Family Dinnertime Tip

Start the New Year off right!
Forgive and forget. Set an attainable goal for the New Year.
Call an old friend to catch up. Be thankful for what you have.
Make more time for family. Vow to make a difference in the world.
Laugh. Thank God every day for the gift of love He sent for you and me!

Ana Lisa Cookies

1½ cups butter
1 cup sugar
1 egg
1 teaspoon almond extract
3¼ cups sifted flour
Lingonberries
Chopped almonds

Glaze:
2½ cups powdered sugar
2 tablespoons water
1 tablespoon butter, softened
1 tablespoon light corn syrup
½ teaspoon almond extract

Cream butter with sugar. Add egg and almond extract; mix well. Stir in flour until completely blended. Refrigerate at least 4 hours or overnight. Roll out dough about ⅜ inch thick. Using two round cookie cutters (one smaller), cut circular shapes. Place larger circles on ungreased cookie sheets. Place small amount of berries and almonds in center of each circle. Use smaller circles to cover filling. Gently press around edges, keeping filling inside. Bake at 375 degrees for 6 to 8 minutes. Cool completely. For glaze, combine powdered sugar, water, butter, corn syrup, and almond extract in small mixing bowl; mix until moistened. Beat at medium speed until smooth, adding additional water if necessary to reach desired glazing consistency.

Yield: 2 dozen cookies

Be a Helper

*Then the LORD God said, "It is not good for the man to be alone.
I will make a helper who is just right for him."*
GENESIS 2:18 NLT

Maybe you've helped clean up after an event or you've helped someone complete an important project. Perhaps you enjoyed that job much more because you had someone to work with. That's how God looks at marriage. A husband marries his wife because she is just right for him. She makes the job God gave him more enjoyable. The same goes for families. Everyone in a family can pitch in to make jobs easier. Today consider how you can bless your family and be a helper.

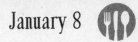

Ambrosia

3 (15 ounce) cans fruit cocktail, drained
1 (11 ounce) can mandarin oranges, drained
1 cup miniature marshmallows
1 cup sweetened, flaked coconut
2 bananas, sliced
½ cup maraschino cherries, drained and halved
1 (5 ounce) can evaporated milk

Combine all ingredients in large bowl. Refrigerate for at least 1 hour before serving.

Yield: 6 servings

Be Joyful!

After his baptism, as Jesus came up out of the water,
the heavens were opened and he saw the Spirit of God descending
like a dove and settling on him. And a voice from heaven said,
"This is my dearly loved Son, who brings me great joy."
Matthew 3:16–17 NLT

Jesus brought God great joy. Why? He was God's own Son, and don't we find great joy in our family? You're probably thinking *not always*, because we're human and not fully perfect like Jesus was. Of course, that is true. So what can we do about that? When we are tempted to feel less than joyful, be it about a person or a situation, we can consider these words: "This is my dearly loved Son, who brings me great joy." God found great joy in Jesus and so can we.

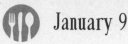

Baked Pizza Sandwich

2 tablespoons butter, softened
1½ teaspoons Italian seasoning
1 teaspoon minced garlic
1 (16 ounce) prepared Italian
    bread shell, sliced in half
    horizontally

4 ounces sandwich pepperoni
4 green bell pepper rings
4 tomato slices
6 slices provolone cheese

Combine butter, Italian seasoning, and garlic in small bowl. Spread mixture on one half of bread shell. Layer with pepperoni, green pepper, tomato, and cheese. Top with remaining half of bread shell. Wrap in aluminum foil and place on baking sheet. Bake at 350 degrees for 18 minutes or until cheese is melted. Cut into 4 sections and serve warm.

Yield: 4 servings

Do Not Fear

Be strong and of a good courage, fear not, nor be afraid of them:
for the LORD thy God. . .he will not fail thee, nor forsake thee.
DEUTERONOMY 31:6 KJV

Are you a worrier? Perhaps you find yourself fretting about things or fearful of events that have not yet happened. The Bible is full of reminders from God not to be afraid. Why? Because God never fails us. Never. Not even once. You and your family are safe in His hands. So what's the cure for fear? Trust. Trust that God will not leave you. Trust that even when you may not feel His presence, God is right there beside you. Do not fear!

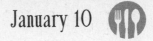

Almond Rice

1¾ cups water
½ cup orange juice
½ teaspoon salt
1 cup uncooked long-grain rice
2 tablespoons butter or
   margarine

2 tablespoons brown sugar,
   packed
½ cup sliced natural almonds
1 teaspoon minced crystallized
   ginger
¼ teaspoon grated orange rind
Additional orange rind (optional)

In medium saucepan, bring water, orange juice, and salt to a boil; gradually add rice, stirring constantly. Cover, reduce heat, and simmer for 20 to 25 minutes or until rice is tender and liquid is absorbed. Meanwhile, melt butter and brown sugar in small skillet over medium heat. Stir in almonds and ginger; sauté for 2 minutes or until almonds are lightly browned. Add almond mixture and grated orange rind to rice; stir gently to combine. Garnish with additional orange rind if desired.

Yield: 4 servings

Just Look

*Now faith is confidence in what we hope for
and assurance about what we do not see.*
HEBREWS 11:1 NIV

We believe birds can fly because we can see them soaring overhead. We believe there is wind even though we cannot see it because we can see flags fly and sails billow. Even though there is no visible proof of wind, we know it by its action. The same can be said for God. We humans cannot see God with our eyes, but we can believe in His existence by seeing the results of His actions. The world is full of evidence that God exists. All you have to do is look!

Bacon Cheddar Spread

1½ cups shredded mild cheddar cheese

4 ounces cream cheese, softened

3 tablespoons minced green onions

3 tablespoons mayonnaise

2 teaspoons mustard

½ teaspoon Worcestershire sauce

10 slices bacon, cooked and crumbled

Combine all ingredients in medium mixing bowl until smooth. Chill to blend flavors. Serve with crackers.

Yield: 6 to 10 servings

Fixing Things

*"Repent of your sins and turn to God,
for the Kingdom of Heaven is near."*
MATTHEW 3:2 NLT

Have you ever done something wrong and hoped you wouldn't get caught? Perhaps you thought it was not a big sin but rather just a little one. Guess what? God doesn't think of sin that way. He tells us in His Word that sin is something that separates us from Him. How can you fix this? Maybe you need to tell someone you're sorry. Or perhaps you've got to repair something you've broken, whether that's a relationship or something else. Just ask God what to do. He will tell you. Then do it.

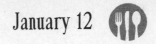

Candy Apple Salad

2 cups water
¼ cup red cinnamon candies
1 (3 ounce) package cherry
   gelatin

½ cup chopped celery
1½ cups chopped tart apples
½ cup chopped walnuts

In saucepan, bring water to boil. Add in cinnamon candies; stir until dissolved. Remove from heat and add gelatin; stir until dissolved. Cool slightly, then refrigerate until gelatin begins to thicken. Add remaining ingredients; blend well. Pour into 8-inch square dish and chill until firm.

Yield: 6 servings

You Can Do This!

I can do all this through him who gives me strength.
PHILIPPIANS 4:13 NIV

Have you ever reached the end of your rope and declared that you had no more strength to continue? Maybe you've been given a task that requires far more than you believe you have to offer. Or maybe you are just so tired you do not know how you will put one foot in front of the other and manage to keep walking. You do not have to do this alone. God sees your struggle. He knows what you need. Through Him, you have strength. Through Him you can do this!

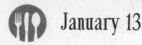
Bierock Casserole

2 pounds lean ground beef
1 medium onion, diced
1 small head cabbage, chopped

Salt and pepper to taste
1 (36 count) package frozen rolls

In large skillet, brown meat with diced onion. Add cabbage; cover and cook until cabbage is tender. Add salt and pepper to taste. Grease two 9x13-inch baking pans. Place eighteen rolls in each pan. Let rise. Press down gently. Spoon cabbage mixture on top of rolls in one pan. Flip rolls from the other pan over top of cabbage. Press down lightly. Bake at 350 degrees for 30 to 35 minutes or until rolls are browned.

Yield: 9 servings

Colors of the Rainbow

Each of you should use whatever gift you have received to serve others, as faithful stewards of God's grace in its various forms.
1 PETER 4:10 NIV

When you look at the faces gathered around your dinner table, do you see any two who are exactly alike? Probably not. Even identical twins have their unique personalities. Why is that? God made us all different so that we can offer our gifts back to Him in our own way. Just as God did not create a rainbow out of just one color, so He has not created your family with just one gift. Celebrate the differences in each of your family's members and offer each of those gifts back to Him!

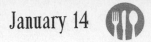

Chicken Diane

4 large boneless chicken breast halves
½ teaspoon salt
½ teaspoon black pepper
2 tablespoons olive oil, divided
2 tablespoons butter or margarine, divided
3 tablespoons chopped fresh chives
Juice of ½ lemon
3 tablespoons chopped fresh parsley
2 teaspoons Dijon mustard
¼ cup chicken broth

Place each chicken breast half between two sheets of waxed paper and pound to flatten slightly. Sprinkle chicken with salt and pepper. Set aside. In large skillet, heat 1 tablespoon each of oil and butter. Cook each chicken breast in skillet for 4 minutes on each side. Transfer to warm serving platter. Add chives, lemon juice, parsley, and mustard to skillet. Cook for 15 seconds, whisking constantly. Whisk in broth and stir until sauce is smooth. Whisk in remaining oil and butter. Pour sauce over chicken and serve immediately.

Yield: 4 servings

Sweet Words Win Every Time

Gracious words are a honeycomb,
sweet to the soul and healing to the bones.
PROVERBS 16:24 NIV

How many times has someone in your family said something that made you want to respond with a less than sweet retort? Some days it almost seems as though certain family members are just trying to get you to snap at them, doesn't it? Resist that temptation and replace those sharp words with sweet ones. The situation will defuse much faster. Why? Because sweet words win every time.

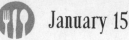

Artichoke Spinach Casserole

1 (8 ounce) carton sour cream
½ cup mayonnaise
3 tablespoons lemon juice
½ teaspoon garlic powder
¼ teaspoon onion powder
¼ teaspoon salt
¼ teaspoon black pepper
2 tablespoons butter or
    margarine
1 pound sliced fresh mushrooms

⅓ cup chicken broth
1 tablespoon flour
½ cup milk
4 (10 ounce) packages frozen
    spinach, thawed and drained
2 (14½ ounce) cans diced
    tomatoes, drained
2 (14 ounce) cans artichoke
    hearts, drained and chopped

In small bowl, combine sour cream, mayonnaise, lemon juice, garlic powder, onion powder, salt, and pepper. Mix thoroughly; set aside. In large skillet, melt butter. Add mushrooms and sauté until they begin to soften. Pour in broth and cook until mushrooms are tender. Remove mushrooms from skillet and set aside. In small bowl, whisk together flour and milk. Add to skillet and bring to boil. Cook for 2 minutes, stirring constantly. Remove from heat and stir in spinach, tomatoes, and mushrooms. Layer half of artichoke hearts in 9x13-inch casserole. Layer half of spinach mixture over artichokes. Spoon half of sour cream mixture on top. Repeat layers. Bake uncovered at 350 degrees for 30 to 35 minutes.

Yield: 12 servings

Saying Grace or Offering Grace?

Let us therefore come boldly unto the throne of grace,
that we may obtain mercy, and find grace to help in time of need.
Hebrews 4:16 KJV

When you sit at the table together as a family, do you say grace? Thanking the Lord for His provision is a great way to recall His care for us. Can you overlook the irritations that are part of living in a family in a fallen world? Do you want to be part of a strong, godly family? Offer grace to the Lord when you sit down and grace to everyone else when you get up.

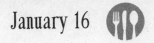

Champagne Salad

1 (8 ounce) package cream
   cheese, softened
¾ cup sugar
1 (20 ounce) can crushed
   pineapple, drained

1 (10 ounce) package frozen
   strawberries, with juice
2 bananas, sliced
½ cup chopped nuts
1 (16 ounce) container frozen
   whipped topping, thawed

Beat cream cheese with sugar. In separate bowl, mix together pineapple, strawberries with juice, bananas, nuts, and whipped topping. Gently combine with cream cheese mixture. Pour into 9x13-inch pan and freeze completely. To serve, thaw slightly and cut into squares. Keep leftovers frozen.

Yield: 12 to 16 servings

Choices

*Choose you this day whom ye will serve. . .but as for me
and my house, we will serve the LORD.*
JOSHUA 24:15 KJV

Choices. We make them every day, from what shoes to wear to what to say and how to behave. Some choices require great deliberation and prayers while other choices, such as what to have for dinner, are much quicker and easier. Take a moment and think of all the choices you've made today. Exhausting to consider, isn't it? And yet there is one choice that is more important than all of those, one choice that literally can mean life or death. Choose whom you will serve. Will your family, your house, serve the Lord? If so, that is the best choice you have ever made.

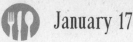

Best Peanut Butter Cookies

½ cup creamy peanut butter
¼ cup crunchy peanut butter
½ cup vegetable shortening
1¼ cups brown sugar, packed
3 tablespoons milk

1 tablespoon vanilla
1 egg
1¾ cups flour
¾ teaspoon salt
¾ teaspoon baking soda

Combine peanut butters, shortening, brown sugar, milk, and vanilla in large mixing bowl. Beat at medium speed until well blended. Add egg. Beat just until blended. Combine flour, salt, and baking soda. Add to creamed mixture at low speed. Mix just until blended. Drop by heaping teaspoonfuls 2 inches apart onto ungreased cookie sheets. Flatten slightly in crisscross pattern with tines of fork. Bake at 375 degrees for 7 to 8 minutes or until set and just beginning to brown. Cool for 2 minutes on baking sheet before transferring to cooling racks to cool completely.

Yield: 3 dozen cookies

Leaving a Legacy

When I call to remembrance the unfeigned faith that is in thee, which dwelt first in thy grandmother Lois, and thy mother Eunice; and I am persuaded that in thee also.
2 TIMOTHY 1:5 KJV

Does your family have a legacy of believing in God? Perhaps you had a grandmother or grandfather, or even a great-grandmother or great-grandfather, who prayed over you as a child. What a privilege to carry on such a lineage. But what if you are the first believer in your family? Then begin leaving that legacy today. Whenever your family is gathered, be sure the Lord is at the table, too. By giving Him the thanks and the glory, you are paving the way for future generations of believers.

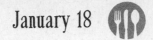

Best Eggnog

6 fresh eggs, beaten well
1 (14 ounce) can sweetened
   condensed milk
1 pinch salt

1 teaspoon vanilla
1 quart milk
⅔ cup heavy whipping cream

In large mixing bowl, use mixer to beat eggs until thick and smooth. Blend in condensed milk, salt, and vanilla; slowly add milk. In small bowl, beat whipping cream until peaks start to form, then use spatula to fold into egg mixture. Serve chilled. Servings may be sprinkled with nutmeg. Note: Please make your guests aware of the use of raw eggs.

Yield: 12 servings

Saying You're Sorry—Again

Then came Peter to him, and said, Lord, how oft shall my brother sin against me, and I forgive him? till seven times?
MATTHEW 18:21 KJV

"He makes me so mad!" How many times have you said that about someone in your family? How many times has someone in your family said that about you? What does Jesus say should be done about this anger at your family member—or anyone with whom you feel this way? He says forgive. No matter how many times this person might make you angry, you are to do as Jesus says and forgive. That's the bad news. The good news? The same applies to those whom you have hurt.
Is there someone you need to forgive? Maybe now is the time to remedy this. Again.

Broiled Shrimp

1 cup butter
2 garlic cloves, minced
¼ cup lemon juice
½ teaspoon salt

¼ teaspoon freshly ground black
 pepper
2 pounds large shrimp, peeled
 and deveined
Chopped fresh parsley

In saucepan over low heat, melt butter with garlic, but don't allow garlic to scorch. Remove from heat and add lemon juice, salt, and pepper. Place shrimp in shallow baking dish and pour sauce over shrimp. Broil shrimp 4 to 5 inches from heating element for 6 to 8 minutes. Turn and baste shrimp halfway through. When done, shrimp should be pink and tender. Garnish with chopped fresh parsley.

Yield: 6 servings

Run Home

The name of the LORD is a fortified tower;
the righteous run to it and are safe.
PROVERBS 18:10 NIV

Family is the heart of the home, and the home is the heart of the family. As much as we all love vacations, doesn't your family love coming home and sleeping in their own beds? In the same way that we run home for comfort, so, too, should we consider God our "home base." It is to Him that we should run when we need that feeling of coming home.

Bacon-Topped Cheese Ball

1 (8 ounce) package cream
cheese, softened
1½ cups sour cream
2 cups (8 ounces) shredded
swiss cheese
2 cups (8 ounces) shredded sharp
cheddar cheese
3 tablespoons grated onion
3 tablespoons sweet pickle relish
1 tablespoon prepared horseradish

¼ teaspoon salt
¼ teaspoon lemon-pepper
seasoning
⅛ teaspoon garlic powder
6 slices bacon, cooked and finely
crumbled
¼ cup chopped fresh parsley
¼ cup almonds, toasted and
finely chopped

Beat together cream cheese and sour cream in large mixing bowl until smooth. Add shredded cheeses, onion, pickle relish, horseradish, salt, lemon-pepper seasoning, and garlic powder; beat on low speed until well blended. Cover and chill thoroughly. Combine bacon, parsley, and almonds; stir well. Shape chilled cheese mixture into ball; roll in bacon mixture, pressing bacon mixture into cheese ball with hands. Wrap cheese ball tightly in waxed paper; chill until ready to serve. Serve with assorted crackers.

Yield: one 6-inch cheese ball

Except the Lord Build the House

Except the LORD build the house, they labour in vain that build it: except the LORD keep the city, the watchman waketh but in vain.
PSALM 127:1 KJV

Have you ever had a house built? There are many decisions that go into the building of a home, but the one that comes first and is most important is the type of foundation upon which the home will sit. Getting the foundation right means getting the house right. The same goes for your family. Taking your orders from the Lord means you will not labor in vain. Your foundation in Christ will keep you and those you love safe and strong—just like a well-built house!

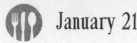

Artichokes au Gratin

2 (9 ounce) packages frozen
    artichoke hearts
¼ cup butter or margarine
⅓ cup flour
¾ teaspoon salt
¼ teaspoon black pepper
1 teaspoon onion powder

¼ teaspoon dry mustard
1½ cups milk
1 egg, lightly beaten
1 cup shredded mild cheddar
    cheese, divided
¼ cup dry bread crumbs
Paprika

Cook artichokes according to package directions. Drain and reserve ½ cup of cooking liquid. Melt butter in saucepan over low heat; stir in flour, salt, pepper, onion powder, and dry mustard. Cook and stir until flour mixture is smooth and bubbly; gradually add reserved cooking liquid and milk. Cook over low heat, stirring constantly until thickened. Remove from heat. Combine beaten egg with ½ cup shredded cheese. Gradually stir sauce mixture into egg and cheese mixture. Place artichokes in greased baking dish in single layer. Pour sauce over artichokes; sprinkle with remaining cheese, bread crumbs, and paprika. Bake at 425 degrees for 20 to 25 minutes.

Yield: 6 servings

God Is Proud of You

Then God looked over all he had made,
and he saw that it was very good!
GENESIS 1:31 NLT

We know God loves us. How? He says it in His Word. Just look at this verse. He looked over all His creation and saw it was very good. Do you know that means you? It does! He created you. He loves you. And He is quite proud of you. If God had a refrigerator, your picture would be on it! Isn't that something to consider? The Creator of the universe loves you. Yes, you!

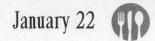

Baked Water Chestnuts

1 (8 ounce) can whole water
   chestnuts
½ cup soy sauce

Sugar
4 slices bacon, cut in half lengthwise and widthwise

Drain water chestnuts. Marinate in soy sauce for 30 minutes. Drain sauce from water chestnuts and roll each water chestnut in sugar. Wrap each chestnut in strip of bacon. Bake at 400 degrees for 30 minutes.

Yield: 8 servings

As Iron Sharpens Iron

As iron sharpens iron, so one person sharpens another.
PROVERBS 27:17 NIV

Do you ever disagree with a friend? Perhaps you work or go to school with people who are sometimes at odds. Or maybe you have a family member with whom you do not see eye to eye. Sometimes the Lord allows these things into our lives so that we can learn from them. Next time you find yourself in one of these situations, ask yourself what God wishes you to learn. The answer just might be surprising.

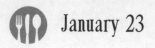

Grape Smoothies

1 pint vanilla ice cream,
   softened
1½ cups milk

1 (6 ounce) can frozen grape
   juice concentrate

Combine all ingredients in blender. Cover and blend until smooth. Serve immediately.

Yield: 4 servings

The Gift of Hospitality

Keep on loving one another as brothers and sisters. Do not forget to show hospitality to strangers, for by so doing some people have shown hospitality to angels without knowing it.
HEBREWS 13:1–2 NIV

Is your home one that is filled with not only the children who live there but seemingly half the neighborhood? Perhaps your kitchen is often filled with friends and family who enjoy spending time there. God loves it when we offer hospitality to others. Make today a day when your family extends the gift of hospitality to someone in need. Offering up something from the bounty the Lord has provided, no matter how large or small, takes our eyes off ourselves and puts them not only on others but also on God.

Family Dinnertime Tip

Tired of preparing the same dishes week after week? Make it a priority to try a new recipe each week. Not only will you expand your culinary skills, but chances are there's a new family favorite waiting to make an appearance on your kitchen table.

Sweet Pecan Roll Rings

2 (8 ounce) tubes refrigerated crescent rolls
4 tablespoons butter, melted and divided
½ cup pecans, chopped
¼ cup sugar
1¼ teaspoons cinnamon
½ teaspoon nutmeg
½ cup powdered sugar
2 tablespoons maple syrup

Separate crescent dough into 8 rectangles; seal perforations. Brush rectangles with melted butter. Mix pecans, sugar, cinnamon, and nutmeg; sprinkle mixture over dough and press lightly. Roll dough up jelly roll-style, beginning at longer end; seal seams. Twist each roll 2 to 3 times. With knife, make 6 shallow diagonal slits in each roll. Shape each roll into ring, pinching ends to seal. Place on greased baking sheet and brush with remaining butter. Bake at 375 degrees for 12 to 14 minutes or until golden brown. Drizzle combination of powdered sugar and maple syrup over warm rolls.

Yield: 8 rings

Calgon Take Me Away!

Casting all your care upon him; for he careth for you.
1 PETER 5:7 KJV

Who doesn't love a bubble bath? There's nothing like a long soak after a hard day to revive a tired soul. But even as wonderful as that might be, nothing takes our care away like leaning on our heavenly Father. Allow Him to be the warm soak that provides relief from anything going on outside your family's front door. He will take up your burdens. Just ask Him.

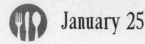

Blueberry-Orange Bread

2 tablespoons butter
¼ cup boiling water
1 tablespoon grated orange rind
½ cup orange juice
1 egg
1 cup sugar

2 cups flour
1 teaspoon baking powder
¼ teaspoon baking soda
½ teaspoon salt
1 cup fresh blueberries

Syrup:
1 teaspoon grated orange rind

2 tablespoons honey
2 tablespoons orange juice

In small bowl, combine butter and boiling water. Add orange rind and orange juice; set mixture aside. Beat egg and sugar with mixer until light and fluffy. Combine flour, baking powder, baking soda, and salt; add to egg mixture alternately with orange juice mixture, beginning and ending with flour mixture. Fold in blueberries. Grease and flour 9x5x3-inch loaf pan. Spoon in bread batter. Bake at 350 degrees for 55 minutes. Cool bread in pan for 10 minutes, then remove to wire rack. Combine syrup ingredients; mix well. Spoon over warm bread; let cool.

Yield: 8 servings

Give Peace a Chance

If it be possible, as much as lieth in you,
live peaceably with all men.
ROMANS 12:18 KJV

Live peaceably? But we're human, Lord. Sometimes we just get upset and want to let that other person know exactly how we feel. Yes, maybe we want to, but should we? God says we are called to something better than fussing and fighting. What would happen in your family if for just one day each family member chose to live peaceably with the others? Try it and see!

European Salad

Dressing:
1 cup rice vinegar
½ cup wine vinegar
4 tablespoons sugar
3 garlic cloves, minced
Salt and pepper to taste
1 cup canola oil

Salad:
8 cups spring salad mix
¾ cup chopped green onions
½ red onion, chopped
6 ounces feta cheese, crumbled
1 cup dried cranberries
1 cup sliced fresh mushrooms
3 hard-boiled eggs, sliced
1 cup toasted pine nuts

Prepare dressing the night before salad is to be served. Whisk together vinegars, sugar, garlic, and salt and pepper. Gradually whisk in oil. Chill. The following day, toss salad ingredients in serving bowl. Drizzle dressing over salad just before serving. Toss to coat.

Yield: 8 to 10 servings

Because God Says So!

Children, obey your parents in the Lord: for this is right.
EPHESIANS 6:1 KJV

"But I don't want to!" We've all said it at one time or another. But if the command came from your parent, then God says it does not matter what you want. You must obey. And what parent among us hasn't said, "Because I said so!" to a child? In the same way, the Lord is a loving parent to all of us, and what He says goes. Every member of your family, whether parent or child, must listen to the words of their Father in heaven and obey. Why? Because God says so!

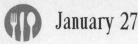

Minestrone Salad

4 ounces uncooked angel hair
   pasta, broken into 2-inch pieces
1 cup julienned carrots
¼ cup chopped fresh parsley
3 medium Roma tomatoes,
   seeded and chopped
1 cup julienned zucchini

1 (15 ounce) can garbanzo beans,
   rinsed and drained
1 (6 ounce) jar marinated
   artichoke hearts, drained,
   liquid reserved
1 cup mozzarella cheese, cut into
   ½-inch cubes

Dressing:
Reserved artichoke liquid
2 tablespoons cider vinegar

½ teaspoon garlic salt
⅛ teaspoon black pepper

Cook pasta according to package directions. Rinse with cold water; drain and set aside. Meanwhile, in medium saucepan, combine carrots and enough water to cover. Bring to full boil and continue cooking until carrots are crisp-tender (1 to 2 minutes). Rinse with cold water; drain. In large bowl, combine pasta, carrots, parsley, tomatoes, zucchini, beans, artichokes, and cheese. In small jar with tight-fitting lid, combine reserved artichoke liquid, vinegar, garlic salt, and pepper; shake well to blend. Pour dressing over salad; toss to coat. Cover; refrigerate at least 2 hours before serving.

Yield: 6 servings

Enjoy the Meal

*Better a dinner of herbs where love is,
than a stalled ox and hatred therewith.*
PROVERBS 15:17 KJV

Sometimes a nice salad hits the spot. But what if that was all you had—ever? What if there was nothing to eat except for whatever herbs you could gather from the garden? After a while, that meal might no longer sound appetizing. God says that a meager meal with a family you love is better than a bountiful banquet with stubborn, hateful people. If you and your family are enjoying a nice meal tonight, give thanks to Him for that.

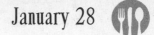

Butterscotch Cookies

1 cup butter or margarine,
  softened
2 cups brown sugar, packed
2 eggs, lightly beaten
1 teaspoon vanilla

3½ cups flour
½ teaspoon salt
1 teaspoon baking soda
1 teaspoon cream of tartar

In large mixing bowl, cream butter, sugar, and eggs. Stir in vanilla. Sift together dry ingredients and blend into creamed mixture. Shape into 2-inch log. Wrap in waxed paper and chill overnight. To bake, slice log into ¼-inch-thick rounds. Place on ungreased cookie sheet and bake at 350 degrees for 10 to 12 minutes.

Yield: 2 to 3 dozen cookies

Answer the Door

Behold, I stand at the door, and knock: if any man hear my voice, and open the door, I will come in to him, and will sup with him, and he with me.
REVELATION 3:20 KJV

"Answer the door!" How many times have you heard one family member call out as the doorbell rings only to find a chorus of reasons why no one else can be interrupted? Would this change if you knew it was Jesus standing on the other side of that door? Would you all ignore the bell and continue with what you were doing? Of course not! The same can be said of other opportunities to spend time with Jesus. Sometimes this means setting aside what you're doing to take up such an opportunity. How can you and your family find time for Jesus in a busy day? Start by answering the door. He is knocking!

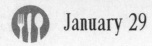

Chicken Divan Casserole

4 boneless, skinless chicken
   breasts
1 fresh rosemary sprig
1 teaspoon salt, divided
¼ teaspoon black pepper
2 tablespoons butter or
   margarine
¼ cup flour
1 cup milk
1 egg yolk, beaten

1 (8 ounce) carton sour cream
½ cup mayonnaise
½ teaspoon grated lemon rind
2 tablespoons lemon juice
¼ teaspoon curry powder
2 (10 ounce) packages frozen
broccoli spears, thawed and
   drained
⅓ cup grated Parmesan cheese
Paprika

Place chicken breasts, rosemary, ½ teaspoon salt, and pepper in large saucepan; add water to cover. Bring water to boil. Cover, reduce heat, and simmer for 10 to 15 minutes or until chicken is tender. Drain, reserving ½ cup broth. Discard rosemary. Cool chicken slightly, then cut into bite-sized pieces; set aside. Melt butter in heavy saucepan over low heat; add flour, stirring until smooth. Cook for 1 minute, stirring constantly. Gradually add milk and reserved broth; cook over medium heat, stirring constantly until thickened and bubbly. Stir small amount of hot mixture into egg yolk; add back into remaining hot mixture, stirring constantly. Cook for 1 minute. Remove from heat; stir in sour cream, mayonnaise, lemon rind, lemon juice, ½ teaspoon salt, and curry. Layer half each of broccoli, chicken, and sauce in greased 2-quart casserole. Repeat layers. Sprinkle with Parmesan cheese and paprika. Bake uncovered at 350 degrees for 30 to 35 minutes.

Yield: 4 to 6 servings

God's Hugs

And thou shalt love the Lord thy God with all thine heart.
DEUTERONOMY 6:5 KJV

When someone in your family stops to give you a hug, doesn't that make you feel loved, especially if she hugs you tight? God wants you to feel that way about Him. You can't hug God, but you can offer up all of your heart and soul to Him. He loves that. And He loves you.

Blue Cheese–Stuffed Dates

2 ounces blue cheese
Milk
12 dried dates, pitted and cut in
   half lengthwise

24 blanched almonds, toasted
Cayenne pepper

In small bowl, mix cheese with hand mixer until creamy. Add a few drops of milk if cheese is too crumbly. Place dates on serving platter. Spread about 1 teaspoon of cheese on cut side of each date. Top with 1 almond. Sprinkle stuffed dates with dash of cayenne pepper. Serve.

Yield: 6 to 8 servings

God's Day Planner

Many are the plans in a person's heart,
but it is the LORD's purpose that prevails.
PROVERBS 19:21 NIV

What does your family's calendar look like? Are your days filled with events, appointments, and other important things? Do you make lists? Perhaps you color-code your calendar so that each family member has his or her own plan. What is your purpose in all of this? To get every family member to the right place at the appointed time. Isn't that what God's purpose is in your life? Be willing to set your plans aside for His. You and your family will not regret it, and I promise you'll end up where you're supposed to be at exactly the right time.

Family Dinnertime Tip

Invite a friend over for dinner and then to stay after for coffee, tea, or dessert. You'll find that the conversation and company will lift your spirit and rejuvenate your soul.

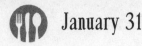

Cheesy Onion Casserole

2 tablespoons butter or
    margarine
3 large sweet onions, sliced into
    rings
2 cups shredded swiss cheese,
    divided
Black pepper to taste

1 (10¾ ounce) can condensed
    cream of chicken soup
⅔ cup milk
1 teaspoon soy sauce
8 slices French bread, buttered
    on both sides

Melt butter in large skillet. Add onions and sauté until clear and beginning to brown. Layer onions, 1⅓ of cheese, and pepper in greased 2-quart casserole. Set aside. In saucepan, combine soup, milk, and soy sauce. Heat and stir until well blended. Pour soup mixture over onions and stir gently. Top with French bread slices. Bake at 350 degrees for 15 minutes. Remove from oven and carefully press bread slices into casserole until sauce covers bread. Sprinkle with remaining cheese and return to oven for 15 minutes.

Yield: 8 servings

Specializing in the Impossible

The things which are impossible with men are possible with God.
LUKE 18:27 KJV

Has anyone in your family ever declared, "I cannot do this"? Probably at one time or another, all of you have. What happens next? If your family is like mine, the next step is that other family members pitch in to help and somehow that impossible task gets done. But what happens when the task is too much even for all of you? That's where God comes in. He specializes in the impossible!

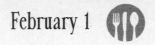
Corned Beef Dip

1 (12 ounce) can corned beef
1 (5 ounce) jar prepared
  horseradish
1 cup mayonnaise

1 medium onion, minced
Black pepper to taste
Worcestershire sauce to taste
Party rye bread or crackers

Chop corned beef finely. In mixing bowl, combine beef, horseradish, mayonnaise, onion, pepper, and Worcestershire sauce. Chill for at least 3 to 4 hours to blend flavors. Spoon into serving bowl and serve with party rye or crackers.

Yield: 3 cups

Everything from Nothing

In the beginning God created the heavens and the earth.
GENESIS 1:1 NLT

Don't you love reading about how God created everything out of nothing? Do you sew? Then you know what it's like to create a quilt or a garment out of thread and cloth. Are you a woodworker? An artist? A cook? Then you've created a piece of furniture, a painting, or a meal in a way that others could not. Think for a moment of how our sovereign God created everything, the seen and the unseen. Can you even imagine it? What a creative God we serve!

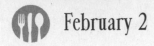

Chocolate Marshmallow Bars

¾ cup butter or margarine, softened
1½ cups sugar
3 eggs
1 teaspoon vanilla
1⅓ cups flour
½ teaspoon baking powder
½ teaspoon salt
3 tablespoons cocoa

4 cups miniature marshmallows

Topping:
1⅓ cups (8 ounces) milk chocolate chips
1 cup crunchy peanut butter
3 tablespoons butter or margarine
2 cups crisp rice cereal

In large mixing bowl, cream butter and sugar. Add eggs and vanilla; beat until fluffy. Combine flour, baking powder, salt, and cocoa; gradually add to creamed mixture. Spread in greased jelly roll pan. Bake at 350 degrees for 15 to 18 minutes. Sprinkle marshmallows evenly over cake; return to oven for 2 to 3 minutes. Dip knife or spatula in water and spread melted marshmallows evenly over cake. Cool completely.

For topping, combine chocolate chips, peanut butter, and butter in medium saucepan. Cook over low heat, stirring constantly until melted and well blended. Remove from heat and stir in cereal. Spread evenly over bars. Chill.

Yield: 3 dozen bars

Behave!

If ye love me, keep my commandments.
JOHN 14:15 KJV

"Behave!" How many times did you hear that from your mother or father? Too many, you might say. And yet your parent never gave up on trying to teach you the proper way to act. Now you can pass that on to your children. In the same way, God asks that you obey Him, that you respect His rules and behave in the way He wants you to behave. He loves you and wants the best for you. To show you love Him in return, all He asks is that you behave.

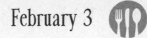
Hot Turkey Salad

3 cups diced cooked turkey
4 hard-boiled eggs, chopped
2 cups diced celery
1 cup sliced fresh mushrooms
2 tablespoons diced onion

¾ cup mayonnaise
1 tablespoon lemon juice
½ cup cornflake crumbs
2 tablespoons butter or
    margarine, melted

In large bowl, combine turkey, eggs, celery, mushrooms, onion, mayonnaise, and lemon juice. Transfer to 9x13-inch baking dish. Top with cornflake crumbs and drizzle with melted butter. Bake at 350 degrees for 30 minutes.

Yield: 6 to 8 servings

You Are Loved!

We love him, because he first loved us.
1 JOHN 4:19 KJV

When you were a child, your mother and father loved you before you ever were capable of loving them back. So did your grandparents and maybe even your great-grandparents. You were precious in their sight well before you could respond equally to them. In much the same way, God loved us before we were ever able to realize who He was and what He meant to us. Think of how much the Lord loves you and your family as you sit down together to this meal. He considers each of you His precious son or daughter. Aren't you glad you are so loved?

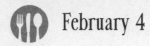

Nutty Pear Salad

2 cans (45 ounces total) pear
    halves in syrup
Lemon juice
1 (8 ounce) package cream
    cheese, softened

1 tablespoon sugar
¼ cup chopped walnuts
Maraschino cherries, halved

Drain pear halves, reserving 1 tablespoon syrup. Brush each pear with lemon juice. In small bowl, beat cream cheese, sugar, and reserved syrup until smooth. Fold in walnuts. Spoon mixture into each pear half. Top with halved maraschino cherry.

Yield: 8 servings

Learning to Learn

There is no wisdom, no insight,
no plan that can succeed against the LORD.
PROVERBS 21:30 NIV

From an early age, we learn to value education. Children go from playing school to attending school. Adults finish their education but never stop learning. Even so, true wisdom comes not from school but from the Lord. God is sovereign. His plans never fail, while plans made without Him never succeed. What does your family seek, education or wisdom? The best answer is both!

Blue Cheese Green Beans

2 ounces blue cheese, crumbled
  and divided
3 tablespoons half-and-half
2 tablespoons white wine vinegar
1 tablespoon grated Parmesan
  cheese
½ teaspoon dried oregano
¼ teaspoon coarsely ground
  black pepper

⅛ teaspoon sugar
¼ cup vegetable oil
1 pound fresh green beans
¼ teaspoon salt
Black pepper to taste
1 (2 ounce) jar diced pimiento,
  drained
4 slices bacon, cooked and
  crumbled

In blender, combine 1 ounce blue cheese, half-and-half, vinegar, Parmesan cheese, oregano, pepper, and sugar. Cover and process until smooth. With blender running, add vegetable oil in slow, steady stream. Process just until blended; set dressing mixture aside. Wash beans; trim ends and remove strings. Cook beans in small amount of boiling salted water for 15 to 20 minutes or until tender. Drain and arrange beans on serving platter. Sprinkle with salt and pepper. Pour blue cheese dressing mixture over beans. Top with pimiento, 1 ounce crumbled blue cheese, and crumbled bacon.

Yield: 4 servings

Pursuing God

Where there is no vision, the people perish.
PROVERBS 29:18 KJV

Are you a planner? Planning an organized day means that your family knows where to be and when. Do you consider your pursuit of God with as much enthusiasm as you arrange your calendar? What would happen if your family began today to make time for the Lord, specific and purposeful time to spend with Him?

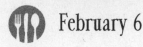

Mini Pizza Delights

1 English muffin, sliced in half
Tomato sauce (or pizza sauce)
Mozzarella cheese, shredded

Toppings of your choice
(pepperoni, mushrooms,
onion, green pepper, etc.)

Top English muffin halves with tomato sauce, cheese, and toppings of your choice. Cook in microwave until cheese is melted.

Yield: 2 servings

Amazing Love

And now these three remain: faith,
hope and love. But the greatest of these is love.
1 CORINTHIANS 13:13 NIV

The greatest of these is love! When you and your family sit down to a meal, do you talk about the things you love? Maybe you're serving someone's favorite dish. It's so easy to say you love the meal or even to say you love your family. Take a minute, however, and think of how much God loves us. He sent His only Son to save us. Just consider the depth of that kind of love. Amazing, isn't it?

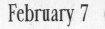

Debbie's Cheese Ball

1 (5 ounce) jar Old English
cheese spread
1 (5 ounce) jar Roka Blue cheese
spread

1 (8 ounce) package cream
cheese, softened
1 small onion, minced
1 dash Worcestershire sauce
¾ cup chopped pecans

With fork, thoroughly blend cheese spreads, cream cheese, onion, and
Worcestershire sauce. Sprinkle chopped pecans onto sheet of waxed
paper. Spoon cheese mixture onto pecans. Roll cheese mixture in pecans
and form into ball. Wrap ball in plastic wrap and chill thoroughly before
serving with crackers.

Yield: 12 to 15 servings

Plans for You

"For I know the plans I have for you," declares the Lord,
"plans to prosper you and not to harm you,
plans to give you hope and a future."
Jeremiah 29:11 NIV

As you sit around the table at any meal, you could easily say that you know
these people. You know their quirks, what makes them happy or sad, and
even what foods they prefer. How is that? Because you love them and have
taken the time to know them. God feels the same about you. He knows you
inside and out—quite literally—and He has created a life
plan that suits you perfectly. Trust that plan and
know He wants only the best for you.

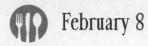

Coconut Butterballs

1 cup butter, softened
   (no substitutions)
½ cup powdered sugar
2 cups flour

1½ cups sweetened, flaked
   coconut, coarsely chopped
Powdered sugar

In large bowl, cream butter and ½ cup powdered sugar. Gradually blend in flour. Fold in coconut. Roll dough into 1-inch balls. Roll in powdered sugar and place 1 inch apart on ungreased cookie sheets. Bake at 350 degrees for 18 to 20 minutes, until lightly browned. Roll in powdered sugar again and cool on wire racks.

Yield: 4 dozen cookies

Listen and Obey

We know that we have come to know him
if we keep his commands.
1 JOHN 2:3 NIV

"Mind your mother!" How many times have you said this? How many times did you hear it growing up? Plenty, I'm sure. Have you ever thought of why we obey? Sure, part of it is because we want to avoid punishment, but beyond that, we do as we are asked because we care about the person asking. In the same way, obedience to God shows we love Him.

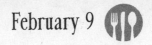

Italian Turkey

1½ pounds ground salt pork
1 garlic clove, minced
3 teaspoons ground sage

2½ to 3⅓ teaspoons chili powder
Salt and pepper to taste
1 (10 to 12 pound) turkey

Combine first five ingredients and spread over turkey. Bake at 350 degrees for 4½ hours or until done. Remove pork mixture from turkey and place in large bowl; crumble mixture with fork. Debone turkey and chop meat into small pieces. Blend turkey with pork mixture. Serve as loose meat or with rolls for sandwiches.

Yield: 25 to 30 servings

Hurry Up, God!

The Lord is not slow in keeping his promise, as some understand slowness. Instead he is patient with you, not wanting anyone to perish, but everyone to come to repentance.
2 PETER 3:9 NIV

How many times have you felt like God was moving far too slow for your liking? Have you decided things would turn out much better if He would just hurry? But His timing is perfect, no matter how it seems, and He sees the situation in a way that you never could. Next time you're tempted to ask the Lord what's taking so long, consider the fact that He has your very best interests at heart, and moving at His speed and not yours is what's best for you.

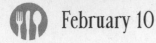

Festive Cauliflower

1 large head cauliflower
2 cups water
½ teaspoon salt
1 tablespoon minced onion
1 tablespoon minced green pepper
1 tablespoon minced sweet red pepper
4 tablespoons butter or margarine, divided

3 tablespoons flour
1 cup milk
1 cup shredded cheddar cheese
¼ teaspoon dry mustard
1 dash ground white pepper
2 slices cooked bacon, crumbled
1 tablespoon sliced natural almonds, toasted

Remove and discard outer leaves and stalk of cauliflower. Wash cauliflower well, leaving head whole. Place cauliflower in large saucepan; add water and salt. Bring to boil; cover, reduce heat to medium, and cook for 10 to 12 minutes or until tender. Drain well. Place cauliflower on serving platter; keep warm. Sauté onion and green pepper in 1 tablespoon butter in skillet until tender; drain well and set aside. Melt remaining butter in heavy saucepan over low heat; add flour, stirring until smooth. Cook for 1 minute, stirring constantly. Gradually add milk; cook over medium heat, stirring constantly until mixture is thickened and bubbly. Add cheese, mustard, and pepper, stirring until cheese melts. Remove from heat; stir in reserved vegetable mixture. Spoon sauce over cauliflower. Sprinkle with bacon and almond slices. Serve immediately.

Yield: 6 servings

Overcooked Popcorn

Do not be misled: "Bad company corrupts good character."
1 CORINTHIANS 15:33 NIV

Have you ever overcooked a batch of popcorn? Even though only some of the kernels are blackened, the entire batch tastes burned. So, too, is the company we keep. God wants us to love everyone but only be close friends with others who are also following Jesus. That way we lift one another up rather than pull one another down.

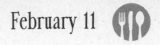

Anytime Egg Fajitas

2 tablespoons vegetable oil
2 cups frozen hash browns
½ pound spicy sausage
5 eggs

½ cup green bell pepper, chopped
¼ cup onion, chopped
8 large flour tortillas
1 cup shredded cheddar cheese

Heat oil in skillet. Add hash browns and cook over medium heat, stirring constantly until lightly browned. Add sausage and stir until cooked. Beat eggs in small bowl and add to hash brown mixture along with green pepper and onion. Cook, stirring occasionally, until eggs are set and thoroughly cooked. Microwave tortillas on high for 25 to 30 seconds to soften. Spoon egg mixture onto center of softened tortillas and top with cheese. Roll up tortillas.

Yield: 8 servings

Road Trip!

*"In your unfailing love you will lead the people you have redeemed.
In your strength you will guide them to your holy dwelling."*
EXODUS 15:13 NIV

Road trip! When you hear those words do you cringe or celebrate? Some families love getting in the car and heading off on adventures. If yours is one of those families, then you know the preparation it takes to make a successful trip. You wouldn't leave home without a destination in mind and a way to get there, would you? Much as the map and GPS will get your family where you are going, so will God see that we reach our destination in His holy dwelling. Let Him be the guide, and you are guaranteed to get there.

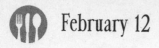

Hot Crab Dip

1 (8 ounce) package cream
   cheese, softened
½ teaspoon prepared horseradish
2 tablespoons minced green
   onions

1 tablespoon Worcestershire
   sauce
1 (6½ ounce) can crabmeat,
   drained
⅓ cup slivered almonds
Paprika

In mixing bowl, blend together cream cheese, horseradish, onions, Worcestershire sauce, and crabmeat. Spread into 3-cup baking dish. Sprinkle with almonds, then with paprika. Bake at 350 degrees for 30 minutes. Serve with wheat or rye crackers.

Yield: 8 servings

Strength for the Tasks

She gets up while it is still night; she provides food for her family. . . . She sets about her work vigorously; her arms are strong for her tasks.
PROVERBS 31:15, 17 NIV

In our modern world, time is a precious commodity. Our days and the tasks they include are ordered by God, but do you ever wonder where the strength to do everything comes from? Guess what? It comes from the Lord. Aren't you glad God has prepared you for the tasks He has assigned to you?

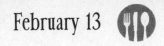

World's Best Cocoa

¼ cup cocoa
½ cup sugar
⅓ cup hot water

⅛ teaspoon salt
4 cups milk
¾ teaspoon vanilla

Mix cocoa, sugar, water, and salt in saucepan. Over medium heat, stir constantly until mixture boils. Continue to stir and boil for 1 minute. Add milk and heat (do not boil). Remove from heat and add vanilla; stir well. Pour into four mugs and serve immediately.

Yield: 4 servings

Speak Up!

Speak up for those who cannot speak for themselves, for the rights of all who are destitute. Speak up and judge fairly; defend the rights of the poor and needy.
PROVERBS 31:8–9 NIV

The loudest voice in a room is the one we are most likely to hear. But what of the others who are speaking? We see them, but do we hear what they say? Sometimes we do, but not always. And what about those who aren't saying a word? God says every person is a child of His, a child whose words should be heard. He charges each of us to speak up for those who are quiet, to stand for those who are forgotten. How will you do that today?

Family Dinnertime Tip

Make your meal times your "God time." Who says you can't talk with God and about God while you're cooking with the family, eating together, or while you're working together to clean up afterward?

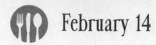

Coconut Macaroons

3 large egg whites
⅛ teaspoon salt
⅛ teaspoon cream of tartar
¾ cup sugar

1 teaspoon vanilla
1¼ cups sweetened, flaked
    coconut
1 tablespoon cornstarch

Lightly grease two cookie sheets. Combine egg whites, salt, and cream of tartar in bowl; beat until soft peaks form. Beat in sugar one tablespoon at a time until egg whites are stiff and shiny. Fold in vanilla. Toss coconut with cornstarch and fold mixture into egg whites. Drop by teaspoonfuls onto cookie sheets. Bake at 325 degrees for 20 minutes, until edges are browned. Cool completely on wire racks.

Yield: 3 dozen cookies

How Long Is Forever?

Give thanks to the Lord, for he is good.
His love endures forever.
PSALM 136:1 NIV

One hundred years is a very long time, but it is easy to imagine. One thousand is even more difficult to consider. Can you even begin to imagine how long forever is? Stretching all the way back to the beginning of time and all the way forward to the end of time, the Lord promises His love will endure, that He will endure, that we will give Him thanks for His goodness.

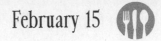

Lemon-Herb Turkey Breast

1 (8 to 9 pound) bone-in turkey breast
3 tablespoons fresh lemon juice, divided
2 tablespoons olive oil, divided
2 garlic cloves, crushed
1¼ teaspoons salt
1 teaspoon grated lemon rind
1 teaspoon dried thyme
1 teaspoon freshly ground black pepper
½ teaspoon ground sage
Lemon-pepper seasoning to taste

Rinse turkey in cold water and pat dry. Loosen skin from turkey with fingers, but leave skin attached to meat. In small bowl, combine 1 tablespoon lemon juice, 1 tablespoon oil, garlic, salt, lemon rind, thyme, pepper, and sage. Spread evenly under turkey skin. Combine remaining lemon juice and oil; set aside. Place turkey on rack in shallow roasting pan sprayed with cooking spray. Bake uncovered at 350 degrees for 2½ to 3 hours or until meat thermometer reads 170 degrees, basting every 15 to 20 minutes with lemon juice and oil mixture. Let stand for 10 to 15 minutes before carving.

Yield: 16 servings

Run Devil!

Submit yourselves, then, to God.
Resist the devil, and he will flee from you.
JAMES 4:7 NIV

Christians have an enemy who wants to see them fail. This enemy tries his hardest to hit you just where you are most vulnerable and at the time when you are the weakest. The best defense against this enemy, the devil, is to stand firm in God's power. The devil cannot exist in a place filled with the Lord. The power of God bests the enemy every time!

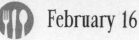

Oriental Ramen Noodle Salad

2 tablespoons butter or
  margarine
1 (3 ounce) package oriental-
  flavor ramen noodle soup,
  seasoning packet reserved
½ cup sliced almonds
⅔ cup evaporated milk
⅔ cup vegetable oil

3 tablespoons white vinegar
2 tablespoons sugar
2 (10 ounce) packages
  romaine-radicchio lettuce
2 green onions, thinly sliced
1 (10 ounce) can mandarin
  oranges, drained

Melt butter in large skillet. Crumble ramen noodles and add to skillet with almonds; cook, stirring constantly until noodles are golden. Remove from pan; cool completely and set aside. In blender, combine evaporated milk, oil, vinegar, ramen seasoning packet, and sugar. Cover and blend until smooth.

    Combine salad greens, noodle mixture, green onions, oranges, and dressing in large bowl; toss to coat. Serve immediately.

Yield: 8 servings

Drifting Away

We must pay the most careful attention, therefore, to what we have heard, so that we do not drift away.
HEBREWS 2:1 NIV

Don't you love a nice day at the beach or lake, especially one where you can lie back on a float and just enjoy a relaxing afternoon? Have you ever fallen asleep on your float only to awaken quite a distance away from where you started? What happened? You let your guard down and drifted away. That can happen in life as well. Don't lose sight of where you are and where you need to be and you will not drift away.

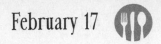
French-Style Green Beans

⅔ cup slivered almonds
6 tablespoons butter or
    margarine

2 (10 ounce) packages frozen
    French-style green beans,
    thawed
½ teaspoon salt

In large skillet, sauté almonds in butter until lightly browned, about 1 to 2 minutes. Stir in beans and salt; cook and stir for 1 to 2 minutes or until heated through.

Yield: 8 servings

A Life Worthy of the Call

So we keep on praying for you, asking our God to enable you to live a life worthy of his call. May he give you the power to accomplish all the good things your faith prompts you to do.
2 THESSALONIANS 1:11 NLT

What does a worthy life look like to you? Is it filled with good things? God says we are to live a life filled with God things. When your life is filled with His purpose and His people, then you are living a life worthy of the call. How do we manage this? Prayer, of course—ours and the prayers of those who love us!

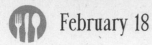

Mexican Sandwich Rolls

3 pounds ground beef
1 medium onion, chopped
3 cups shredded cheddar cheese

1 (15 ounce) can tomato sauce
1 (4 ounce) jar salsa
2 dozen hard rolls

Brown ground beef and onion; drain. Add remaining ingredients except rolls. Remove pinch of bread from center of rolls, then fill with beef mixture. Wrap each in foil. Bake at 350 degrees for 30 minutes.

Yield: 24 rolls

Busy, Busy

"Martha, Martha," the Lord answered, "you are worried and upset about many things, but few things are needed—or indeed only one. Mary has chosen what is better, and it will not be taken away from her."
LUKE 10:41–42 NIV

Have you ever been working while everyone else is enjoying themselves? It's easy to look at the others play and complain that we are the only ones working. Jesus watched this happen with two sisters: Martha and Mary. While Martha busied herself in the kitchen, Mary sat at Jesus' feet and listened. Both were good things, but Jesus says being busy, even with good things, should never get in the way of spending time with Him.

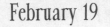

Party Meatballs

½ pound ground beef ·
⅓ cup lemon-lime soda
½ cup Italian bread crumbs
1 egg, beaten

½ teaspoon garlic salt
½ teaspoon onion salt
18 stuffed green olives

In medium bowl, combine ground beef, lemon-lime soda, bread crumbs, egg, garlic salt, and onion salt. Mix well. Form small amount of mixture into ball around 1 olive. Repeat with remaining mixture. Place under broiler for about 10 minutes or until browned.

Yield: 18 meatballs

Night-Light

"You, LORD, are my lamp; the LORD turns my darkness into light."
2 SAMUEL 22:29 NIV

When you were a child, did you find it hard to go to sleep in the dark without worrying about what sort of scary things were lurking in the shadows? Funny how a simple night-light solved the problem and chased all the monsters away. In the same way, God is our lamp—our night-light—that sheds light on all the dark corners of our world.

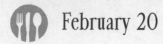

Cranberry-Pecan Bars

1 cup flour
2 tablespoons sugar
⅓ cup butter or margarine,
   softened
1 cup finely chopped pecans,
   divided
1¼ cups sugar
2 tablespoons flour

2 eggs, beaten
2 tablespoons milk
1 tablespoon finely grated orange
   rind
1 teaspoon vanilla
1 cup chopped cranberries
½ cup sweetened, flaked coconut

In medium mixing bowl, combine 1 cup flour and 2 tablespoons sugar. With pastry blender, cut butter into flour mixture until mixture resembles coarse crumbs. Stir in ½ cup pecans. Press flour mixture into bottom of ungreased 9x13-inch baking pan. Bake at 350 degrees for 15 minutes. Meanwhile, combine 1¼ cups sugar and 2 tablespoons flour. Add eggs, milk, orange rind, and vanilla. Fold in cranberries, coconut, and remaining pecans. Spread over partially baked crust. Bake for 25 to 30 minutes, until top is golden. Cool completely in pan on wire rack. Cut into bars while warm.

Yield: 3 dozen bars

Walking with Jesus

We did not follow cleverly devised stories when we told you about the coming of our Lord Jesus Christ in power, but we were eyewitnesses of his majesty.
2 PETER 1:16 NIV

Can you imagine being an eyewitness to the events of Jesus' life? Imagine being there when He performed miracles or when He walked on water! What if you were there to see Him multiply the loaves and fishes or to carry the cross for Him on the way to the crucifixion? The Bible is filled with the testimony of those who walked alongside Jesus and saw these things. While we cannot walk in their shoes, we can imagine what it must have been like. What a gift!

Mediterranean Chicken

½ cup feta cheese
¼ cup minced green onions
Black pepper to taste
4 boneless chicken breasts
3 tablespoons butter
2 small shallots, minced
¼ teaspoon minced fresh basil

3 small garlic cloves, minced
1 teaspoon dried oregano
1 cup sliced fresh mushrooms
1 tablespoon flour
¾ cup chicken stock
½ cup diced tomatoes
1 tablespoon feta cheese

In small bowl, combine ½ cup feta cheese, green onions, and pepper. Place chicken breasts between sheets of waxed paper and pound to flatten slightly. Divide cheese filling equally between chicken breasts. Fold chicken around filling and place in shallow baking dish. Bake at 350 degrees for 35 to 40 minutes.

Meanwhile, melt butter in small skillet. Add shallots, basil, garlic, oregano, and mushrooms. Sauté briefly. Add flour and stir until blended. Slowly pour in half of chicken stock. Stir constantly until sauce is smooth and begins to thicken. Add remaining chicken stock, then stir in tomatoes and 1 tablespoon feta cheese. Simmer for 10 minutes. Serve sauce over baked chicken breasts.

Yield: 4 servings

The Family That Learns Together

By wisdom a house is built, and through understanding it is established; through knowledge its rooms are filled with rare and beautiful treasures.
PROVERBS 24:3–4 NIV

How blessed is the family that learns together. From an early age, an emphasis on learning is key. God encourages us to be curious and to seek knowledge and wisdom, and He provides ample opportunities for doing so. The Lord refers to knowledge as rare and beautiful treasure that fills the rooms of our home. Seek those treasures! God will most certainly be pleased.

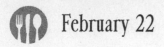

Pink Salad

1 (24 ounce) carton cottage
   cheese
1 (3 ounce) package strawberry
   gelatin

1 (8 ounce) carton frozen
   whipped topping, thawed
½ cup miniature marshmallows
½ cup nuts (optional)

Mix cottage cheese and gelatin. Gently fold in whipped topping and marshmallows. Stir in nuts if desired. Spoon into serving dish and chill until set.

Yield: 8 servings

Hard Work

Those who work their land will have abundant food,
but those who chase fantasies will have their fill of poverty.
PROVERBS 28:19 NIV

Farming is hard work. If you've lived the life of a farmer or know someone who has, you can appreciate just how difficult it is to plant the seeds and then tend them until they grow into a product that can be eaten or sold. God encourages us to work hard at everything we do, whether it's growing the things we eat, studying to do well in school, or earning an honest living to care for ourselves and our families. Take heart, those of you who are working hard. God knows and He is pleased.

Family Dinnertime Tip

Enhance a plain roll or slice of bread with extra flavor.
Soften a stick of butter, then whip in your choice of garlic,
rosemary, lemon juice, or honey. Be creative.

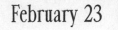

Fruited Wild Rice

1 (6 ounce) package long-grain
   and wild rice mix
2 cups water
1 tablespoon butter or margarine
2 teaspoons grated orange rind,
   divided

¼ cup halved green grapes
¼ cup chopped Red Delicious
   apple
¼ cup golden raisins
¼ cup slivered almonds, toasted

Combine rice mix, water, butter, and 1 teaspoon orange rind in medium saucepan. Bring to boil; cover, reduce heat, and simmer for 20 to 25 minutes or until rice is tender and liquid is absorbed. Combine grapes, apple, raisins, almonds, and remaining 1 teaspoon orange rind in large bowl; stir gently. Add rice mixture; toss gently to combine. Serve immediately.

Yield: 6 servings

Sweet Treats

*Gracious words are a honeycomb,
sweet to the soul and healing to the bones.*
PROVERBS 16:24 NIV

Have you ever seen honey dripping from a real honeycomb? It is golden and delicious, a sweet treat that God Himself created for His people to enjoy. In the same way, sweet words from a friend at just the right time are also a treat we all enjoy. If you see a friend or family member in need of something sweet, offer pleasant words. It works every time!

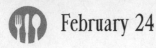

Family-Size Gyro

1 (8 inch) loaf round bread,
    unsliced
½ cup butter
4 ounces roast beef, thinly sliced
8 slices American cheese

¼ cup Thousand Island dressing,
    divided
6 lettuce leaves
1 medium tomato, sliced
4 ounces pastrami, thinly sliced
16 slices Monterey Jack cheese

Cut bread loaf horizontally into 4 slices. Spread all cut surfaces with butter. Place bottom slice of loaf on platter; top with roast beef and American cheese. Top with 2 tablespoons Thousand Island dressing. Place second bread slice on top of beef and cheese; top with lettuce and tomato. Place third bread slice on top of tomato; top with pastrami and Monterey Jack cheese. Top with remaining Thousand Island dressing. Add remaining bread slice. Cut into 8 wedges.

Yield: 8 servings

Like a Child

*He called a little child to him, and placed the child among them.
And he said: "Truly I tell you, unless you change and become like
little children, you will never enter the kingdom of heaven."*
MATTHEW 18:2–3 NIV

Children are brutally honest. They love, they laugh, and they cry easily. They also ask questions, consider answers, and make up their own minds without worrying about much other than what they believe about any particular topic. Jesus tells us we should be like children when we approach our Christian life. God wants no artifice when we stand before Him. The faith of a child, oh how precious it is. Oh how like them we should be!

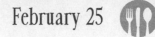

Ravioli Bites

2 tablespoons milk
1 egg, lightly beaten
1 cup Italian bread crumbs
1 (25 ounce) package frozen
   cheese-filled ravioli

Olive oil cooking spray
2 tablespoons grated Parmesan
   cheese
1 cup spaghetti sauce

Combine milk and egg in small bowl. Place bread crumbs in another shallow bowl. Dip each ravioli in milk mixture, then coat with bread crumbs. Place on baking sheet. Spray each ravioli liberally with cooking spray; recoat with bread crumbs and spray a second time with cooking spray. Bake at 450 degrees for 8 to 10 minutes or until golden brown. Sprinkle with Parmesan cheese and serve with spaghetti sauce.

Yield: 9 servings

Consider Our God

Our Redeemer—the LORD Almighty is his name—
is the Holy One of Israel.
ISAIAH 47:4 NIV

When was the last time you stopped to consider exactly who God is? Can you even fathom the grandness, the perfectly amazing magnificence of our Creator and Redeemer? Today as you walk through your ordinary day, take time to consider our completely extraordinary God. He is holy, the Holy One of Israel.

Cream Cheese Walnut Kiffels

1 pound butter (no substitutions)
1 (8 ounce) and 1 (3 ounce)
   package cream cheese,
   softened
3 egg yolks
4 cups flour

Walnut Filling:
3 egg whites
½ cup sugar
1 pound ground walnuts
½ teaspoon vanilla

In mixing bowl, cream butter and cream cheese. Add egg yolks and mix well. Stir in flour and combine thoroughly. Divide dough into four sections. Wrap in plastic wrap and refrigerate overnight. The next day, beat egg whites until soft peaks form. Add sugar and beat until stiff. Fold in walnuts and vanilla. Set aside.

Roll each section of dough into circle about ¼ inch thick. Using a pizza cutter, divide circle into eight triangles. Place 1 to 1½ teaspoons of filling at widest end of each section. Fold top two corners of triangle inward to touch and seal in filling. Roll top down toward narrow point of triangle. Place cookies on ungreased cookie sheets and bake at 350 degrees for 13 to 15 minutes, until kiffels are golden. Remove from cookie sheets while still warm.

Yield: 32 kiffels

To Speak or Remain Silent

A time to be silent and a time to speak.
ECCLESIASTES 3:7 NIV

Quiet! How many times have you had to shout over the noise to bring silence to a room? Sometimes our noisy chattering is a blessing, a sign there are happy people in the home. Other times, the din is less pleasant. In either case, there is a time to speak and a time to be quiet. God clearly tells us to be mindful of both.

Orange Duck

½ cup orange juice
½ cup apple jelly
1 dash pepper
1 (5 pound) dressed duck
Salt and pepper to taste
1 large stalk celery, cut into
   2-inch pieces

1 small onion, quartered
⅔ cup long-grain rice, uncooked
1 (12¾ ounce) package instant
   wild rice
⅓ cup chopped fresh parsley

Combine orange juice, jelly, and pepper in small saucepan. Cook over medium heat until jelly melts and mixture bubbles, stirring frequently. Remove from heat and keep warm. Rub cavity of duck with salt and pepper; place celery and onion pieces in cavity. Place duck, breast side up, on rack in roasting pan. Baste lightly with melted jelly mixture. Bake uncovered at 375 degrees for 1 hour, basting frequently with jelly mixture. If duck starts to brown too much, cover loosely with aluminum foil. Bake, basting frequently, for an additional 1 to 1½ hours or until meat thermometer registers 185 degrees when placed in thickest part of duck breast. Prepare long-grain rice and wild rice according to package directions. Combine cooked rice and parsley; stir well. Spoon onto serving platter. Place duck on top of rice.

Yield: 4 servings

Marathon Running

I consider my life worth nothing to me; my only aim is to finish the race and complete the task the Lord Jesus has given me— the task of testifying to the good news of God's grace.
ACTS 20:24 NIV

Have you ever run a long-distance race? First there is the preparation: months of planning and then finally the warm-up and the stretching before putting your feet onto the racetrack. All that planning pales in comparison to the feeling of crossing the finish line, doesn't it? Life is like running a marathon. God calls us to prepare, to endure, and not to give up until we reach the finish line. And who is waiting at that finish line to cheer us on? The Lord Himself!

Sauerkraut Salad

1 (27 ounce) can sauerkraut, drained and rinsed
1 large sweet onion, chopped
1 green pepper, chopped
1 cup chopped celery

2 teaspoons diced pimiento
1 cup sugar
½ cup salad oil
½ cup white vinegar

In large bowl, mix together sauerkraut, onion, green pepper, celery, and pimiento. In small bowl, whisk together sugar, oil, and vinegar. Pour oil and vinegar mixture over vegetables and mix to coat. Chill thoroughly.

Yield: 8 to 10 servings

The Golden Rule

"So in everything, do to others what you would have them do to you, for this sums up the Law and the Prophets."
MATTHEW 7:12 NIV

"Do unto others as you would have them do unto you." We learn the Golden Rule when we are very young, but how often do we forget this important command? The Lord reminds us in His Word that how we treat others is very important. Watch your words. They count. They can lift up or tear down. What changes can you make to better live by the Golden Rule? Start today!

Family Dinnertime Tip

It may sound odd, but I've found that the dishwasher is a great place for letting bread dough rise. Place dough in a bowl and cover with a towel. Set the bowl on the bottom rack of the dishwasher, then set the dishwasher to the dry heat cycle. The warm, moist air is perfect for a quick rise. Be sure to let your family know what you are doing so no one tries to help and accidentally "washes" the bread!

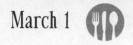

Ginger Carrots

1½ pounds carrots, pared and
   sliced
1 cup chicken broth
1 (3 inch) piece fresh ginger,
   peeled and cut into ¼-inch
   slices

1 tablespoon butter
1 dash red pepper flakes
2 tablespoons honey
1 garlic clove, minced

Combine all ingredients in medium saucepan. Bring to boil; reduce heat and simmer carrots uncovered for 10 to 15 minutes or until carrots are soft and evenly glazed.

Yield: 8 servings

I Can't Help It!

*Like a city whose walls are broken through
is a person who lacks self-control.*
PROVERBS 25:28 NIV

"I just can't help it!" How many times have you felt that way? Maybe you've started an exercise program only to decide you don't have enough time to do it regularly. Or perhaps it's a sport you want to play or a program of Bible reading you plan to take up. Self-control is essential to a life well lived. What steps can you take today to bring more self-control to your life?

Best Cinnamon Sticky Buns

1 cup brown sugar, packed
½ cup corn syrup
½ cup butter
1 cup pecans, coarsely chopped

½ cup sugar
¼ cup cinnamon
2 (17.3 ounce) tubes large
   refrigerated biscuits

Mix brown sugar, corn syrup, and butter in saucepan. Heat over low to medium heat until sugar dissolves, stirring constantly. Add pecans to mixture. Spoon into greased cake pan. In shallow bowl, combine sugar and cinnamon. Cut each biscuit in half and dip into cinnamon mixture; place in cake pan. Bake at 375 degrees for 25 to 30 minutes or until golden brown. Invert pan on platter and serve.

Yield: 12 to 16 servings

Remember!

Praise the LORD, my soul, and forget not all his benefits.
PSALM 103:2 NIV

At the time we are standing in awe of His goodness up on the mountaintop, we believe we will always remember that moment. However, once we are back down in the valley again, it is so easy to forget the good things God has done for us, isn't it? Are you on the mountain? What can you do today to better recall these moments? Perhaps a thankfulness journal is in order. You and your family could create one together. What better way to recall our heavenly Father's goodness?

Family Dinnertime Tip

Buy some spring bulbs for daffodils, tulips, or hyacinths and put them in the coldest corner of your refrigerator for 2 to 4 weeks. Fill over half a bucket or large vase with gravel, pebbles, or marbles. Nestle the bulbs among the top pebbles, points facing upward. Add water just to the tops of the pebbles. In a few weeks there will be blossoms for all to enjoy.

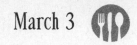

Sausage and Apple Bites

2½ cups baking mix
1 pound mild breakfast sausage
1½ cups shredded sharp cheddar cheese
¼ cup finely chopped celery

2 tablespoons minced onion
1 pinch garlic powder
2 medium tart apples, finely chopped

In mixing bowl, combine all ingredients; knead until well blended. Roll into 1-inch balls and place on greased cookie sheet. Bake at 350 degrees for 15 to 20 minutes or until browned, turning each ball after 10 minutes.

Yield: 36 appetizers

True and Perfect

"Every word of God is flawless;
he is a shield to those who take refuge in him."
PROVERBS 30:5 NIV

How many times have you said something only to have to take it back later? Maybe you thought you knew what was true and correct, but later you find out that you were mistaken. Unlike human words, God's Word never has to be retracted or corrected. Everything the Lord says in the Bible is true and perfect. How comforting to know we can always rely on God's Word!

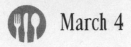

Instant Cappuccino

⅔ cup instant coffee   ½ cup sugar
1 cup powdered sugar   ½ teaspoon cinnamon
1 cup powdered chocolate milk ½ teaspoon nutmeg
   mix   Boiling water

Create a fine texture to instant coffee by putting it through blender or coffee grinder. Combine all dry ingredients and mix well. Use 1 to 2 heaping tablespoons per cup of boiling water. Store drink mix in airtight container.

Yield: two 12-ounce jars of drink mix

Trust Him

When I am afraid, I put my trust in you.
PSALM 56:3 NIV

Can you remember the last time you were afraid? Given our imperfect human nature, it probably was not all that long ago. While fear is an automatic response to a threat, our next response should be to turn that fear over to the Lord and let Him handle the issue. The shadows of fear vanish in the light of God's love. Trust Him! He knows what He's doing!

Family Dinnertime Tip

Find you're often distressed over a messy kitchen? Instead of focusing on the yucky part of cleanup, remember that the dirty pots and pans, the sticky table, the crumbs on the floor. . .all mean that you have a family who needs your love and care. Now doesn't that just make it all worthwhile?

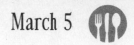

Gingersnaps

2 cups flour
2 teaspoons baking soda
¼ teaspoon salt
1 teaspoon cinnamon
1 teaspoon ground cloves
1 teaspoon ground ginger

¾ cup butter or margarine
1 cup sugar
1 egg
¼ cup molasses
Additional sugar

In small bowl, sift together flour, baking soda, salt, cinnamon, cloves, and ginger. Set aside. In mixing bowl, cream together butter and 1 cup sugar. Add egg and molasses and beat well. Gradually mix in dry ingredients. Mix well. Chill dough. Form dough into 1-inch balls and roll in additional sugar. Place balls 2 inches apart on ungreased cookie sheets. Bake at 375 degrees for 10 minutes or until cookies are set and tops are beginning to crack. Cool on wire racks.

Yield: 4 dozen cookies

Gone!

"Come now, let us settle the matter," says the LORD.
"Though your sins are like scarlet, they shall be as white as snow;
though they are red as crimson, they shall be like wool."
ISAIAH 1:18 NIV

It is so easy to carry around the heavy weight of guilt, isn't it? Some of us feel that punishing ourselves will somehow show the Lord how sorry we are for what we've done. God says to reason through this and allow Him to decide our punishment. When we give our sins and our sorrow to Him, He takes them completely away. Gone. No more guilt. What do you need to hand over to God today?

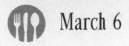
Oven-Fried Chicken

¼ cup butter or margarine, melted and divided
⅓ cup cornmeal
⅓ cup flour
¼ teaspoon paprika
¼ teaspoon salt

¼ teaspoon garlic powder
2 tablespoons grated Parmesan cheese
4 to 6 boneless, skinless chicken breasts

Pour half of butter in long baking dish and set aside. Combine next six ingredients in sealed plastic bag. Shake each piece of chicken in mixture to coat. Place chicken pieces in baking dish, and pour remaining butter over chicken. Bake at 350 degrees for 1 hour and 15 minutes.

Yield: 4 to 6 servings

Watch What He Does

*Dear children, let us not love with words
or speech but with actions and in truth.*
1 JOHN 3:18 NIV

"Don't listen to what he says, watch what he does." Good advice, isn't it? We can say anything, but that does not make it so. A claim of love isn't proven to be true unless it's backed up by loving behavior. In the same way, God tells us to put our love for Him into action. What can you do today to back up what you say about the Lord?

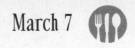

Strawberry-Orange Salad

2 cups boiling water
2 (3 ounce) packages strawberry
  gelatin
1 (10 ounce) package frozen
  strawberries, thawed and
  drained, juice reserved

⅓ cup orange juice
1 (11 ounce) can mandarin
  oranges, drained
⅓ cup sour cream

In large bowl, pour boiling water over gelatin; stir until gelatin is dissolved. Combine reserved strawberry juice and orange juice in small bowl; stir into gelatin. Reserve 1 tablespoon of mixture; set aside. Cover gelatin mixture and chill until slightly thickened. Gently stir in strawberries and oranges. Pour into gelatin mold. Cover and refrigerate until set. Meanwhile, blend sour cream and reserved gelatin mixture in small bowl. Cover; refrigerate until serving time. Serve sour cream mixture with salad.

Yield: 8 servings

When We Are Weak

But he said to me, "My grace is sufficient for you, for my power is made perfect in weakness." Therefore I will boast all the more gladly about my weaknesses, so that Christ's power may rest on me. That is why, for Christ's sake, I delight in weaknesses, in insults, in hardships, in persecutions, in difficulties. For when I am weak, then I am strong.
2 CORINTHIANS 12:9–10 NIV

When I am weak, then I am strong. That sounds impossible, doesn't it? Delighting in insults and hardships? In persecutions and difficulties? Also impossible, right? Absolutely not! When we give those things to God, He gives us the ability to persevere in all these circumstances. When we are weak, He is strong. Rest assured that the Lord is fully capable!

Green Bean Bundles

2 (15 ounce) cans whole green
    beans, drained

1 cup Italian salad dressing
9 slices bacon, cut in half

In medium bowl, combine green beans and dressing; toss gently. Cover; chill overnight. When ready to prepare, preheat oven to 375 degrees. Drain beans; arrange in bundles of 10 to 12 beans each. Wrap half slice of bacon around each bundle; secure with toothpick. Bake for 30 minutes or until bacon is done.

Yield: 8 to 10 servings

The Distracted Life

Since, then, you have been raised with Christ, set your hearts on things above, where Christ is, seated at the right hand of God. Set your minds on things above, not on earthly things.
Colossians 3:1–2 niv

How easy it is to be distracted by day-to-day life. Between the troubles and the triumphs, the stress and the success, we do well to take a breath some days. And yet God says we are not to set our hearts on these things, not to let the events of our earthly life take precedence over what awaits us in heaven. Where is your emphasis today? Where should it be?

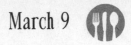

Hawaiian Sweet Bread

¾ cup sugar
½ cup butter, softened
1½ teaspoons vanilla
2 eggs
2 cups flour
1 teaspoon baking soda

½ teaspoon salt
1 cup bananas, mashed
¼ cup orange juice
1 cup sweetened, flaked coconut
¾ cup macadamia nuts, coarsely
   chopped

In large mixing bowl, mix sugar, butter, and vanilla; add eggs. In another large bowl, blend flour, baking soda, and salt; stir into sugar mixture. Use mixer to beat at low speed for 2 minutes until well blended. Add bananas and orange juice. Continue beating, scraping bowl often, until well mixed. Use spoon to fold in coconut and nuts. Pour into 1 greased loaf pan or 3 greased mini loaf pans. Bake loaf at 350 degrees for 60 to 65 minutes (mini loaves for 35 to 45 minutes) or until tester comes out clean. Cool for 10 minutes; remove from pan.

Yield: 8 servings

An Anxious Heart

Anxiety weighs down the heart, but a kind word cheers it up.
PROVERBS 12:25 NIV

Don't you love it when someone puts a smile on your face by saying something nice? It doesn't take much to change a person's day. Just a kind word or maybe a sweet statement timed just right will go a long way toward removing the weight of sadness and putting a spring in someone's step. What can you do today to cause someone to say, "Thanks, I needed that!"?

Stuffed Mushrooms

12 medium fresh mushrooms
2 tablespoons butter or
   margarine, divided
¼ cup finely chopped green
   pepper

¼ cup finely chopped celery
¼ cup finely chopped onion
Salt and pepper to taste

Wipe mushrooms with damp cloth to clean. Remove stems and chop stems finely. Melt 1 tablespoon butter in skillet. Sauté mushroom caps on bottom side only for 2 to 3 minutes. Remove from skillet and arrange, round side down, in shallow baking dish. Sauté stems, green pepper, celery, and onion in remaining butter until tender, about 4 to 5 minutes. Season with salt and pepper. Spoon mixture into mushroom caps. Bake at 350 degrees for 15 minutes or until heated through.

Yield: 6 servings

Let Your Light Shine

"In the same way, let your light shine before others."
MATTHEW 5:16 NIV

Are you shy? Do you hesitate to stand up and be noticed? Maybe you do not know what this sort of feeling is like but someone in your family does. Running from the spotlight is second nature to this family member. But God says stand up. Find that spotlight and then let your light shine. What light is that? The light of Jesus that shines through you!

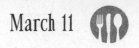
Lemon Wafers

½ cup butter, softened
½ cup sugar
2 large eggs, lightly beaten
1 teaspoon vanilla

Grated rind of 2 lemons
1 teaspoon lemon juice
1¼ cups sifted flour
⅛ teaspoon salt

Cream butter and sugar in large bowl until light and fluffy. Add eggs, vanilla, lemon rind, and juice; mix well. Fold in flour and salt. Chill for at least 1 hour. Heat oven to 350 degrees. Lightly grease cookie sheets. Drop dough by teaspoonfuls about 1½ inches apart onto prepared cookie sheets. Bake for 6 to 7 minutes, until edges are very lightly browned. Cool on pans for 2 to 3 minutes. Transfer to wire racks to cool completely.

Yield: 4 dozen cookies

Tending the Flock

Be shepherds of God's flock that is under your care,
watching over them—not because you must, but because you
are willing, as God wants you to be.
1 PETER 5:2 NIV

We know that Jesus is the Shepherd, that He cares for His flock and watches over them day and night. We also know that we are His flock. But did you realize that God has also given you a flock to care for and watch over: your family? Perhaps you do not yet have children. Who is your flock then, you might add? Your flock is always those whom the Lord has caused to live in your world, be they extended family, friends, or someone else. Ask Him and He will show you!

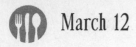
Porcupine Meatballs

1 (10¾ ounce) can condensed
   tomato soup
1 pound ground beef
½ cup uncooked white rice
½ cup water
1 teaspoon salt

½ teaspoon black pepper
1 small onion, minced
½ tablespoon dried parsley
   flakes
1 teaspoon Worcestershire sauce

Mix tomato soup with one soup can of water. Set aside. In large mixing bowl, combine remaining ingredients. Form meat mixture into 1½-inch balls. Place meatballs in greased casserole. Pour soup and water mixture over meatballs. Cover and bake at 350 degrees for 45 minutes.

Yield: 4 servings

Let Go and Let God

Do not repay anyone evil for evil.
Be careful to do what is right in the eyes of everyone.
ROMANS 12:17 NIV

How many times have you wanted to exact revenge on someone who has hurt you or someone you love? It would be so easy to just pay that person back for the wrong that has happened, wouldn't it? God understands that we humans wish for injustice to be handled swiftly and fairly. However, God tells us revenge is not ours to take, but rather it is for Him to handle. Let go and let God; that's the best way to right a wrong.

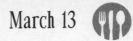

Strawberry Pretzel Salad

¾ cup butter or margarine, melted
3 tablespoons sugar
2 cups crushed pretzels
1 (8 ounce) package cream
 cheese, softened
¾ cup sugar
1 (8 ounce) carton frozen
 whipped topping, thawed

2 (3 ounce) packages strawberry
 gelatin
2 cups boiling water
1 (16 ounce) package frozen
 strawberries
1 (8 ounce) can crushed
 pineapple, drained

Mix butter, 3 tablespoons sugar, and crushed pretzels, then press mixture into 9x13-inch pan. Bake at 350 degrees for 10 minutes. Cool completely. In mixing bowl, beat cream cheese with ¾ cup sugar. Fold in whipped topping. Spread evenly over cooled pretzel crust. Combine gelatin with boiling water. Stir to dissolve. Mix in frozen strawberries and pineapple. Allow gelatin to set slightly. Pour gelatin over cream cheese mixture. Refrigerate until completely set.

Yield: 12 to 15 servings

No More Fishing

Then Jesus said to Simon, "Don't be afraid;
from now on you will fish for people."
LUKE 5:10 NIV

Simon had always been a fisherman and knew no other occupation. When Jesus came along, He demanded that Simon walk away from the one thing he had known, fishing, to join Him. It is so easy to see that Simon made the right choice. After all, this is Jesus bidding him leave. Did you ever wonder if Simon was worried that he might miss this familiar life he was leaving? Has God called you to do something that will cause you to step out in faith and perhaps even shake up your familiar life? Trust Him. Simon did, and look what an adventure he found!

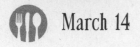

Green Onion and Bacon Mashed Potatoes

4 to 5 large baking potatoes, peeled and cubed

2 cups shredded sharp cheddar cheese

6 bacon slices, cooked and crumbled, divided

4 green onions, chopped

2 garlic cloves, pressed

½ cup sour cream

¼ cup butter or margarine, softened

1½ teaspoons salt

½ teaspoon black pepper

Place potatoes in large dutch oven and cover with water; bring to boil and cook for 25 minutes or until tender. Drain. Mash potatoes; stir in cheese, ¾ of crumbled bacon, onions, garlic, sour cream, butter, salt, and pepper. Sprinkle remaining crumbled bacon on top. Serve immediately.

Yield: 6 to 8 servings

When Life Is Unfair

"So then, it was not you who sent me here, but God."
GENESIS 45:8 NIV

Joseph was betrayed by his jealous older brothers and sold into a life that included slavery, betrayal, and finally a place of honor that allowed him to save not only his adopted country but also those same brothers. Through it all, Joseph kept his eyes on God and not his circumstances. He knew that no matter how it might feel at the moment, the Lord had a plan. Can you say the same when life seems unfair? Look at the life of Joseph and find encouragement.

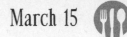
Kansas Muffins

2 cups flour
⅓ cup sugar
4 teaspoons baking powder
¼ cup shortening

Milk
Jelly
Dates, nuts, or raisins (optional)

Sift flour, sugar, and baking powder; cut in shortening. Add just enough milk to make dough drop easily from spoon. In paper-lined muffin tin, drop 1 teaspoon of dough then 1 teaspoon of jelly (mixed with dates, nuts, or raisins if desired), followed by spoonful of dough to fill tin ¾ full. Bake at 375 degrees for 25 minutes.

Yield: 12 muffins

Take Heart

The Lord blessed the latter part of Job's life
more than the former part.
JOB 42:12 NIV

If you know anything about Job's story, you surely know that of all the men and women in the Bible, his is not the story you wish to live. Everything Job held dear was taken from him, and yet he refused to curse God. Instead, he continued to believe. Have you ever felt like God was allowing circumstances into your life that you surely would never survive? Take heart. God knows and He sees, and He just may be about to bless you if you will just persevere.

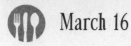

Sweet Snack Mix

1 cup salted roasted peanuts   ¼ cup whole almonds
¼ cup semisweet chocolate chips   ¼ cup raisins
1 tablespoon sunflower seeds,
    shelled

Combine all ingredients in large bowl. Serve.

Yield: 4 to 6 servings

He Is Waiting

" 'I will give them a heart to know me, that I am the Lord.
They will be my people, and I will be their God,
for they will return to me with all their heart.' "
JEREMIAH 24:7 NIV

Don't you love how God not only gives us the need to know Him, but
He also loves us no matter what we do? That kind of unconditional love
is something a human heart just cannot manage. As parents, we come
close to that level of caring, but we are human and fail sometimes. God
will never fail, and He will never cease to offer unconditional love. All you
have to do is return to Him. He's waiting!

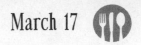

Meringue Kisses

2 egg whites
⅛ teaspoon salt
⅔ cup powdered sugar

⅔ cup semisweet chocolate chips
⅓ cup chopped pecans

In mixing bowl, beat egg whites until foamy. Add salt, then gradually add sugar, one tablespoon at a time, beating until very stiff peaks form. Fold in chocolate chips and pecans. Drop by teaspoonfuls onto lightly greased cookie sheets. Put in 350-degree oven and turn off heat. Leave overnight. These are best served the same day.

Yield: 2 dozen cookies

God's Special Gifts

To these four young men God gave knowledge and understanding of all kinds of literature and learning. And Daniel could understand visions and dreams of all kinds.
DANIEL 1:17 NIV

Daniel and his friends were young men chosen by God and set apart with special gifts. When the time came for them to be tested, these special gifts enabled them to not only excel but to literally walk through fire and bypass the danger of being lion food. The same God who made Daniel and the others made you, and He put into you your own special set of gifts. Do you know what those gifts are? If not, ask Him and He will show you.

Reuben Casserole

8 slices rye bread, cubed and
   divided
1 cup sour cream
1 large onion, diced
1 (16 ounce) can sauerkraut,
   drained

1 (12 ounce) can corned beef
12 to 16 ounces shredded swiss
   cheese
½ cup butter or margarine,
   melted

Layer half of bread cubes in greased 9x13-inch casserole. Blend sour
cream and onion; spread over bread. Spread sauerkraut on top. Crumble
corned beef over sauerkraut. Add shredded cheese, then top with remaining bread; drizzle with melted butter. Bake at 350 degrees for 45 minutes.

Yield: 6 to 8 servings

Change of Heart

*Rend your heart and not your garments. Return to the LORD your
God, for he is gracious and compassionate, slow to anger and
abounding in love, and he relents from sending calamity.*
JOEL 2:13 NIV

How do you feel when someone you love isn't behaving as you wish he or
she would? Perhaps your loved one is making harmful choices. Know that
God is ready and waiting to draw that person back to Him. Or perhaps
it is you who has moved away from the Lord. There's an easy fix for that.
Change your heart and return to the Lord. He is gracious and waiting for
your return.

Family Dinnertime Tip

Use an egg slicer to slice olives. This tool also works great with
slicing strawberries, mushrooms, boiled potatoes,
cooked and peeled beets, and much more.

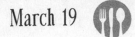

Tortellini Salad

1 (9 ounce) package frozen cheese tortellini
1 (10 ounce) package tricolored rotini
1 (6 ounce) package salami, chopped
1 (10¾ ounce) can sliced black olives, drained
1 cup sliced green olives

1 green pepper, chopped
1 cup chopped cucumber
½ cup chopped celery
1 cup Italian dressing
1 dash salt
1 dash pepper
1 dash garlic salt
Freshly grated Parmesan cheese

Cook tortellini and rotini according to package directions. Drain. Rinse with cold water; combine pastas in large bowl. Add salami, black olives, green olives, green pepper, cucumber, and celery to pasta. In small bowl, whisk together Italian dressing, salt, pepper, and garlic salt. Pour dressing over salad ingredients and toss to coat. Top with grated Parmesan cheese.

Yield: 12 to 16 servings

The Belly of a Fish

From inside the fish Jonah prayed to the Lord his God.
JONAH 2:1 NIV

Did you catch that? Jonah prayed to God from *inside* the fish. He hadn't ended up in the belly of this fish by following God. Rather, it was the opposite that caused him to find his current trouble. Have you ever found yourself in a bind because you chose not to do what God told you to do? It's no fun ending up in the belly of a fish. Likely it's pretty nasty and dark in there. Next time you find yourself in a fix, do what Jonah did and call on God. He can hear you from anywhere, even in the belly of a fish!

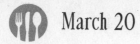

Mariann's Stuffing Balls

2 (1 pound) loaves bread
2 stalks celery, finely chopped
1 small to medium onion, finely
  chopped
½ cup butter
2 eggs, slightly beaten
⅛ to ¼ teaspoon poultry seasoning
Garlic powder to taste

Freshly ground black pepper to
  taste
1 (10¾ ounce) can condensed
  cream of chicken soup
1 (15 ounce) can chicken broth
1 packet chicken gravy mix
1 cup milk

Roast bread in 200-degree oven until dry and crusty but not dark. Cool and cube into very large mixing bowl or roaster pan. Microwave celery, onion, and butter on high power for 2 minutes; stir and microwave for 2 more minutes or until onions look transparent. Cool completely. Mix well with bread cubes. Add eggs to bread mixture, stirring to distribute evenly. Sprinkle in seasonings. Add soup and mix well. Stir chicken broth throughout mixture. Let stand a few minutes to allow moisture to soak in. Mixture should be somewhat wet. Form into 2- to 3-inch balls. Place in 9x13-inch pan sprayed with cooking oil.

Make gravy, adding milk instead of water. Cook according to package directions. Spoon over each ball. Cover and bake at 325 degrees for approximately 30 minutes.

Stuffing balls can be made ahead and prebaked without gravy then frozen individually. You can enjoy quick single servings this way. Prepare gravy and spoon over stuffing balls before warming.

Yield: 24 to 26 stuffing balls

He Is There

"If I only touch his cloak, I will be healed."
MATTHEW 9:21 NIV

There was once a woman who was so desperate that she was willing to do anything to reach Jesus, even to snatch a handful of His cloak as He passed. Have you ever been so desperate for God that you would do anything to catch His attention? All you have to do is reach out. He's there!

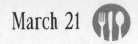

Granny's Zucchini Bread

3 cups flour
3 eggs
1 cup vegetable oil
2 cups sugar
1 teaspoon vanilla
2 cups zucchini, peeled and
  grated

1 cup walnuts, chopped
1 cup raisins
¼ teaspoon baking powder
1 teaspoon cinnamon
1 teaspoon salt
1 teaspoon baking soda
½ cup sour cream

Place flour in large bowl. Beat eggs and add to flour with remaining ingredients. Beat well for several minutes. Pour into 2 greased loaf pans. Bake at 350 degrees for 55 minutes to 1 hour.

Yield: 16 servings

Who Are You?

A good name is more desirable than great riches;
to be esteemed is better than silver or gold.
PROVERBS 22:1 NIV

Think of the things in your home that would be considered valuable. Perhaps you have a big-screen TV with a gaming system or a jewelry box filled with gold and silver jewelry given to you by that special someone. While these things have value to the world, God says our good name—the reputation we carry—is much more valuable. Who you are matters even more than what you have!

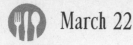

Ultimate Snack Mix

2 cups wheat squares cereal
  (such as Wheat Chex)
2 cups toasted oats cereal
3 cups mini pretzel sticks
½ cup sunflower seeds, shelled
1½ tablespoons butter
¼ cup honey

2 tablespoons vegetable oil
¼ cup sugar
¾ teaspoon cinnamon
½ cup dried cranberries
8 ounces mozzarella cheese
  cubes

Toss cereals, pretzel sticks, and sunflower seeds in large mixing bowl; set aside. Melt butter in small saucepan. Stir in honey, vegetable oil, and sugar. Bring to boil, stirring occasionally. Remove from heat, then stir in cinnamon and mix well. Pour over cereal mixture, stirring until evenly coated. Spread cereal mixture in baking pan and bake at 325 degrees for 20 minutes (stirring after 10 minutes). Remove from oven and cool on waxed paper. Add dried cranberries and store in airtight container until ready to serve. Toss in cheese cubes just before serving.

Yield: 10 servings

Love Each Other

"This is my command: Love each other."
JOHN 15:17 NIV

God loves all His children, and He calls us to do the same. Sometimes that is easy. Other times it is not. Do you have people in your life who make it difficult to love them? Do it anyway, if not for yourself, then for God. Do not wait until you feel like showing love to someone. Just do it. God commands it. Can you think of someone in your life who needs to feel loved? What will you do about that?

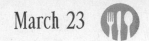

No-Bake Date Balls

1 cup chopped dates
1 cup sugar
3 tablespoons butter
1 egg, beaten
1 teaspoon vanilla

2 cups crisp rice cereal
¾ cup chopped pecans
1 cup sweetened, flaked coconut,
   chopped

Combine dates, sugar, butter, and egg in heavy saucepan. Cook over low heat, stirring constantly until dates are softened and mixture is thickened and bubbly. Remove from heat and cool slightly. Mix in vanilla, rice cereal, and pecans. When mixture is cool enough to handle, form into 1-inch balls and roll in chopped coconut.

Yield: 15 date balls

Finding Honor

Humble yourselves, therefore, under God's mighty hand,
that he may lift you up in due time.
1 PETER 5:6 NIV

We all love to be lifted up, don't we? Finding ourselves at the receiving end of a celebration is something to be cherished, especially when people we love are honoring us. But far better than this sort of honor is the honor that comes from God. How do we get that sort of honor? By humbling ourselves. How can you humble yourself before God today?

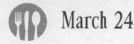

Roasted Leg of Lamb

1½ tablespoons fresh rosemary
  leaves
½ cup fresh mint leaves
4 garlic cloves, crushed
½ cup raspberry vinegar
¼ cup soy sauce

½ cup beef stock
3 tablespoons crushed
  peppercorn, divided
1 (5 to 6 pound) leg of lamb
2 tablespoons Dijon mustard

In shallow dish, combine rosemary leaves, mint leaves, garlic, vinegar, soy sauce, beef stock, and 1 tablespoon crushed peppercorn. Place lamb in mixture and marinate for 8 to 9 hours, turning occasionally. Remove lamb from dish and drain, reserving marinade. Roll roast and tie with string. Spread mustard over lamb and sprinkle with remaining peppercorn. Bake at 350 degrees for 1½ hours. Bake for additional 15 minutes for well-done meat. Let lamb stand for 15 minutes before serving.

Yield: 6 to 8 servings

Strength to Carry On

He gives strength to the weary and increases the power of the weak.
ISAIAH 40:29 NIV

Have you ever reached the end of a very long day and decided you absolutely could not move another muscle if you had to? Perhaps you've had a string of days like this and are ready for a break. What do you do? Go to the Lord, of course. Better than any break is the strength you will receive from God, strength to carry on! Just try and see!

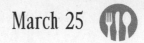

Wilted Spinach Salad

8 slices bacon, diced
1 tablespoon brown sugar, packed
⅓ cup thinly sliced green onions
Salt to taste

3 tablespoons white vinegar
¼ teaspoon dry mustard
1 pound fresh spinach, washed, dried, and chilled
1 hard-boiled egg, chopped

In heavy skillet, fry diced bacon until crisp. Reduce heat; stir in brown sugar, onions, salt, vinegar, and mustard; bring to boil. Pour hot mixture over spinach. Toss lightly. Sprinkle chopped egg over salad. Serve immediately.

Yield: 6 servings

Prayer Is Warfare

And pray in the Spirit on all occasions with all kinds of prayers and requests. With this in mind, be alert and always keep on praying for all the Lord's people.
EPHESIANS 6:18 NIV

God says prayer is warfare. Let the Holy Spirit guide you as you use this form of communication like a wartime walkie-talkie to communicate with headquarters on behalf of yourself and your family. Never give up! The battle may be long—likely all your life—but oh how the end result is worth it!

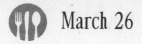

Orange–Sweet Potato Casserole

4 large sweet potatoes
½ cup brown sugar, packed,
   divided
2 tablespoons butter or margarine,
   divided
1 (11 ounce) can mandarin
   oranges, drained
½ cup orange juice

Topping:
½ cup chopped walnuts
¼ cup sweetened, flaked coconut
1 tablespoon brown sugar,
   packed
½ teaspoon cinnamon
2 tablespoons butter or
   margarine

Boil whole potatoes for 30 to 40 minutes. Cool, then peel and slice into ¼-inch slices. Arrange half of potato slices in greased casserole. Sprinkle with ¼ cup brown sugar. Dot with butter. Arrange half of oranges on top. Repeat layers. Pour orange juice over all. Cover and bake at 350 degrees for 45 minutes. While casserole is baking, mix together walnuts, coconut, 1 tablespoon brown sugar, and cinnamon. Cut butter into mixture and set aside. Remove casserole from oven, uncover, and sprinkle topping over potatoes. Return to oven uncovered for 10 minutes.

Yield: 8 servings

How God Made You

Now you are the body of Christ, and each one of you is a part of it.
1 CORINTHIANS 12:27 NIV

God made us all so very different! Even among the members of your family there is great diversity. Why did the Lord choose to make some of us good at some things while others excel in different areas? Because all the gifts He gives are chosen to complement each other and to work together to form one body in Christ. Celebrate your differences. That's how God made you, and He is never wrong!

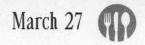

Monkey Bread

1 cup sugar

2 teaspoons cinnamon

3 packages refrigerated biscuits, cut into quarters

½ cup nuts, chopped

½ cup butter

1 cup brown sugar, packed

Place sugar and cinnamon in large plastic bag. Add biscuits and shake. Grease Bundt pan. Place coated biscuits in Bundt pan with nuts. Boil butter with brown sugar for 1 minute; pour over biscuits. Bake at 350 degrees for 30 to 35 minutes. Remove from Bundt pan immediately. This bread is best when served warm.

Yield: 14 to 16 servings

Be Bold!

"Enable your servants to speak your word with great boldness."
ACTS 4:29 NIV

After threats and imprisonment, the apostles Peter and John should have been afraid to speak out. They had been released from prison only on the provision that they keep quiet about this Jesus fellow. How easy it would have been to do as they were told, but instead these men prayed that God would make them bold. Bold! Have you ever prayed for God to make you bold in speaking about Him? Try it and see what happens!

Family Dinnertime Tip

A simple kindness, like baking an extra cake and giving it away to a neighbor, has the potential to make a big impact. Reaching out to others leaves lasting imprints on hearts.

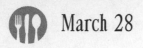
Trail Mix

½ cup walnuts, coarsely chopped
½ cup raisins
½ cup dates, chopped
½ cup dried apple slices,
    chopped

½ cup dried apricots, chopped
½ cup semisweet chocolate chips
½ cup round oats cereal (such as
    Cheerios)

Combine all ingredients in large bowl. Store in airtight container.

Yield: 8 to 10 servings

Brag on God

"My God sent his angel, and he shut the mouths of the lions."
DANIEL 6:22 NIV

Daniel was certainly in a fix when he was thrust into the lions' den. Not
only were those lions hungry, but they were also closed up in a place small
enough to easily capture and devour their prey. The odds looked poor for
Daniel, and yet when the sun rose on that cage, there Daniel was to testify
to the power of the Lord. You might not have had to face down hungry
lions, but there have been times when God has brought you through
something that looked hopeless. Share that now. Brag on God, and do not
forget to thank Him!

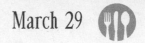

Peanut Butter Kiss Cookies

1¾ cups flour
1 teaspoon baking powder
¾ teaspoon baking soda
¼ teaspoon salt
½ cup butter or margarine
½ cup creamy peanut butter

½ cup sugar
½ cup brown sugar, packed
1 egg
1 teaspoon vanilla
Additional sugar
48 chocolate kisses

In small bowl, mix first four ingredients. Set aside. In mixing bowl, cream butter, peanut butter, and sugars. Add egg and vanilla; blend well. Stir in flour mixture. Form dough into 1-inch balls and roll in sugar. Place balls on greased cookie sheets. Bake at 375 degrees for 10 minutes or until just golden brown. Place unwrapped chocolate kiss in center of each cookie while cookies are still warm.

Yield: 4 dozen cookies

Clenched Hands

*"Those who cling to worthless idols turn
away from God's love for them."*
JONAH 2:8 NIV

I read a story once about a monkey that would not let go of a bunch of bananas even though it meant choosing between being rescued and falling down a steep cliff. The harder he held on to that thing of value, the more precarious his position became. Only when he finally let go of those bananas did he manage to save his life. In the same way, we hang on to the things we think will make us happy, not realizing that those very things are not only weighing us down but could cost us our lives. What can you release from your clenched hands today? Tell God about it. He's waiting to hear.

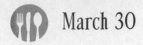

Rotisserie-Style Chicken

1 (4 to 5 pound) whole chicken
2 teaspoons salt
1 teaspoon paprika
½ teaspoon onion powder
½ teaspoon ground thyme

½ teaspoon black pepper
½ teaspoon dried oregano
¼ teaspoon cayenne pepper
¼ teaspoon garlic powder
1 onion, quartered

Remove giblets from chicken. Rinse out chicken cavity and pat chicken dry. Set aside. In small bowl, mix together spices and herbs. Rub spice mixture on inside and outside of chicken. Place onion inside chicken cavity. Place chicken in sealable bag and refrigerate overnight. Remove chicken from bag and place in roasting pan. Bake uncovered at 250 degrees for 5 hours or until internal temperature reaches 180 degrees.

Yield: 4 servings

A Brave Prayer

"Yet not as I will, but as you will."
MATTHEW 26:39 NIV

Jesus called out to God before He was led to the cross and begged that He might be spared from the cross. Even as He called out, though, He offered up His choice in the matter and turned it all over to the Father. Whatever God wanted was what Jesus wanted, even though that might mean death. Are you so dedicated to God that you are willing to lay down your will for His? Would you let Him do the choosing even if it meant that you might not like the outcome? This is a brave prayer, but one that God honors.

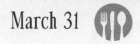

Vineyard Chicken Salad

1 pound boneless, skinless chicken
    breasts, cooked and finely
    chopped
1 cup mayonnaise
1 cup grapes, quartered
½ cup dates, chopped

1 (8 ounce) can crushed
    pineapple, drained
1 stalk celery, finely chopped
1 to 1½ teaspoons seasoned salt
    (low sodium)

Combine all ingredients in large bowl, adding more mayonnaise if mixture is too dry. Chill for 2 hours to allow flavors to blend. Serve on bread, croissants, or crackers.

Yield: 8 servings

The Little Things

*"Whoever can be trusted with very little can also be trusted
with much, and whoever is dishonest with very
little will also be dishonest with much."*
LUKE 16:10 NIV

"It's just a little lie." How often have you heard this saying? But little lies don't exist for God. God says if you are dishonest in the small things, He will not trust you with the big things. Who among us does not want God to give us great things to do for Him? Then start by being trustworthy with those things that do not appear to mean much. Trust me. They do.

Potluck Potatoes

9 medium russet potatoes, peeled and cubed

1 (8 ounce) package cream cheese, softened

2 tablespoons butter or margarine

½ cup sour cream

2 cups (8 ounces) shredded cheddar cheese, divided

1 teaspoon garlic salt

1 teaspoon onion salt

1 (10 ounce) package frozen chopped spinach, thawed and squeezed dry

Place potatoes in large saucepan; cover with water. Cover and bring to boil. Cook for 20 to 25 minutes until tender. Drain. Transfer to mixing bowl and mash with cream cheese and butter. Stir in sour cream, 1 cup cheddar cheese, garlic salt, onion salt, and spinach. Spoon into greased 2-quart baking dish. Bake at 350 degrees for 30 to 35 minutes or until thoroughly heated. Sprinkle with remaining cheese; bake 5 minutes longer or until cheese is melted and bubbly.

Yield: 10 to 12 servings

No Trick to It

"Everyone who calls on the name of the Lord will be saved."
ROMANS 10:13 NIV

There is no trick to it. Just call on the name of the Lord and He will save you. It is that simple, and that difficult. Because to call on the name of Jesus means you give all your heart and soul and trust to the Lord who created you. It means you turn away from your former life and look forward to a life lived here on earth with Him and then someday a reward in heaven. Have you taken that step? If not, then now is your time. No trick!

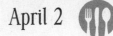

Sugar Nut Rolls

1 cup milk
½ cup sugar
1 teaspoon salt
½ cup shortening
1 package dry yeast
3 eggs, beaten
4½ cups flour

Butter
1¼ cups brown sugar, packed,
    divided
1 cup pecans, chopped
½ cup butter, softened
1 cup maple syrup, divided

In saucepan, combine milk, sugar, salt, and shortening; heat mixture until shortening melts. Cool to lukewarm. Add yeast and let stand 20 minutes. In large mixing bowl, combine milk mixture with eggs, then add flour and beat until dough is smooth and soft. Knead mixture lightly on floured board. Place in greased bowl to rise until doubled in size (approximately 1 hour). Grease 3 pans of muffin tins (9 tins each) with butter. Combine ½ cup brown sugar with pecans and divide into each tin. Turn dough out onto floured board and divide into 3 portions. Roll each portion into long rectangle no more than 3 inches wide and ½ inch thick. Spread dough with generous portion of butter blended with ¾ cup brown sugar. Roll dough up starting at narrow end. Cut each rolled portion into three 1-inch slices and place one in each tin. Let rise. Cover each slice with ½ teaspoon maple syrup. Bake at 400 degrees for 25 minutes.

Yield: 27 rolls

Choices

"As you have done, it will be done to you;
your deeds will return upon your own head."
OBADIAH 1:15 NIV

Have you ever heard the saying "What goes around comes around"? God says that, too, in His Word. The things you have done, good or bad, will someday be answered for. The Lord sees. He knows. He wants you to be aware that there are consequences for your choices. When you consider this, what does that make you want to change about your life? About your behavior toward one another?

Spinach Dip

1 envelope dry onion soup mix
1 (16 ounce) container sour
  cream

1 (16 ounce) package frozen
  chopped spinach, thawed and
  drained

Combine all ingredients. Refrigerate for 2 hours before serving. Serve with veggies of your choice.

Yield: 8 to 10 servings

Hurry Up!

*"Though it linger, wait for it;
it will certainly come and will not delay."*
HABAKKUK 2:3 NIV

How many times have you wished that God would move faster? That He would somehow stop His stalling and come through in a big way, and fast? Have you considered that the Lord just might know better about when things should happen? Of course you have, and yet it is so hard to wait, isn't it? Trust God. He is worth the wait!

• •

Family Dinnertime Tip

Egg-based foods can be hard to clean off plates and utensils.
Sprinkle the dishes with some salt right after the meal.
The salt reacts with the egg and makes for easier cleanup.

Molasses and Cream Coffee

1½ cups (12 ounces) hot coffee   ⅛ cup light cream
1 teaspoon molasses

Combine coffee and molasses in large mug; stir until molasses dissolves.
Add cream and serve.

Yield: 1 serving

God's Plans Are Best

*Do not let your heart envy sinners, but always be zealous for
the fear of the LORD. There is surely a future hope
for you, and your hope will not be cut off.*
PROVERBS 23:17–18 NIV

Have you ever looked around and wished you had someone else's life?
Does it seem like you work hard and do all the right things while others
seem to get all the glory? God says do not envy others but rather look to
Him. He has plans for you that only He knows. Put your trust and hope in
His plan and don't take your eyes off Him.

Scottish Shortbread

1 cup butter, softened
(no substitutions)
½ cup plus 2 tablespoons sugar,
divided

2 cups sifted flour
¼ teaspoon salt
¼ teaspoon baking powder

Beat butter until light and creamy. Add ½ cup sugar and beat until mixture is fluffy. Sift flour with salt and baking powder; stir into butter mixture. Place dough on ungreased baking sheet and pat into ½-inch-thick rectangle. Score dough into 1x2-inch bars with point of knife. Sprinkle with remaining sugar and bake in center of oven at 350 degrees for 15 minutes, until edges are lightly browned. Cool shortbread on baking sheet for 15 minutes; cut into bars as marked.

Yield: 2 dozen bars

What You Cannot Change

*For sin shall no longer be your master, because you are
not under the law, but under grace.*
ROMANS 6:14 NIV

"I can't help it!" Have you ever said this? Maybe you feel like there are areas of your life in which you lack the power to make changes. Guess what? You have all the power you need at your fingertips. All you need to do to access this power is to call on the Lord. What you cannot change, He can!

Raspberry Chicken

4 boneless, skinless chicken
   breasts
2 tablespoons butter
¼ cup finely chopped onion
¼ cup raspberry vinegar

¼ cup chicken broth
¼ cup heavy cream
1 tablespoon canned crushed
   tomatoes
¼ cup frozen raspberries

Between sheets of waxed paper, pound chicken to flatten slightly. In large skillet, melt butter. Cook each chicken breast in melted butter for 3 minutes on each side. Transfer from skillet to warmed platter. Add onion to skillet and sauté until onions are translucent. Add vinegar and cook until syrup is reduced to approximately 1 tablespoon. Whisk in chicken broth, cream, and tomatoes. Simmer for 1 minute. Return chicken breasts to skillet and simmer gently in sauce, basting frequently, until chicken is done, about 5 minutes. Remove chicken and add raspberries to skillet. Cook over low heat for 1 minute. Pour sauce over chicken and serve immediately.

Yield: 4 servings

A Do-Over

For we live by faith, not by sight.
2 CORINTHIANS 5:7 NIV

Have you ever wanted a do-over? There's nothing like a fresh start to breathe life into a sagging faith, is there? And God has given you everything you need for a fresh start in His Word. When you give Him your old life, He trades it for a brand-new one—one created especially for you.

Cucumbers with Cream Dressing

1 cup mayonnaise
  (no substitutions)
¼ cup sugar

¼ cup vinegar
¼ teaspoon salt
4 cups cucumbers, sliced

Blend mayonnaise, sugar, vinegar, and salt. Add cucumbers and toss. Cover and refrigerate for at least 2 hours.

Yield: 6 to 8 servings

When No One Is Watching

*Whatever you do, work at it with all your heart,
as working for the Lord, not for human masters.*
Colossians 3:23 niv

What do you do when no one is watching? Do you work as hard at your office when your supervisor is away as you do when he or she is in? God reminds us in His Word that He is always watching, always there. So whatever you do, do it with the knowledge that your heavenly Father is supervising.

Family Dinnertime Tip

You don't need to cry over your onions. Try one of these solutions:
  • Keep them in the refrigerator. Warm onions easily release their fumes.
  • Peel and cut the onion under running water.
  • Don't cut off the bloom end of the onion, as that is where the fumes are stored.

Rye Stuffing

1 pound day-old light rye bread, cubed

½ pound day-old dark rye bread, cubed

1 pound mild bulk sausage

1½ cups chopped onion

2 large cooking apples, peeled and chopped

1 cup chopped celery

3 garlic cloves, minced

½ cup butter or margarine

¾ cup chopped pecans

2 tablespoons dried parsley flakes

2 teaspoons salt

2 teaspoons ground thyme

1½ teaspoons ground sage

¾ teaspoon dried rosemary, crushed

½ teaspoon black pepper

¼ teaspoon nutmeg

3 to 3½ cups chicken broth

Combine bread cubes in large bowl. In skillet, cook and crumble sausage; drain. To same skillet, add onion, apples, celery, garlic, and butter. Sauté until apples and vegetables are tender. Add onion mixture and sausage to bread. Add pecans, seasonings, and enough broth to moisten. Cover and refrigerate until ready to bake. Stuff turkey just before baking and bake according to package directions, or spoon stuffing into greased 9x13-inch baking dish and bake at 325 degrees for 1 hour.

Yield: 10 to 12 servings

Are You a Rule Breaker?

Praise the LORD. Blessed are those who fear the LORD,
who find great delight in his commands.
PSALM 112:1 NIV

Are you a rule follower? Do you cringe at the thought of breaking just one rule? Perhaps you've got a bit of a rebellious streak. Though you're not out doing terrible things, you do on occasion let a rule or two slide. But God says we are to delight in His commands, in His rules. Why? Because they come from Him and are meant for our good. Consider the God who loves us next time you think about ignoring a protection He has put in place for you.

Mom's Gingerbread

½ cup butter, melted
1 cup sugar
1 cup molasses
⅔ cup milk
2 eggs
¼ teaspoon salt

3 cups flour
2 teaspoons baking soda
2 teaspoons cinnamon
2 teaspoons ginger
Whipped topping (optional)

Mix all ingredients together except whipped topping; pour into greased loaf pan. Bake at 325 degrees until loaf springs back when lightly touched (approximately 45 minutes). Serve plain or with whipped topping.

Yield: 8 servings

Give Thanks!

Give thanks to the LORD, for he is good; his love endures forever.
1 CHRONICLES 16:34 NIV

"Thank You, Jesus." How many times do you say that each day, either out loud or mentally? Plenty, I hope, because God loves it when we acknowledge His loving gifts. What if you don't feel like thanking Him? Maybe you're feeling as though He's no longer there or maybe He's just no longer on your side. Thank Him anyway. Eventually this will pass and you will see why He did what He did or allowed what He allowed. While I cannot promise you will have an answer this side of heaven, you will at least know what to do while you wait. And what is that? Give thanks!

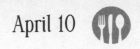

Cucumber Spread

1 cucumber, chopped
1 small onion, chopped

1 (8 ounce) package cream
cheese, softened

Place cucumber and onion in blender or food processor; puree. Drain most of juice from vegetables through strainer, then blend vegetables into cream cheese. Refrigerate for at least 12 hours. Serve on crackers or party rye bread.

Yield: 2 cups

Remember the Sabbath

"Remember the Sabbath day by keeping it holy. Six days you shall labor and do all your work, but the seventh day is a Sabbath to the LORD your God. On it you shall not do any work, neither you, nor your son or daughter, nor your male or female servant, nor your animals, nor any foreigner residing in your towns."
EXODUS 20:8–10 NIV

Don't you just love the weekend? Seems like those two days end up so crammed with activities that by Sunday night you're exhausted and have no idea where the time has gone. God tells us to remember the Sabbath by keeping it holy. What would happen if you emptied your Sunday calendar of everything except that which keeps the day holy? Try it and see.

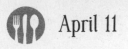

Sesame Seed Cookies

1 cup sesame seeds
½ cup sweetened, flaked coconut
½ cup butter, softened
1 cup brown sugar, packed
1 large egg
2 teaspoons vanilla

Grated rind of 1 lemon
2 cups flour
1 teaspoon baking powder
½ teaspoon baking soda
⅛ teaspoon salt

Toast sesame seeds and coconut in oven on ungreased cookie sheet at 350 degrees for 7 to 8 minutes, stirring 2 to 3 times. Remove from oven; stir and set aside. Cream butter and sugar until light and fluffy. Stir in egg, vanilla, lemon rind, and cooled sesame seeds and coconut. Sift together flour, baking powder, baking soda, and salt. Fold into butter mixture. Shape dough into ½-inch balls. Place on lightly greased cookie sheets and bake for 10 minutes or until lightly browned. Cool completely on wire racks.

Yield: 3 dozen cookies

Avoid the Fight

*How good and pleasant it is when God's
people live together in unity!*
PSALM 133:1 NIV

Do you have a brother or sister? Maybe you have several. If so, you understand what this verse is saying about living together pleasantly, don't you? Fighting, especially among siblings, is most unpleasant to God. Next time you're tempted to squabble with a family member, remember what the Lord says about that and see if you can avoid a fight. God will be most pleased.

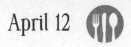

Shrimp with Pasta

16 ounces vermicelli
Salt and pepper to taste
½ cup butter
½ cup olive oil
4 garlic cloves, minced

24 large shrimp, peeled and
   deveined
8 large fresh mushrooms, sliced
1 cup chopped fresh parsley
Romano cheese

Cook vermicelli in boiling water for 10 minutes. Drain and rinse in cold water. Toss noodles with salt and pepper and set aside. In large skillet, heat butter and oil. Add garlic, shrimp, and mushrooms. Cook until shrimp turns pink, about 5 minutes. Toss in vermicelli and heat through. Transfer to warmed platter and sprinkle with parsley and cheese.

Yield: 4 servings

Take Heart

"I have told you these things, so that in me you may have peace.
In this world you will have trouble. But take heart!
I have overcome the world."
JOHN 16:33 NIV

Some days it just seems like trouble follows you everywhere you go, doesn't it? From someone leaving homework at home to the car getting a flat, it just seems as though you cannot catch a break. God says, *Do not worry*. He sees and He knows. These temporary troubles are nothing compared to what He has for you. Take heart!

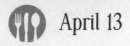

Spaghetti Slaw

1 (16 ounce) package angel hair
    pasta
1 small onion, chopped
1 small green bell pepper,
    chopped

1 (1.8 ounce) package coleslaw
    mix
2 cups prepared coleslaw
    dressing

Cook pasta according to package directions; drain, rinse in cold water,
and drain completely. Place in large serving bowl and add onion, green
pepper, and coleslaw mix. Stir in dressing. Refrigerate for 2 hours before
serving.

Yield: 8 to 10 servings

If God Is for Us

What, then, shall we say in response to these things?
If God is for us, who can be against us?
ROMANS 8:31 NIV

Have you ever felt like you've been ganged up on? Like there is no one
you can call on to take your side? Remember that you have an advocate
greater than any person whose number might be in your phone book,
someone you can call at any hour of the day or night and experience no
delays. Who is that special someone? God, of course! And if God is for us,
who can be against us?

Twice-Baked Sweet Potatoes

6 medium sweet potatoes
2 tablespoons butter, softened
½ cup orange juice

1 (8 ounce) can crushed
    pineapple, drained
2 tablespoons brown sugar,
    packed

Pierce sweet potatoes with fork. Bake at 400 degrees until tender, 45 to 60 minutes. Let potatoes cool slightly. Cut thin slice off top of each potato and scoop out pulp, leaving thin shell. In large bowl, mash potato pulp; stir in butter, orange juice, and pineapple. Refill potato shells. Sprinkle with brown sugar. Bake at 400 degrees for 15 to 20 minutes, until heated through.

Yield: 6 servings

Great and Glorious God

*"What is mankind that you are mindful of them, a son of man
that you care for him? You made them a little lower than
the angels; you crowned them with glory and honor
and put everything under their feet."*
HEBREWS 2:6–8 NIV

Have you ever stopped to consider exactly who God is? Of course, He is unfathomable, His greatness and glory unimaginable to mere humans. And yet this great and glorious God cares about us. The sovereign Lord of the universe wants a relationship with us. With you.
Just let that soak in.

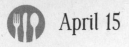

Poppy Seed Bread

3 cups flour
2¼ cups sugar
1½ cups milk
1⅛ cups vegetable oil
3 eggs
1½ teaspoons poppy seeds
1½ teaspoons salt
1½ teaspoons baking powder
1½ teaspoons almond flavoring
1½ teaspoons butter flavoring

Glaze:
¾ cup sugar
¼ cup orange juice
½ teaspoon butter flavoring
½ teaspoon vanilla
½ teaspoon almond flavoring

Mix all bread ingredients. Pour into 2 greased loaf pans. Bake at 350 degrees for 1 hour. Cool for 5 to 10 minutes then remove bread from pans. Mix all glaze ingredients and pour over hot bread.

Yield: 16 servings

Timing Is Everything

*Let us not become weary in doing good, for at the proper time
we will reap a harvest if we do not give up.*
GALATIANS 6:9 NIV

Timing is everything, isn't it? The best comedians know that an integral part of joke telling is knowing exactly when to say the punch line. Too soon or too late, and the laughter may not come. In the same way, we must know that God has timing that is perfect, timing that may not be the same as ours. Keep doing what you're doing and wait on His perfect timing. He is never too soon and never too late. Wait and see!

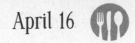

Dill Pickle Fryers

1 cup flour
¼ teaspoon salt
1 egg

½ cup milk
1½ cups dill pickle slices, drained
Vegetable oil

Combine flour and salt in shallow mixing bowl. In separate bowl, beat egg and milk. Remove excess moisture from pickle slices by blotting with paper towel. Coat pickles with flour mixture, dip in egg mixture, then dip in flour mixture one more time. In deep skillet, heat oil to 375 degrees. Fry pickles for approximately 3 minutes or until golden brown, turning once during frying. Drain. Serve with ranch dressing if desired.

Yield: 2 to 4 servings

Sweet Dreams

I will lie down and sleep, for you alone,
LORD, make me dwell in safety.
PSALM 4:8 NIV

Who doesn't love a good night's sleep? There's just something wonderful about climbing under the covers and resting your head on your favorite pillow. But what about those nights when you cannot sleep, nights when you lie awake and allow the cares of the world to roll around in your head and keep you from finding slumber? God says to release all those cares to Him. Give Him your worries, and He will give you a good night's sleep. Try it!

Iced Berry Burst

1 (10 ounce) package frozen
   raspberries
½ cup sugar
½ cup water
10 cups cold, brewed coffee

1 pint half-and-half
Chipped ice
1 cup whipped topping
Mint sprigs
Whole raspberries

Place frozen raspberries, sugar, and water in blender and mix until smooth. Strain mixture into large mixing bowl, eliminating seeds. Add coffee and half-and-half and blend well. Fill chilled glasses half-full with chipped ice and pour berry mixture over ice. Garnish with whipped topping, mint sprigs, and whole raspberries.

Yirled: 8 to 12 servings

Stop Grumbling

Do everything without grumbling or arguing.
PHILIPPIANS 2:14 NIV

If you have children, you've probably said these words: "Stop complaining and do what I said!" Maybe you've heard those words yourself. Or maybe you're the silent type, the kind who grumbles under your breath or complains silently while offering the world no hint of your discontent. God says put all that aside and do everything without complaining or arguing. Can you try that today? I promise it will make a big difference in your day.

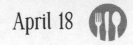

Sour Cream Walnut Cookies

½ cup butter, softened
¼ cup sugar
1 large egg yolk
½ cup sour cream
1½ cups sifted flour

½ teaspoon baking soda
½ teaspoon ground cloves
½ cup ground walnuts
Grated rind of 1 orange

Cream butter and sugar in large bowl until light and fluffy. Blend in egg yolk and sour cream. Sift flour with baking soda and cloves; fold into butter mixture. Stir in walnuts and orange rind. Shape dough into ball and chill for at least 1 hour. Grease cookie sheets. Form chilled dough into 1-inch balls. Place balls on cookie sheets and flatten gently with fork. Bake at 325 degrees for 10 minutes or until edges are lightly browned. Transfer cookies to wire racks to cool.

Yield: 2 dozen cookies

Rest in God

*In vain you rise early and stay up late, toiling for food
to eat—for he grants sleep to those he loves.*
PSALM 127:2 NIV

Have you ever wanted to linger just a little longer under the covers? To ignore the alarm and stay home from work or school to slumber away the day? Maybe you feel like you never get enough sleep. Between rising early and working late, there's barely time to do anything, much less find some rest. God says rest is found in Him. He loves you and wants the best for you. Fall into His arms and fall asleep.

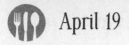

Spicy Honey-Citrus Cornish Hens

4 Cornish game hens
1 orange, unpeeled and quartered
1 lemon, unpeeled and quartered
¼ cup apricot preserves
¼ cup honey
1 tablespoon grated orange rind
1 tablespoon grated lemon rind

1 tablespoon lemon juice
1 tablespoon Dijon mustard
1 teaspoon ground ginger
½ teaspoon cayenne pepper
Salt and freshly ground pepper
   to taste

Remove giblets from hens. Rinse and pat dry. Place one orange wedge and one lemon wedge in each hen and place in roasting pan. Combine remaining ingredients in small saucepan and simmer for 5 minutes. Brush hens with mixture and bake at 350 degrees for approximately 1¼ hours, until hens are tender. While baking, brush hens occasionally with sauce.

Yield: 4 servings

Just Give

"Give, and it will be given to you. A good measure, pressed down, shaken together and running over, will be poured into your lap. For with the measure you use, it will be measured to you."
LUKE 6:38 NIV

Have you heard it said that you cannot outgive God? He says right here in His Word that if you give, He sees and rewards you. Not only will He give back to you, but He will give back well beyond your wildest dreams. The more you give, the more He gives back. That's God's economy, God's promise. All you have to do is give. He will do the rest. Beware, however, because the reverse is also true. If you shy away from giving back to God, do not be surprised if He does the same. Whatever measure you use, He will use.

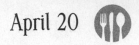

Waldorf Salad

3 apples, cut into medium
    chunks
1 stalk celery, chopped
4 to 5 dates, chopped
¼ cup walnuts, chopped

½ cup mini marshmallows
⅔ cup mayonnaise or salad
    dressing
1 tablespoon sugar
1 tablespoon lemon juice

In large bowl, combine apples, celery, dates, walnuts, and marshmallows. In separate bowl, blend mayonnaise, sugar, and lemon juice; spread over apple mixture, coating well.

Yield: 4 servings

The Great Equalizer

God is not unjust; he will not forget your work and the love you have shown him as you have helped his people and continue to help them.
HEBREWS 6:10 NIV

Have you ever felt as though you toil away day in and day out and no one notices? Maybe you feel like others are being promoted ahead of you or are getting raises that you should get. Perhaps you are in a situation that just isn't fair. God says to take heart. Though this imperfectly human world may be unjust, God is not. He is the great equalizer. Wait and see!

Family Dinnertime Tip

Make it a priority to include your entire family around the table for dinner at least one night a week. Discuss one another's activities of the day and revel in the warmth this togetherness brings to your heart.

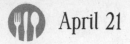

Two-Cheese Broccoli Casserole

2 tablespoons butter or
   margarine
2 tablespoons flour
1 cup milk
3 ounces cream cheese, softened

¼ cup blue cheese, crumbled
2 (10 ounce) packages frozen
   chopped broccoli
½ cup soft bread crumbs

Melt butter in saucepan. Stir in flour and cook for 1 minute. Gradually add milk and continue cooking, stirring constantly until thickened and bubbly. Add cheeses; cook until cheese melts and mixture is smooth. Cook broccoli according to package directions; drain. Stir cheese mixture into broccoli. Turn into buttered ½-quart casserole dish. Sprinkle with bread crumbs and bake uncovered at 350 degrees for 30 minutes.

Yield: 6 servings

Consider It Joy

Consider it pure joy, my brothers and sisters, whenever you face trials of many kinds, because you know that the testing of your faith develops perseverance. Let perseverance finish its work so that you may be mature and complete, not lacking anything.
JAMES 1:2–4 NIV

Who in their right mind would ask for problems? Maybe you say you've already got more than enough. But God uses those problems you wish you did not have to teach you to have faith. With faith you can continue down the road the Lord has set you on, and you can and will persevere. When all this testing is done, God will have brought you to a place where He is rightly pleased with you. Until then, do not give up when trials come your way. Know this is part of the process.

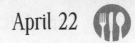

Pull-Apart Cheesy Mushroom Bread

1 loaf French bread
1 pound baby swiss cheese, sliced
1 large can sliced mushrooms,
   drained

1½ to 2 sticks butter
¼ cup onion, chopped
2 teaspoons poppy seeds
½ teaspoon dry mustard

Cut 3 slits lengthwise into bread, down to bottom crust. Stuff with cheese slices and mushrooms. Place bread on aluminum foil. Melt butter; add chopped onion, poppy seeds, and mustard. Pour over bread. Wrap bread in foil and bake at 350 degrees for 40 minutes. Slice before serving.

Yield: 12 servings

Giving Back to God

"In everything I did, I showed you that by this kind of hard work we must help the weak, remembering the words the Lord Jesus himself said: 'It is more blessed to give than to receive.'"
ACTS 20:35 NIV

Are you the type who shies away from putting money in the offering plate? Maybe you figure enough people give and no one will notice if you do not go along with the rest of them and give your offering. God wants you to give cheerfully, to offer not only your treasure but also your time to His people. What would happen if you and your family made an effort to give every day? Maybe this means making a donation on Sunday or perhaps it means you will be donating your time to help someone during the week. Look for ways to give back. You'll get more than you ever could give.

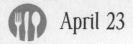

Vegetable Roll-Ups

1 (8 ounce) package cream cheese
1 (8 ounce) package sour cream
1 cup cheddar cheese, shredded
1 package ranch dressing mix

½ cup onion, chopped
½ cup carrots, chopped
1 cup broccoli, chopped
1 cup cauliflower, chopped
Flour tortillas

Mix first 8 ingredients and spread on tortillas. Roll up tight and place in plastic wrap. Refrigerate overnight. When ready to serve, unwrap covering and slice into pinwheels.

Yield: 16 servings

The Ultimate Craftsman

For we are God's handiwork, created in Christ Jesus to do good works, which God prepared in advance for us to do.
EPHESIANS 2:10 NIV

Have you ever stopped to think about how God created you? Like a potter crafting a pot or a carpenter building a piece of furniture, He began with a special plan that fit you perfectly. Unlike any mere human, however, God's handiwork is beyond impeccable. It is perfect. Stop and think a minute about how you were created by God, the ultimate craftsman. Can you imagine it? Try!

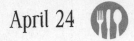

Sweet-and-Sour Chops

4 loin-cut pork chops, excess fat
   trimmed
4 medium potatoes, cut into
   ¾-inch slices
2 (10¾ ounce) cans condensed
   cream of mushroom soup
1 small onion, diced
1 garlic clove, minced
3 tablespoons honey

3 tablespoons mustard
3 tablespoons lemon juice
½ teaspoon Worcestershire
   sauce
½ teaspoon dried parsley flakes
½ teaspoon ground sage
½ teaspoon ground thyme
Salt and pepper to taste

In large skillet, quickly brown pork chops on both sides. Place pork chops in large baking dish and set aside. Boil potatoes in salted water until slightly softened. Drain well and layer over pork chops. In large bowl, combine remaining ingredients; stir until thoroughly combined. Pour mixture over potatoes and chops. Bake at 350 degrees for 25 to 30 minutes or until pork chops are done.

Yield: 4 servings

Knowing God

*For, "Who has known the mind of the Lord so as to
instruct him?" But we have the mind of Christ.*
1 CORINTHIANS 2:16 NIV

How many times have you looked at a situation and tried to guess what God was up to? Maybe you're the type who feels you need to have everything explained. You want the Lord to tell you at every step of the way exactly what He's about to do along with why He's doing it. Figuring out what God is thinking might be a fun game to play, but truly no mortal will ever be able to know the mind of the Lord. And yet this same unknowable God has given us the ability to communicate with Him. Hard to believe, isn't it?

Banana Nut Cake

2½ cups flour
1⅔ cups sugar
1¼ teaspoons baking soda
1¼ teaspoons baking powder
1 teaspoon salt
⅔ cup shortening
1¼ cups mashed banana
⅓ cup buttermilk
2 eggs, lightly beaten
1 cup chopped walnuts

Frosting:
1 (1 pound) box powdered sugar
½ cup butter, softened
⅛ teaspoon salt
1 teaspoon vanilla
2 tablespoons milk
½ banana, mashed

Combine dry ingredients. Add shortening and mashed banana and mix with large spoon for 2 minutes. Add buttermilk and eggs; blend well. Fold in walnuts. Pour batter in greased and floured 9x13-inch pan. Bake at 350 degrees for 40 minutes or until cake tests done with toothpick. Cool completely. For frosting, cream together powdered sugar, butter, and salt. Blend in vanilla, milk, and mashed banana. Beat until creamy. Spread on cooled cake.

Yield: 15 servings

The Good Life

"I know your afflictions and your poverty—yet you are rich!"
REVELATION 2:9 NIV

Money and good health are often taken for granted until they are gone. Having a nice income certainly makes it easier to live a comfortable life, doesn't it? And who doesn't prefer to feel good rather than to feel poorly or be sick? But what if you are both poor and sick? God says even then you are rich. Stop and think about that a moment. God is saying that even if the two things most wanted by us are taken away, you still have Him. You are rich in the love of the Lord, and that is the kind of richness that can never disappear.

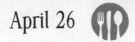

Layered Lettuce Salad

1 head lettuce, torn into small
   pieces
½ cup celery, chopped
½ cup green bell pepper,
   chopped
1 can sliced water chestnuts
½ cup onion, chopped

1 (10 ounce) package frozen peas,
   thawed
2 cups mayonnaise or salad
   dressing
2 tablespoons sugar
1½ cups cheddar cheese,
   shredded

In 10x15-inch dish, layer lettuce, celery, green pepper, water chestnuts, onion, and peas in order given. Spread with mayonnaise, then sprinkle with sugar and top with cheddar cheese. Cover with plastic wrap and refrigerate for one day. Serve at room temperature.

Yield: 8 to 10 servings

Praise God

"Return home and tell how much God has done for you."
So the man went away and told all over town
how much Jesus had done for him.
LUKE 8:39 NIV

It is so easy to praise God at the time He is doing something amazing in our lives, isn't it? We want to shout His goodness and glory from the rooftops. But what happens shortly after? Most of us return to our lives and forget all about what He did for us. Don't let that happen to you. Keep shouting His glory. What has He done in your life that is worth telling about today? Consider making bragging on the Lord a regular part of your family's day.

Zesty Carrots

6 to 8 carrots, cut into ¼-inch
　slices
½ cup mayonnaise
2 tablespoons minced onion
1 tablespoon prepared
　horseradish

¼ cup shredded cheddar cheese
1 teaspoon salt
¼ teaspoon black pepper
½ cup crushed cornflakes
1 tablespoon butter or margarine,
　melted

Place carrots in saucepan and cover with water. Cook for 5 minutes. Drain, reserving ¼ cup water. Pour reserved liquid into mixing bowl. Stir in mayonnaise, onion, horseradish, cheese, salt, and pepper. Mix well. Add carrots; transfer to greased 2-quart casserole. Sprinkle with crushed corn-flakes and drizzle with butter. Bake at 350 degrees for 20 to 25 minutes.

Yield: 8 servings

Whom Can You Serve?

"The greatest among you will be your servant."
MATTHEW 23:11 NIV

It is so easy to see who is most important in a gathering of humans. The greatest of the group will be adorned in fancy clothes or standing at the front of the line. There may be servants waiting on him or her. God says in His world the greatest are not the ones who wear the finest garments or stand at the head of lines with underlings forced to follow behind. The greatest of those who love the Lord are the ones who serve others. When you serve, you show Him you love Him. Whom can you serve today?

Baking Powder Biscuits

2 cups flour, sifted

4 teaspoons baking powder

1 scant teaspoon salt

1 teaspoon sugar

5 tablespoons shortening

¾ cup milk

Sift dry ingredients together. Cut in shortening, then add milk all at once. Stir with fork until mixture begins to leave sides of bowl. Turn out onto board and knead for 30 seconds. Roll out to ½ inch thick. Cut with round biscuit cutter and place in baking pan. Bake at 425 degrees for 15 minutes.

Yield: 10 servings

You're an Overcomer

Do not be overcome by evil, but overcome evil with good.
ROMANS 12:21 NIV

God says you are an overcomer. What is an overcomer? Someone who does not look at the situation or the odds and lament about what to do, but rather looks to God and asks what He will do. An overcomer knows he will win the fight, even if he might lose a battle or two along the way. An overcomer knows there is evil in the world, and he also knows that the Lord has overcome evil. What do we do when confronted with evil? Overcome with good. Try it today and see what happens.

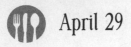

Bacon Roll-Ups

1 (12 ounce) package chicken stuffing mix

1 cup chicken broth, undiluted
1 package bacon

Mix stuffing and chicken broth. Cut bacon slices in half. Spoon stuffing mixture onto each bacon half; roll up and secure. Place on broiler pan and bake at 350 degrees for 30 minutes. Serve hot.

Yield: 16 roll-ups

Be Nice!

Offer hospitality to one another without grumbling.
1 PETER 4:9 NIV

Don't you love a party? There's nothing more fun that having a gathering filled with people you love, complete with good food and great conversation. But what happens when you are forced to entertain people you don't like? Perhaps people who are not the nicest or the easiest to talk to? God says they, too, are deserving of your hospitality. Offer up your nicest plates and food; find a way to converse and enjoy these people. God says so!

....

Family Dinnertime Tip

Kitchens aren't just for creating palate-pleasing meals. . .
Maybe even more important are some of the loveliest memories
that are created there. Spend time together talking, laughing,
and bonding. Family ties are strengthened during these moments.

Turkey Scaloppine

½ to ¾ pound turkey cutlets
½ cup flour
½ teaspoon salt
¼ teaspoon black pepper
¼ teaspoon dried basil
3 tablespoons butter or
   margarine, divided

2 tablespoons olive oil
1 garlic clove, minced
¼ pound sliced fresh mushrooms
2 tablespoons lemon juice
⅓ cup chicken broth
¼ cup white wine or additional
   chicken broth

Between sheets of waxed paper, pound cutlets to ⅛-inch thickness. Combine flour, salt, pepper, and basil. Dredge cutlets in seasoned flour and shake off excess. In skillet, melt 2 tablespoons butter. Add oil and stir in garlic. Brown each cutlet until golden, approximately 3 minutes. Place browned meat in ovenproof casserole. Melt remaining tablespoon butter in skillet; add mushrooms. Sauté until mushrooms have softened; spoon over meat. In same skillet, combine lemon juice with broth and wine. Cook until heated through. Pour over casserole. Bake at 325 degrees for 30 to 35 minutes.

Yield: 4 servings

Don't Test God

Jesus answered him, "It is also written:
'Do not put the Lord your God to the test.'"
MATTHEW 4:7 NIV

How many times each day do you put God to the test? Maybe you say you don't know what that means. Satan tried several different ways to get the best of Jesus. He tempted Him with things, with power, and even tried twisting God's own words. You probably don't do any of those things, at least not regularly, but we, too, can stand between what God wants and what we want and end up putting God to the test. Be mindful of what you do and what you say. Consider what God wants. That's always the safest path.

Banana Pudding Cake

2 small ripe bananas, mashed
1 package yellow cake mix
1 (4 serving size) package instant
   vanilla pudding mix
4 eggs, lightly beaten

1 cup water
¼ cup vegetable oil
½ cup finely chopped nuts
   (optional)
Whipped topping (optional)

Mash bananas in mixing bowl. Add cake mix, pudding mix, eggs, water, and vegetable oil. Beat at medium speed for 2 minutes. Fold in nuts. Pour into greased and floured 9x13-inch cake pan and bake at 350 degrees for 50 to 55 minutes. Top with whipped topping if desired.

Yield: 12 to 15 servings

Say Thank You!

Give thanks in all circumstances,
for this is God's will for you in Christ Jesus.
1 THESSALONIANS 5:18 NIV

"Say thank you!" From our youngest days, our parents rarely let us forget that we were to be grateful and express our thanks to anyone who offered a kindness. Doesn't it feel good to be on the receiving end of a thank-you? God also loves it when we thank Him, and He tells us no matter the circumstances, we should always give thanks. No matter the circumstances? Yes, absolutely!

Alfredo Pasta Salad

8 ounces rotini
  (corkscrew-shaped pasta)
1 cup red bell pepper, chopped
1 cup frozen peas, slightly thawed
¼ cup onion, chopped
4 to 5 hard-boiled eggs, peeled
  and chopped

Dressing:
1 cup plain nonfat yogurt
1 cup mayonnaise
⅓ cup grated Parmesan cheese
1 teaspoon dried basil
2 teaspoons garlic salt
⅛ teaspoon white pepper

Cook rotini for 10 to 12 minutes until done; drain and rinse with cool water. While rotini is cooking, blend dressing ingredients in small bowl. In large bowl, gently combine rotini, red pepper, peas, and onion. Stir dressing into pasta. Gently fold eggs into salad. Cover and refrigerate until ready to serve.

Yield: 8 servings

Slow to Speak

My dear brothers and sisters, take note of this:
Everyone should be quick to listen,
slow to speak and slow to become angry.
JAMES 1:19 NIV

Have you ever said about someone, "He's just impatient"? "He says his mind and that's just to be expected." Or perhaps you have excused another's bad behavior—or your own—by saying that's just the way God made him. God says you should be slow to speak and slow to anger. Keep an even temper and listen: two good things to remember when dealing with the imperfect people in your world. Try it today and see what happens.

Cheesy Chicken Potatoes

4 large potatoes
2 tablespoons vegetable oil
2 boneless, skinless chicken
   breasts, cut into chunks

1 cup broccoli florets
1 (10¾ ounce) can condensed
   cheddar cheese soup

Cook potatoes in microwave until done (approximately 4 to 6 minutes per potato on high). Place vegetable oil and chicken in skillet and cook until chicken is browned; add broccoli florets. Cook 5 minutes over medium-high heat. Place baked potatoes on microwave-safe plate. Cut open and fluff potatoes with fork. Top with broccoli and chicken. Spoon cheese soup over top. Microwave on high for 4 minutes.

Yield: 4 servings

Playing Favorites

My brothers and sisters, believers in our glorious
Lord Jesus Christ must not show favoritism.
JAMES 2:1 NIV

There once was a pair of brothers who had a successful comedy act based on the allegation that their mother liked one brother better than the other. It was a joke, of course, but the pair could make what is not funny seem hilarious. Perhaps you've been on the receiving end of that sort of joke. Maybe you're the one who isn't the favorite. God says take heart. He shows no favorites, nor should you. Be like Jesus. Love everyone and do not play favorites.

Cheddar Bay Biscuits

1¼ pounds biscuit baking mix
3 ounces cheddar cheese,
   shredded
1⅓ cups water
1 teaspoon garlic powder

¼ teaspoon salt
⅛ teaspoon onion powder
½ cup butter, melted
⅛ teaspoon dried parsley flakes

Grease baking sheet. In mixing bowl, combine baking mix, cheese, water, garlic powder, salt, and onion powder, forming stiff dough. Drop by spoonfuls onto baking sheet. Bake at 375 degrees for 10 to 12 minutes. Combine butter and parsley; brush over browned biscuits while still warm.

Yield: 20 servings

You Are Not Alone

The eyes of the LORD keep watch over knowledge,
but he frustrates the words of the unfaithful.
PROVERBS 22:12 NIV

You are not alone. No matter where you go or what you do, God is always there, always watching and waiting to come to His people's aid. So even though you may hit a troubled patch, know He is there and in His own timing, He will come to your aid. In the same way, He may allow those who are evil to succeed for a season, but rest assured He will frustrate them in due time.

Tortilla Rolls

2 (8 ounce) packages cream
   cheese
1 cup sour cream
1 bunch green onions, diced

1 small jar jalapeño peppers
   or black olives, diced
1 package flour tortillas
1 jar picante sauce

In mixing bowl, combine cream cheese, sour cream, onions, and peppers until smooth. Spread thin layer of mixture onto each tortilla and roll up. Place tortillas in pan; cover and refrigerate overnight. Cut each roll into bite-sized pieces. Serve with picante sauce for dipping.

Yield: 16 servings

The Gift of Children

Train up a child in the way he should go:
and when he is old, he will not depart from it.
PROVERBS 22:6 KJV

Have you ever owned a puppy or kitten? If you have, you know that when they were very small these baby animals needed your guidance and love to learn right from wrong. In the same way, children need parents to teach them how to grow into strong and faithful believers. Sometimes this training might be unpleasant, but children are learning lessons now that God will someday ask them to teach their own children. Isn't it fun to consider that someday the kids will be the mom or dad? God has already planned for this and is waiting and watching for you to complete your training!

Family Dinnertime Tip

Give an anonymous gift to someone in need. A gift certificate for groceries, toys, a donation of money—the possibilities are endless. Let God receive all the praise and honor for your thoughtfulness.

Tropical Fruit Punch

1 cup sugar
1 cup water
3 cups grapefruit juice
3 cups orange juice
3 cups pineapple juice

½ cup lemon juice
½ cup lime juice
1 (2 liter) bottle ginger ale,
   chilled

Combine sugar and water in saucepan. Heat until boiling. Boil for 2 minutes, stirring constantly. Remove from heat to cool. Pour into punch bowl and add juices. Cover and refrigerate until ready to serve. Add ginger ale immediately before serving.

Yield: 12 to 16 servings

Bold!

For the Spirit God gave us does not make us timid,
but gives us power, love and self-discipline.
2 TIMOTHY 1:7 NIV

Be bold! You are a child of the King! Though you may feel shy or introverted, you were created with an innate power to proclaim the glory of your Creator. Perhaps your quiet personality causes you to feel uncomfortable about shouting from the rooftops. But God also gave you a deep capacity to love Him and the self-discipline to know how to properly behave in all circumstances. So, the next time you feel an urge to brag on God, go for it! He has more than equipped you with a boldness that just may surprise you.

Super-Easy Chicken Pot Pie

1 (10¾ ounce) can condensed
   cream of chicken soup
1 (9 ounce) package frozen mixed
   vegetables, thawed

1 cup chicken, cooked and cubed
½ cup milk
1 egg
1¼ cups all-purpose baking mix

Mix soup, vegetables, and chicken in 9-inch pie plate. In separate bowl, mix milk, egg, and baking mix; pour over chicken mixture. Bake at 400 degrees for 30 minutes or until golden brown.

Yield: 4 servings

No Worries!

They will have no fear of bad news;
their hearts are steadfast, trusting in the LORD.
PSALM 112:7 NIV

Do you have a tendency to worry? Perhaps you come from a family of worriers, a long line of men and women who can create scenarios that will keep a person up at night out of concern that one of them might actually happen. Well, you can be the first of your family to break that cycle. You do not have to worry. Rest assured that you need have no fear if your heart is steadfast and your trust is in the Lord. He's got this. Yes, He really does. He says so in His Word.

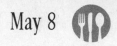

Best Carrot Cake with Cream Cheese Frosting

4 eggs
1½ cups vegetable oil
2 cups sugar
2 teaspoons vanilla
2 cups flour
2 teaspoons baking powder
2 teaspoons baking soda

3 teaspoons cinnamon
1 teaspoon salt
3 cups shredded carrots
½ cup chopped walnuts
½ cup golden raisins
½ cup sweetened, flaked coconut

Frosting:
½ cup butter, softened
1 (8 ounce) package cream
  cheese, softened

1 teaspoon vanilla
1 pound powdered sugar
1 to 2 tablespoons milk

In large mixing bowl, lightly beat eggs. Add oil. Stir in sugar and vanilla. In separate bowl, combine flour, baking powder, baking soda, cinnamon, and salt. Gradually blend dry ingredients into egg mixture. Stir in carrots, walnuts, raisins, and coconut. Divide batter evenly between three greased and floured 9-inch round baking pans. Bake at 350 degrees for 20 to 25 minutes or until toothpick inserted in center comes out clean. Allow cake to cool in pans for 10 minutes, then transfer from pans to wire racks to cool completely. For frosting, beat butter with cream cheese. Add vanilla. Gradually beat in powdered sugar. Beat in enough milk to reach fluffy consistency. Frost cooled cake.

Yield: 12 to 16 servings

Promises

"The LORD he will never leave you nor forsake you."
DEUTERONOMY 31:8 NIV

When you gave your heart to the Lord, He gave you back a promise in return. Just as a parent cares for a child, whether biological or adopted, that parent cares for that child's well-being as long as that child lives. Our God will do the same thing for you. Trust Him. He's always on the job.

Heavenly Broccoli Salad

½ cup celery, finely chopped
½ cup golden raisins, rinsed and drained
½ (3 ounce) jar bacon bits
⅓ cup unsalted sunflower seeds, shelled
1 bunch broccoli, cut into small florets

1 small red onion, finely chopped
½ cup seedless red grapes, halved

Dressing:
½ cup mayonnaise
¼ cup sugar
1 tablespoon cider vinegar

In large bowl, combine celery, raisins, bacon bits, sunflower seeds, broccoli, onion, and grapes; mix thoroughly. Blend dressing ingredients in separate bowl; pour over salad. Cover and refrigerate until ready to serve.

Yield: 4 to 6 servings

Soaking Up Knowledge

Teach me knowledge and good judgment,
for I trust your commands.
PSALM 119:66 NIV

God created His people to be like sponges. In the same way that a sponge soaks up any liquid it's immersed in, the Lord means for us to soak in His knowledge and still yearn for more of Him. How do we do this? First and foremost, by going straight to the book of knowledge He wrote to us: the Bible. Read something you don't understand? Ask Him to explain. How? By the second means of gaining knowledge from God: prayer. Soak in His Word and listen for His instructions, and He will teach you!

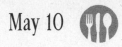

Fruitcake

1 pound pitted dates, cut into
    pieces
1 pound glazed cherries, halved
2 pounds chopped pecans
½ pound shredded coconut

1 pound glazed pineapple, cut
    into pieces
1 (14 ounce) can sweetened
    condensed milk
2 teaspoons vanilla

Grease three 8x4-inch loaf pans well. Mix dates, cherries, pecans, coconut, and pineapple in large bowl. Add sweetened condensed milk and vanilla; blend well. Pack tightly in prepared pans. Bake at 275 degrees for 1½ hours.

Yield: 3 (2 pound) fruitcakes

A Down-in-the-Dumps Day?

*"Have I not commanded you? Be strong and courageous.
Do not be afraid; do not be discouraged, for the LORD
your God will be with you wherever you go."*
JOSHUA 1:9 NIV

Have you ever had one of those down-in-the-dumps days where nothing goes right? One of those days when everything seems to conspire against you to create one disaster after another until you just want to go home and hide your head under the covers? When we become Christians, God does not promise all our troubles will leave us. Indeed, He warns us that just the opposite may happen. So what do we do? We do what the Lord tells us to do: be strong and courageous. God is with us!

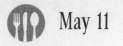

Country Breakfast Casserole

½ pound spicy bulk pork
   sausage
½ cup onion, finely chopped
4 cups diced hash brown
   potatoes

1½ cups Colby/Monterey Jack
   cheese, shredded
3 eggs, beaten
1 cup milk
¼ teaspoon pepper
Salsa

In large skillet, brown sausage and onion; drain. In 8-inch square baking dish, layer potatoes, half of cheese, sausage mixture, and remaining cheese. Combine eggs, milk, and pepper; pour over cheese. Bake uncovered at 350 degrees for 50 to 55 minutes or until knife inserted near center comes out clean. Let stand for 10 minutes. Slice into squares and serve with salsa.

Yield: 4 servings

The Ultimate Superhero

*Jesus looked at them and said, "With man this is impossible,
but not with God; all things are possible with God."*
MARK 10:27 NIV

Do you like superhero movies? Don't you wish you had your own personal superhero who would pop in when you need him and fix anything that's going wrong? Guess what? You already have one, or rather one who is infinitely more powerful than any character the comic book writers can create. Unlike the superheroes you see on the big screen, the Lord has no kryptonite. He is the ultimate power, the ultimate superhero. With Him, anything is possible!

Corn Skillet Fritters

1 cup flour
1 tablespoon sugar
1 teaspoon salt
1 teaspoon baking powder
½ cup milk
2 egg yolks

2 tablespoons butter, melted
2 cups whole-kernel corn,
   drained
2 egg whites, stiffly beaten
Vegetable oil
Maple syrup

Sift dry ingredients together; set aside. In mixing bowl, combine milk, egg yolks, butter, and corn. Add dry ingredients. Fold in beaten egg whites. Drop batter by spoonfuls into hot oil (1 inch deep) in skillet. Cook until golden brown (3 to 4 minutes). Serve hot with maple syrup.

Yield: 10 to 12 servings

Holding Hands

Though he may stumble, he will not fall,
for the LORD upholds him with his hand.
PSALM 37:24 NIV

How many times have you walked through a dark room and stubbed your toe on a table leg or jabbed your foot by stepping on the sharp edge of a toy? Maybe you've slid on a wet towel or hit your funny bone on a doorknob. With each jabbing pain, you promise yourself you won't do that again. But you do. And why? Because without light for a guide, you can't see where you're going. In the same way, walking through life without the light of the Lord means you will fall. However, God promises His people that though we might stumble, we will never fall. Why? Because He is holding our hands.

Veggie Pizza

2 (8 ounce) packages refrigerated crescent rolls
1 (8 ounce) package cream cheese
1 cup mayonnaise
1 envelope buttermilk ranch dressing mix
Vegetables of your choice, chopped
½ cup cheddar cheese, shredded

Pat crescent roll dough out to cover jelly roll pan. Bake at 375 degrees for 7 minutes. Cool. Blend cream cheese, mayonnaise, and ranch dressing mix. Spread over crust. Top with chopped vegetables and cheese.

Yield: 6 servings

The One Treasure

"Provide purses for yourselves that will not wear out,
a treasure in heaven that will not fail,
where no thief comes near and no moth destroys."
LUKE 12:33 NIV

Most women own more than one purse. Many make purse shopping a favorite way to pass an afternoon. Others go so far as to collect purses in many colors and often with extremely high price tags. To these women, their purses are their treasures. Likewise, some men have their own affinity for collecting items of value, be it cars or golf clubs or something else. God says those things are fine, but if they are not taken or destroyed, they will still someday pass away. The one treasure that will not fail, will not be stolen, and certainly will never be destroyed awaits you in heaven. Consider that and be thankful. What a gift!

Curried Honey Chicken

¼ cup butter
1 cup honey
¼ cup Dijon mustard
2 teaspoons curry powder

1 teaspoon salt
1½ pounds boneless, skinless
   chicken breasts, cut into
   chunks

In saucepan, melt butter and whisk in honey, mustard, curry, and salt. Add chicken and stir to coat. Place chicken mixture in 2-quart baking dish. Bake at 375 degrees for 45 minutes, basting occasionally. Chicken will be golden when done. Serve over hot cooked rice.

Yield: 4 servings

God Listens

*Do not be anxious about anything, but in every situation,
by prayer and petition, with thanksgiving,
present your requests to God.*
PHILIPPIANS 4:6 NIV

When bad things are happening, what do you do first? Do you complain? Perhaps you worry. God says to skip those things and do the one thing that works: take your concerns to Him. Tell Him how you feel about your current situation. Even though He already knows, He wants to hear it from you. Then, ask Him to change things. He might, or He might not. Tell Him you're fine with whichever result happens. Most importantly, though, do not forget to thank Him for being there to hear your prayer and to act. God listens. He really does.

Butterscotch-Pumpkin Bundt Cake

1 (11 ounce) package
  butterscotch chips, divided
2 cups flour
1¾ cups sugar
1 tablespoon baking powder
1½ teaspoons cinnamon
1 teaspoon salt

½ teaspoon nutmeg
1 cup pumpkin puree
½ cup vegetable oil
3 large eggs
1 teaspoon vanilla
3 tablespoons powdered sugar

Prepare 12-cup Bundt pan. Melt 1 cup butterscotch chips in small microwave-safe bowl, on medium power for 1 minute; stir. Microwave at additional 10-second intervals, stirring until chips are completely melted. Cool to room temperature. In medium bowl, combine flour, sugar, baking powder, cinnamon, salt, and nutmeg. In large mixing bowl, whisk together melted chips, pumpkin, oil, eggs, and vanilla. Stir in dry mixture. Blend in remaining chips. Pour batter into prepared Bundt pan. Bake at 350 degrees for 40 to 50 minutes or until wooden toothpick inserted in cake comes out clean. Cool in pan on wire rack for 30 minutes; remove from pan to cool completely. Sprinkle with powdered sugar.

Yield: 16 servings

There Is a Time

*There is a time for everything,
and a season for every activity under the heavens.*
Ecclesiastes 3:1 niv

"It's not time yet!" How many times as a child did you hear that from your parents on Christmas morning? Perhaps you've been pregnant with a baby that ignored due dates and lingered longer than you and your anxiously awaiting family wanted. Perhaps you've been praying for something and it feels like God is ignoring you. He isn't. However, His time schedule is the only one that matters. There is a time. Wait for it. God is never late.

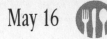

Taco Salad

1 pound ground beef
1 envelope taco seasoning
1 large or 2 small heads lettuce, shredded
1 (15 ounce) can kidney beans, drained and rinsed
2 cups shredded cheddar cheese

1 to 2 large tomatoes, chopped (optional)
1 cup sliced black olives (optional)
1 large bottle spicy french dressing
1 small bag tortilla chips

Brown ground beef; drain. Add taco seasoning with water as called for on package and cook until thickened. Cool. Place meat with lettuce, kidney beans, cheese, tomatoes, and olives in large bowl. Coat with dressing. Just before serving, crumble chips on top and toss into salad.

Yield: 6 to 8 servings

What Is Faith?

Though you have not seen him, you love him; and even though you do not see him now, you believe in him and are filled with an inexpressible and glorious joy.
1 PETER 1:8 NIV

What does faith look like for you? Is it a belief that God is who He says He is? Perhaps it is a deep knowing that He will do what He says He will do. Maybe it is both—and more. Beyond all this, it is the understanding that despite the fact we cannot see or touch this God of the universe who rules over us and yet loves us like His own children, we are still filled with a deep and abiding joy at the fact that He is ours. And He always will be.

Sausage 'n' Cheese Grits Casserole

4 cups water
1 teaspoon salt
1 cup quick grits
4 eggs, beaten
1 pound sausage, browned

1½ cups shredded cheddar
  cheese, divided
1 cup milk
½ cup margarine

Grease 3-quart baking dish and set aside. Bring water and salt to boil in large saucepan. Slowly stir in grits; cook for 4 to 5 minutes, stirring occasionally. Remove from heat. Stir grits mixture into eggs; return all to saucepan. Add sausage, 1 cup cheese, milk, and margarine; blend well. Pour into baking dish; sprinkle with remaining cheese. Bake at 350 degrees for approximately 1 hour. Let stand for 10 minutes before serving.

Yield: 6 servings

Nothing Is Too Hard for God

"I am the LORD, the God of all mankind. Is anything too hard for me?"
JEREMIAH 32:27 NIV

Sometimes things are just hard. Whether you're a child learning to ride a bike or tie a shoe or an adult figuring out how to understand God's will for your life, difficulties are a part of living. They are also meant to be overcome, aren't they? While a little boy may have trouble learning to ride a bike, he will someday manage the feat and move on to other things. Soon the little girl who is frustrated at trying to tie her shoes will forget that she ever had such a problem. And that adult who is wondering about God's will? The Lord Himself will answer that question. It's too hard, you say? Nothing is too hard for God.

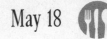

Linda Germany's Yeast Bread

½ cup butter
2 cups milk
2 packages dry yeast
1 tablespoon sugar
1 cup water

2 eggs
2½ teaspoons salt
½ cup sugar
7 to 8 cups flour

Melt butter in milk on low heat (don't scald). Dissolve yeast and 1 tablespoon sugar in water. Mix eggs, salt, and ½ cup sugar. Combine buttery milk and liquid yeast. Gradually work in flour, kneading until elastic and velvety. Let rise for 30 minutes, then knead again. Let rise for 1 hour, then form into 4 loaves. Let rise for additional 1 to 2 hours and bake at 350 degrees for 25 to 30 minutes.

Yield: 4 loaves of bread

The Mighty Warrior

When the angel of the LORD appeared to Gideon, he said, "The LORD is with you, mighty warrior." "Pardon me, my lord," Gideon replied, "but if the LORD is with us, why has all this happened to us?" . . . . The LORD turned to him and said, "Go in the strength you have and save Israel out of Midian's hand. Am I not sending you?" "Pardon me, my lord," Gideon replied, "but how can I save Israel? My clan is the weakest in Manasseh, and I am the least in my family." The LORD answered, "I will be with you."
JUDGES 6:12–16 NIV

Are you like Gideon? He was a mighty warrior, even God said so, and yet when God speaks to him, he sounds defeated. Yes, things had happened to Gideon's tribe that he hadn't expected or liked, but given his history with the Lord, why does Gideon question the Lord when He speaks? Had he forgotten? Perhaps, or maybe he was just too tired, too involved in his circumstances to remember that God was sovereign. Have you ever felt like God's mighty warrior Gideon? The same answer God gave him applies to you no matter the situation: the Lord will be with you.

Sausage Balls

3 cups biscuit baking mix
1 pound sausage
4 cups shredded cheddar cheese
½ cup Parmesan cheese

½ cup milk
½ teaspoon dried rosemary
   leaves

Mix all ingredients together until well blended. Mold into 1-inch balls. Bake at 350 degrees for 20 minutes.

Yield: 100 sausage balls

Noah and His Sons

Then God blessed Noah and his sons, saying to them,
"Be fruitful and increase in number and fill the earth."
GENESIS 9:1 NIV

Have you ever planted a garden? First you till the soil to break up the rocks and give the seeds a good place to get their start. Then comes the planting, a purposeful application of seed to soil that is followed by watering and the hope of just enough sunny days and lack of predators to provide a bountiful result at harvest. So it was with Noah. God blessed them so that their lives would produce fruit and their love of the Lord would be passed down through the generations. Perhaps you've prayed that same prayer over your family. If not, maybe today is the day to begin.

Family Dinnertime Tip

Volunteer your time—or your talents—to a worthy cause. You may never know the impact you have on others. After all, kindness is contagious!

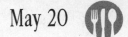

Chicken Waikiki

1 whole chicken, cut up
1 teaspoon salt
¼ teaspoon pepper
½ cup flour
⅓ cup canola oil
1 (20 ounce) can pineapple slices
   in juice

1 cup sugar
2 tablespoons cornstarch
¾ cup cider vinegar
1 tablespoon soy sauce
¼ teaspoon ground ginger
1 chicken bouillon cube
1 large green bell pepper, sliced

Sprinkle each piece of chicken with salt and pepper, dredge in flour, then brown in hot oil. Transfer browned chicken to roasting pan. Drain pineapple juice into 2-cup measuring cup. Add enough water to juice to equal 1¼ cups liquid. In saucepan, combine sugar, cornstarch, pineapple juice and water mixture, vinegar, soy sauce, ginger, and bouillon. Bring liquid to boil, and boil for 2 minutes. Pour sauce over chicken. Bake uncovered at 350 degrees for 30 minutes. Add slices of pineapple and green pepper, and bake for additional 30 minutes. Serve over hot cooked rice.

Yield: 4 servings

The God of Redemption

"But when all goes well with you, remember me and show me kindness; mention me to Pharaoh and get me out of this prison."
GENESIS 40:14 NIV

Joseph was one of the most patient and optimistic men in the Bible, and the most persecuted. First, his own brothers sold him into slavery, and then he was sent to prison after being wrongly convicted of a crime he did not commit. When two of his cellmates are released, he asks them to speak on his behalf, but they forget. Forget! You'd think this would make him finally give up, but instead Joseph continues to believe God will save him. If you've read the story, you know God shows up and redeems Joseph in a mighty way. Are you living a life in need of redeeming? Maybe you or someone you love is in need of a mighty God to do a mighty work. Hold on. Be patient. He will!

Chocolate Cream Cheese Bundt Cake

1¼ cups semisweet chocolate
    chips
2 (8 ounce) packages cream
    cheese, softened
¾ cup sugar
3 tablespoons milk
1 package chocolate cake mix
¾ cup brewed coffee, cooled

¼ cup vegetable oil
3 large eggs, lightly beaten
⅔ cup chopped nuts

Glaze:
½ cup heavy cream
½ cup semisweet chocolate chips

Grease and flour Bundt pan. Microwave chocolate chips on medium power for 1 minute; stir. Continue to heat at 10-second intervals until chocolate is melted completely. Cool to room temperature. In medium mixing bowl, combine cream cheese, sugar, milk, and melted chocolate. Beat until smooth. Set aside. In another bowl, combine cake mix, coffee, oil, and eggs; beat for 4 minutes. Pour into prepared pan and sprinkle with nuts. Spoon cream cheese mixture over cake mix, but do not allow cream cheese mixture to touch sides of pan. Bake at 350 degrees for 55 to 65 minutes, until top springs back when pressed lightly in center. Cool in pan for 1 hour before inverting. For glaze, heat cream in small saucepan over medium heat until cream just begins to boil. Remove from heat and stir in chocolate chips until melted and smooth. Drizzle warm glaze over cooled cake. Store covered in refrigerator.

Yield: 12 servings

An Encouragement Dare

But encourage one another daily, as long as it is called "Today."
HEBREWS 3:13 NIV

To some, the gift of encouragement is second nature. Others must work at it. Perhaps you are the latter. Why not challenge yourself to offer a word of encouragement to at least one person every day? Perhaps this could even be a family project, something you can report about at dinnertime. Think of the smiles you and your family could cause!

Grated Potato Salad

6 cups potatoes, peeled, cooked, and grated

6 hard-boiled eggs, peeled and chopped

1 cup mayonnaise

¾ cup sugar

¼ cup milk

2 tablespoons cider vinegar

2 teaspoons salt

1½ teaspoons mustard

In large bowl, combine potatoes and eggs. In separate bowl, whisk remaining ingredients; pour over potato and egg mixture. Stir until mixed thoroughly. Cover and refrigerate for 4 hours before serving.

Yield: 10 servings

Choose Your Words

My son, if your heart is wise, then my heart will be glad indeed; my inmost being will rejoice when your lips speak what is right.
PROVERBS 23:15–16 NIV

Have you ever said something and then cringed because you knew you should not have said it? Perhaps you wished you could rewind time and change a response or maybe even the lack of a response. Words are mighty things, sometimes sharper than even the sword. Think before you speak. Consider the wisdom you have gained through your study of God's Word and choose words that build up rather than tear down, words that are right in the Lord's eyes. Not only will the recipient of those words be glad, but so will God.

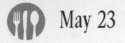

Chicken 'n' Corn Bread Casserole

¼ cup margarine
1 small onion, chopped
2 stalks celery, chopped
1 cup flour, divided
1 teaspoon salt
⅛ teaspoon dried rosemary
2⅔ cups milk, divided
1 cup chicken broth

2½ cups chicken, cooked and cubed
½ cup cornmeal
1 tablespoon sugar
1½ tablespoons baking powder
½ teaspoon salt
1 egg
3 tablespoons vegetable oil

In skillet, heat margarine and sauté onion and celery. Sprinkle ½ cup flour over contents of skillet and blend. Season with salt and rosemary. Over low heat, slowly blend 2 cups milk into margarine. Add broth, stirring constantly until mixture thickens. Add chicken and pour all into 7x12-inch baking dish. Sift together cornmeal, ½ cup flour, sugar, baking powder, and salt. In separate dish, beat egg, then stir in ⅔ cup milk and oil. Blend egg mixture into sifted mixture. Pour over chicken mixture and bake at 425 degrees for 20 minutes or until browned.

Yield: 6 servings

Looking at the Heart

But the LORD said to Samuel, "Do not consider his appearance or his height, for I have rejected him. The LORD does not look at the things people look at. People look at the outward appearance, but the LORD looks at the heart."
1 SAMUEL 16:7 NIV

We love to compare don't we? Women might see an actress on television and think they could never look like her. Men may wonder if they ever have a car like his, a job like his, maybe even a wife or girlfriend like his. For kids, the comparison might be clothes, video games, or bikes. However God says none of those things are important to Him when considering a person's worth. Instead, He looks inside each of us to judge our hearts. Perhaps we should do the same.

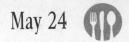

Pizza Spuds

4 potatoes
½ cup pizza sauce
⅔ cup pepperoni, chopped

¼ cup grated Parmesan cheese
¼ cup mozzarella cheese

Poke clean potatoes with fork. Microwave for 6 minutes. Rotate and turn potatoes; microwave an additional 4 to 6 minutes. Let stand 5 minutes. Slice open potatoes. Spoon in pizza sauce, pepperoni, and cheeses. Microwave for 1 to 2 minutes to melt cheeses.

Yield: 4 servings

Syncing Calendars

"So do not worry, saying, 'What shall we eat?' or 'What shall we drink?' or 'What shall we wear?' For the pagans run after all these things, and your heavenly Father knows that you need them. But seek first his kingdom and his righteousness, and all these things will be given to you as well.
MATTHEW 6:31–33 NIV

Are you a planner? Do you have a schedule affixed to your refrigerator that's color coded and broken up into different days of the week and weeks of the month? Perhaps you've got a calendar loaded onto your phone that syncs up with your computers at work and at home. Or maybe you prefer to keep up with things through a spreadsheet or even a paper calendar with lovely photos on it. There's nothing wrong with being organized. However, when organization turns to obsession, God says to take a step back and consider an important fact. He is in control. He decides what will happen tomorrow, next week, next year. Next time you sync your calendars, keep that in mind. And thank Him for today!

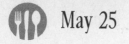

Home-Style Sausage, Cabbage, and Potatoes

4 potatoes, peeled and cut into ¼-inch chunks
½ medium onion, sliced
2 cups cabbage, cut into large chunks

1 pound smoked sausage or ham, cut into chunks
½ teaspoon salt
¼ teaspoon pepper
1 cup water

Combine all ingredients in large saucepan. Bring to boil. Cover and cook over low heat for 15 to 25 minutes or until potatoes are tender.

Yield: 4 to 6 servings

Where No One Walks Alone

So, if you think you are standing firm, be careful that you don't fall!
1 CORINTHIANS 10:12 NIV

Are you a klutz? If there's a pebble anywhere between the front door of the mall and your car, are you the one person who walks through the parking lot that day who will tumble right over it? Maybe you are the opposite. You are sure footed and never miss a chance to step around an obstacle. In the same way that we can fall in a parking lot, so we can fall in our walk with God. It is those who think they are immune to tripping who are at the most risk of landing upside down with their faces in the gravel. So stand firm, but hold tight to God's hand. That way you're not trying to walk alone.

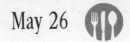
Chocolate Sour Cream Sheet Cake

1 cup water
1 cup butter or margarine
¼ cup cocoa
2 large eggs, lightly beaten
1 (8 ounce) carton sour cream
2 cups sugar
2 cups flour
1 teaspoon baking soda
⅛ teaspoon salt

½ cup semisweet chocolate chips

Icing:
6 tablespoons milk
6 tablespoons cocoa
1 cup butter or margarine
1 pound powdered sugar
1½ teaspoons vanilla

In medium saucepan, combine water, butter, and cocoa. Bring to boil, and boil for two minutes. Set aside to cool slightly. In mixing bowl, blend eggs, sour cream, sugar, flour, baking soda, and salt. Add cocoa mixture and blend well. Stir in chocolate chips. Spread batter into greased and floured 10x15-inch jelly roll pan. Bake at 375 degrees for 20 to 25 minutes. Cool slightly before icing. For icing, in saucepan, boil milk, cocoa, and butter for three minutes. Remove from heat. Beat in powdered sugar and vanilla until icing is smooth and glossy. Pour over warm cake and spread evenly.

Yield: 24 servings

Hearing the Cry of the Poor

*Whoever shuts their ears to the cry of the poor
will also cry out and not be answered.*
PROVERBS 21:13 NIV

It is so easy to turn your head when someone comes to the car and asks for money, isn't it? Just pretend the beggar is not there, wait until the light turns green, and then drive away. What if you knew that ignoring the cry of the poor would result in God ignoring your cry in times of need? That's a sobering thought, isn't it? What can you and your family do to respond to the cry of the poor? Strategize now so that you will be prepared.

Roasted Ranch Potato Salad

4 cups small red potatoes, unpeeled and cut into 1-inch chunks

½ teaspoon garlic powder

¼ teaspoon salt

⅛ teaspoon pepper

½ cup ranch dressing

3 to 4 slices bacon, cooked crisp and crumbled

2 hard-boiled eggs, peeled and chopped

2 tablespoons green onion, sliced

Spray baking sheet with cooking oil. Spread out potato chunks in single layer. Sprinkle with garlic powder, salt, and pepper. Spray with more oil. Bake at 425 degrees for 30 to 35 minutes or until potatoes are tender and golden brown. Stir potatoes halfway through baking. Blend dressing, bacon, eggs, and onion in large bowl. Add potatoes; mix lightly. Enjoy warm or chilled.

Yield: 5 servings

Live like Jesus

Whoever claims to live in him must live as Jesus did.
1 JOHN 2:6 NIV

Do the people who know you well see Jesus in you? Do your neighbors and coworkers see you and think of Jesus? What about your family? Are you walking and talking like Jesus in their presence? And what about when you are alone, just you and God? How then do you behave? God says if you claim to live in Christ, you must do all you can to behave as Christ did. Of course, we are not perfect like Him, but the Lord says we must try our best. What can you do today to begin trying to walk more like Jesus?

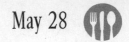

Chicken 'n' Wild Rice Casserole

3 cups cooked chicken, cubed
2½ cups wild rice, cooked
1 (10¾ ounce) can condensed
cream of chicken soup
1 (10¾ ounce) can condensed
cream of mushroom soup

1 cup milk
1 (6 ounce) can sliced
mushrooms, drained
½ cup onion, finely chopped
½ cup green bell pepper,
chopped

Combine all ingredients and pour into large casserole dish. Bake at 350 degrees for 45 minutes.

Yield: 4 to 6 servings

God Stands Firm

*For he spoke, and it came to be;
he commanded, and it stood firm.*
PSALM 33:9 NIV

Can you imagine a God so all-powerful that by His words alone, He created entire worlds? He spoke into existence the skies and the seas, the mountains and the plains, and it is by His command that you and I are here on this earth today. Mere humans cannot understand the power of our Lord, but we can understand this: what He commanded came into being, and what He created stands firm. We serve a God who does not change. In a world where everything seems to change, how reassuring it is to know that!

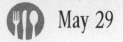

Blue Deviled Eggs

12 eggs
½ cup (2 ounces) blue cheese,
    crumbled
1 tablespoon parsley

¼ teaspoon celery seed
¼ teaspoon pepper
⅓ cup real mayonnaise
½ teaspoon hot sauce

In large saucepan, place eggs in enough water to cover them and bring to boil. Reduce heat to slow boil for 12 minutes. Cool and peel eggs. Cut eggs in half, remove yolks, and set whites aside. In small mixing bowl, mash yolks with fork; stir in blue cheese, parsley, celery seed, and pepper. Blend mayonnaise and hot sauce; add to yolk mixture, mixing until well blended. Evenly fill whites. Refrigerate eggs until ready to serve.

Yield: 24 servings

The Ultimate Judge

"This is what the LORD Almighty said: 'Administer true justice; show mercy and compassion to one another.'"
ZECHARIAH 7:9 NIV

Do you like watching courtroom dramas on television? You might be surprised to know that much of what you see on television is nothing like what actually happens in a courtroom trial. For that matter, most court cases never make it into the courtroom because they are either settled before trial or ruled on by a judge. In the same way, we should use restraint in dealing with those around us. Don't force an argument all the way to the point of no return. Consider the path of reconciliation. Let go and let God handle things. He is the ultimate Judge anyway.

Family Dinnertime Tip

A no-mess method for deviling your eggs is to place your filling ingredients in a plastic bag. Massage the bag to mix, then cut a small hole in one corner of the bag. Squeeze the filling out of the bag and directly into the hollows of the egg whites.

Grandma Shutt's Meat Loaf

4 pounds ground beef
1⅓ cups oats, uncooked
⅔ cup onion, chopped
2 teaspoons salt

½ teaspoon pepper
2 cups tomato juice
2 eggs, beaten

Combine all ingredients; mix thoroughly. Pack firmly into ungreased loaf pan. Bake at 350 degrees for 1 hour and 15 minutes. Let stand for 5 minutes before serving.

Yield: 8 to 10 servings

Tell Him Everything

All my longings lie open before you, Lord;
my sighing is not hidden from you.
PSALM 38:9 NIV

Are you honest with God when it comes to your deepest desires and longings? Do you tell Him everything, leaving out nothing? God understands. He hears every sigh. There is solace in knowing that no matter the situation, you never walk through it alone. Whether you are traveling through the valley or resting on the mountaintop with the whole world at your feet, God is there with you. Tell Him everything. He already knows.

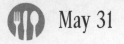

Classic Cherry Cheesecake

1½ cups graham cracker crumbs
2 tablespoons sugar
¼ cup plus 2 tablespoons butter
   or margarine, melted
1 teaspoon grated lemon rind
3 (8 ounce) packages cream
   cheese, softened

1 cup sugar
3 eggs
½ teaspoon vanilla
1 (16 ounce) carton sour cream
3 tablespoons sugar
½ teaspoon vanilla
1 (21 ounce) can cherry pie filling

In medium mixing bowl, combine graham cracker crumbs, 2 tablespoons sugar, butter, and lemon rind. Blend well. Press mixture firmly in bottom and up sides of 9-inch springform pan. Bake at 350 degrees for 5 minutes; set aside. Increase oven temperature to 375 degrees. In large mixing bowl, beat cream cheese until light and fluffy; gradually add 1 cup sugar and beat well. Add eggs, one at a time, beating well after each addition. Stir in ½ teaspoon vanilla. Pour cream cheese mixture into prepared crust. Bake for 30 to 35 minutes or until set.

   Increase oven temperature to 475 degrees. Beat sour cream at medium speed for 2 minutes. Add 3 tablespoons sugar and vanilla; beat 1 additional minute. Spread sour cream mixture evenly over cheesecake. Bake cheesecake for 5 to 7 minutes or until topping is bubbly. Remove from oven and place on wire rack. Let cool in pan to room temperature. Top with pie filling. Chill at least 8 hours. To serve, carefully remove sides of springform pan.

Yield: 10 to 12 servings

Bold, Tenacious Prayers

*Then Jesus used this story to teach his followers
that they should always pray and not give up.*
LUKE 18:1 NIV

God responds to bold, tenacious prayers. He loves hearing from you and when you ask for big things. Be bold for Him. That's what Jesus taught His disciples, and that's still what God asks from us today. What bold, tenacious prayer can you pray today?

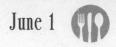

Hawaiian Fruit Salad

¼ cup mayonnaise
1 tablespoon sugar
½ teaspoon lemon juice
¼ teaspoon salt
½ cup whipping cream
1 large red apple, chopped

1 large yellow apple, chopped
1 large banana, sliced
½ cup walnuts, chopped
Lettuce
½ cup flaked coconut, toasted

In large bowl, blend mayonnaise, sugar, lemon juice, and salt; set aside. In separate bowl, whip cream to form soft peaks; fold into mayonnaise mixture. Gently stir in apples, banana, and walnuts; chill. Line bowl with lettuce; add chilled fruit mixture. Garnish with toasted flaked coconut.

Yield: 6 servings

Because He Says So!

Give us aid against the enemy, for human help is worthless.
With God we will gain the victory.
PSALM 108:12–13 NIV

Looking to people to solve problems is never going to work. Perhaps you've already discovered this. Or maybe you believe the opposite is true because you've always had success in joining with someone else to conquer your troubles. In either case, know that going to God is always the best choice. Ultimately, in God you will gain the victory. Why? Because He says so. What can you give to God today?

Tuna Noodle Casserole

1 (10¾ ounce) can condensed
   cream of mushroom soup
½ cup milk
1 cup peas, cooked

2 (6 ounce) cans tuna, drained
   and flaked
2 cups egg noodles, cooked
2 tablespoons dry bread crumbs
1 tablespoon margarine, melted

Mix soup, milk, peas, tuna, and egg noodles in 1½-quart casserole dish. Bake at 400 degrees for 20 minutes. Stir. Mix bread crumbs with margarine and sprinkle on top of casserole. Bake an additional 5 minutes before serving.

Yield: 4 to 6 servings

Perfect Peace

You will keep in perfect peace those whose minds are steadfast, because they trust in you.
Isaiah 26:3 niv

Perhaps you feel that the only way to find peace is to control every facet of your life. You organize everything on your busy schedule and think that you have it all handled. And yet, you just don't feel at peace. There's something missing. Perfect peace is available to all who keep their minds on God. Trust Him to be the one in control. It won't be easy, but it will definitely be worth it!

Family Dinnertime Tip

Nifty napkin rings for your family dinner start with a hodgepodge of old spoons and forks from family collections or flea markets. Use your hands to bend the pliable ones around a paper towel tube. Let the ends meet side by side, and you have a delightful napkin ring. Make an extra set for a gift.

Cinnamon Pears

1 (29 ounce) can Bartlett
   pear halves

4 tablespoons red cinnamon
   candies

Drain juice from pears into small saucepan. Add candies to juice and cook until candy is dissolved. Remove from heat and place pears back in juice. As liquid cools, pears will absorb red coloring.

Yield: 6 servings

Wonderfully Made

*For you created my inmost being; you knit me together in my
mother's womb. I praise you because I am
fearfully and wonderfully made.*
PSALM 139:13–14 NIV

God knew you before you were born. He created you, knit you together in your mother's womb, and knew exactly who you would be and what you would be like before you ever drew a breath outside your mother's body. You are no accident. You were perfectly created and perfectly planned by the God of the universe to be uniquely you. Praise Him for what He has created, and do not forget He made you special!

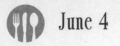

Orange Tea

7 cups water
1 (12 ounce) can frozen orange
   juice concentrate
½ cup sugar

2 tablespoons lemon juice
5 teaspoons instant tea mix
1 teaspoon whole cloves

In large saucepan, combine water, orange juice concentrate, sugar, lemon juice, and tea mix. Place cloves in tea ball or cheesecloth bag and add to saucepan. Simmer for 15 to 20 minutes. Remove cloves and serve hot.

Yield: 8 servings

Be Relevant

Among those who were chosen were some from Judah:
Daniel, Hananiah, Mishael and Azariah.
DANIEL 1:6 NIV

The book of Daniel begins with the mention of the names of three young men, three among many, who were conscripted into the king's service. These young men were the best of the best from across all the lands that had been overtaken by the king, and yet of those only three are named in the Bible. Why do you think that is? Perhaps it is because all the others, and there well might have been thousands, were absorbed into the culture and became irrelevant and unusable by God. They became like the world into which they were living. Our purpose is to be relevant, to be usable by God. Watch that you do not become one of those whose names are not worthy of record. Be relevant and watch Him use you!

Hash

1 to 2 tablespoons canola oil
2 cups potatoes, cooked and
   cubed
1 cup beef roast, cooked and
   chopped
2 tablespoons onion, chopped

2 tablespoons green bell pepper,
   chopped (optional)
1 tablespoon Worcestershire
   sauce
2 eggs
Salt and pepper

Heat oil in skillet. Add potatoes, beef roast, onion, and green pepper to
the skillet. Heat through, then blend in Worcestershire sauce; break eggs
over mixture and stir with spatula until eggs are set. Season with salt and
pepper.

Yield: 2 servings

Do What You're Told!

But you must return to your God,
maintain love and justice, and wait for your God always.
HOSEA 12:6 NIV

In any argument or difficult situation, the first thing the Lord wants you
to do is to go to Him, not your mother or your best friend or your spouse,
but directly to Him. Next, God commands that you are to show love to the
other person whether you feel like it or not. Yes, that is difficult, and yet
the Lord tells us it is essential. Finally, you are called to play fair even if
the other person is not. But that's not fair, you might
say. When you start feeling wronged, remember
God is always there to provide justice for you.
Just wait and see. And while you're waiting, do
what you're told!

Cranberry Bundt Cake

2 cups flour
1 teaspoon baking powder
¾ teaspoon baking soda
½ teaspoon salt
⅔ cup butter or margarine,
  softened
1 cup sugar

3 eggs
1½ teaspoons vanilla
1 (8 ounce) carton sour cream
¾ cup chopped dried cranberries
⅓ cup chopped pecans
Powdered sugar

In small bowl, combine flour, baking powder, baking soda, and salt. Set aside. In mixing bowl, cream butter with sugar. Add eggs one at a time, beating well after each addition. Stir in vanilla. Add dry ingredients to creamed mixture alternately with sour cream. Stir in cranberries and pecans and pour into greased and floured 8-inch Bundt cake pan. Bake at 350 degrees for 45 to 50 minutes or until wooden toothpick inserted in cake comes out clean. Cool for 10 minutes before removing from pan. Dust with powdered sugar.

Yield: 8 to 10 servings

Just a Closer Walk

*He has shown you, O mortal, what is good. And what does
the LORD require of you? To act justly and to love
mercy and to walk humbly with your God.*
MICAH 6:8 NIV

Walk with God. Don't you love that image? Just you and God strolling along together. The Bible tells us God is a walker, not a runner. Could you keep up if He was running through your life? Probably not! So how do you walk with Him? You walk humbly. Do not treat God like His only job is to follow you around and carry your burdens. God always allows us to walk with Him. It is an honor that we should never take lightly. Never forget His authority. It is never our place to dictate the pace. Instead, allow Him to lead. Of the two of you, He is the one who knows the destination.

Cheesy Bacon Cauliflower Salad

1 large head lettuce, chopped
1 head cauliflower, chopped
½ red onion, chopped
1 (10 ounce) bag frozen peas
1 teaspoon sugar

1 (16 ounce) jar mayonnaise
2 cups shredded cheddar cheese
1 pound thin-sliced bacon,
   cooked, drained, and crumbled
6 hard-boiled eggs

In large bowl, mix lettuce, cauliflower, onion, and peas. In separate bowl, mix sugar and mayonnaise; spread on top of salad mixture then sprinkle with cheese and bacon. Cover and refrigerate overnight. When ready to serve, chop hard-boiled eggs and add to salad.

Yield: 12 to 16 servings

Don't Look Away

*Immediately Jesus reached out his hand and caught him [Peter].
"You of little faith," he said, "why did you doubt?"*
MATTHEW 14:31 NIV

Jesus trusted Peter to do the impossible, but only with His help. Peter took that first step toward Jesus in faith because He understood Jesus never fails. Only when he looked away did Peter get into trouble. In the same way, God can do the miraculous in your life if you let Him. All you have to do is get out of the boat and take a step in His direction. Keep your eyes on Him and don't look away!

Family Dinnertime Tip

When boiling eggs, add a tablespoon of vinegar to the water to keep the eggs from cooking out if they crack. Also, remove them from the heat immediately and add cold water to the pan to cool them quickly. They will peel more easily.

Crisp Rice Casserole

2 cups water
1 cup rice, uncooked
4 cups crisp rice cereal, divided
1 pound sausage
1 small onion, chopped

2 cups shredded cheddar cheese
3 eggs
2 (10¾ ounce) cans condensed
   cream of celery soup
Milk

In medium saucepan, bring water to boil. Add rice, cover, and cook over low heat for 20 minutes. Grease 7x12-inch baking dish and cover bottom with 2 cups of cereal. Brown sausage and onion; drain and layer over cereal. Top with cooked rice and cheese. In bowl, beat eggs and blend in soup and half soup can of milk. Pour egg mixture over cheese, poking a few holes down through layers to allow egg mixture to soak through. Add 2 cups cereal on top. Bake at 400 degrees for 30 to 40 minutes or until bubbly.

Yield: 4 servings

The Surest Steps

*The Sovereign LORD is my strength; he makes my feet
like the feet of a deer, he enables me to tread on the heights.*
HABAKKUK 3:19 NIV

Can you imagine having the feet of a deer? If you had them, you could climb mountains and never worry about slipping or falling. You could race through uneven terrain surely and quickly and would never have to be concerned with stumbling. In the same way that God created the deer to easily move through its world, He also created you with the same ability. Through Him, you can reach the heights; you can travel treacherous ground and find a sure spot on the slipperiest slope. Isn't that something to ponder?

Dried Beef Ball

1 (8 ounce) package cream
   cheese, softened
¼ cup grated Parmesan cheese

1 tablespoon prepared
   horseradish
1 cup dried beef, finely cut

Blend cheeses and horseradish; form into ball. Chill overnight. Roll in dried beef pieces. Serve with assorted crackers.

Yield: 8 to 10 servings

Looking Up

Taking the five loaves and two fish and looking up to heaven, he gave thanks and broke them. Then he gave them to the disciples to distribute to the people. They all ate and were satisfied, and the disciples picked up twelve basketfuls of broken pieces that were left over.
LUKE 9:16–17 NIV

Looking up to heaven, He gave thanks. Did you catch that? Jesus paused to make a request to His Father in heaven and then He gave thanks—before God did anything in response—and what happened? Not only were the loaves and fishes multiplied in such numbers that all were fed, but there was an abundance left over after all were finished eating. When Jesus prayed, He expected His Father would answer. In the same way, we, too, should expect we will be heard and God will respond. Thank Him first and then wait for His answer. Step back and watch for the miracle. Your Father in heaven is fully capable to respond just as you are fully capable of asking.

Cheesy Chicken Bake

5 boneless, skinless chicken
   breasts
1 (10¾ ounce) can condensed
   cream of chicken soup

5 slices American cheese
Butter
Garlic salt

Place chicken in shallow baking pan. Pour soup over chicken pieces, then top with cheese slices. Place chunk of butter on each piece and sprinkle with garlic salt. Bake at 350 degrees for 45 to 50 minutes. Serve over rice or noodles, if desired.

Yield: 5 servings

Time to Soar

Those who hope in the LORD will renew their strength.
They will soar on wings like eagles; they will run and
not grow weary, they will walk and not be faint.
ISAIAH 40:31 NIV

Some days it can be hard just to get out of bed. Maybe you had a sleepless night or perhaps worries kept you tossing and turning well into the wee hours. Or maybe you are suffering from an illness that has you wondering if you'll ever get your strength back. Whatever the cause, there is a cure. Hope in the Lord. Turn everything over to Him, from anxiety to sickness. He promises to refresh you, to give you the strength you did not know you have. What are you waiting for? It's time to soar!

Glazed Ham

1 (7 to 10 pound) fully cooked
  ham
1 (2 liter) bottle Dr Pepper
1 tablespoon ground cloves
1 teaspoon cinnamon
Whole cloves

First Basting Mix:
Dr Pepper
1 teaspoon cinnamon
1 teaspoon dry mustard

Second Basting Mix:
1 cup brown sugar, packed
Dr Pepper

Place ham in roasting pan and cover with mixture of Dr Pepper, ground cloves, and cinnamon. Bake ham at 325 degrees for 1½ hours. Remove from oven and score top of ham. Stud ham with cloves.

For first basting, add enough Dr Pepper to form paste with cinnamon and mustard. Brush mixture over scored ham. For second basting, mix together brown sugar and enough Dr Pepper to form paste. Brush final mixture over ham. Bake an additional 1½ hours or until ham reaches an internal temperature of 140 degrees.

Yield: 12 to 14 servings

The Ultimate Sacrifice

*"Greater love has no one than this:
to lay down one's life for one's friends."*
JOHN 15:13 NIV

How often have we heard that a soldier has made the ultimate sacrifice? We all understand what that means, but can we see it from God's perspective? God calls us to think less of ourselves and more of others. Thus, giving up things of value to us, even our very lives, is what He calls us to do. He is a good and just God. There is no unfairness in His economy. After all, He gave us the ultimate sacrifice when His own Son laid down His life for us.

Frog Eye Salad

1 cup sugar
3 egg yolks
2 tablespoons flour
2 cups pineapple juice
1 tablespoon lemon juice
1 (16 ounce) package acini di
   pepe pasta

2 (20 ounce) cans pineapple
   chunks, drained
2 (11 ounce) cans mandarin
   oranges, drained
1 (16 ounce) package miniature
   marshmallows
1 (12 ounce) container frozen
   whipped topping, thawed

In large saucepan over low heat, whisk together sugar, egg yolks, flour, pineapple juice, and lemon juice. Cook and stir until thickened. Remove from heat. Meanwhile, bring large pot of lightly salted water to boil. Add pasta and cook for 8 to 10 minutes or until al dente; drain and rinse with cold water. In large bowl, combine cooked mixture with pasta and gently stir to combine. Refrigerate at least 4 hours or overnight. When chilled, toss pasta with pineapple chunks, mandarin oranges, marshmallows, and whipped topping. Refrigerate until ready to serve.

Yield: 12 servings

Close as Family

Does not he who guards your life know it?
Will he not repay everyone according to what they have done?
PROVERBS 24:12 NIV

The people you know best are the ones you spend the most time with. You and your family are close, not only because you're related, but also because you do things together. In the same way, you know God because of the time you've spent with Him. Even better, just like you keep your family safe, so does He!

Cocktail Wieners

1 (10 ounce) jar chili sauce
1 small jar grape jelly

2 packages smoked cocktail
wieners

Preheat oven to 350 degrees. In small saucepan, combine chili sauce and jelly. Heat until well blended. Place cocktail wieners in casserole dish. Pour jelly mixture over wieners. Bake for 15 to 20 minutes.

Yield: 10 servings

The Old Mirror

Now we see only a reflection as in a mirror; then we shall see face to face. Now I know in part; then I shall know fully, even as I am fully known.
1 CORINTHIANS 13:12 NIV

Have you ever tried to see your reflection in an old mirror, one of those antiques that is scratched and darkened with age? While the shabby chic look might fit with the décor in your home, you certainly would not want to use a mirror like that to see your reflection. God tells us that seeing Him while here on this earth is much like looking in one of those mirrors. You might see parts of Him, but the whole won't be revealed this side of heaven.

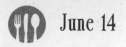

Green Peas with Celery and Onions

2 (10 ounce) packages frozen
   peas
½ cup sliced celery
1 small onion, thinly sliced

3 tablespoons margarine or
   butter, softened
¼ teaspoon salt

Follow directions on package for peas; cook celery, onion, and peas, then drain. Stir in margarine and salt.

Yield: 8 servings

The Wedding Month

And over all these virtues put on love,
which binds them all together in perfect unity.
COLOSSIANS 3:14 NIV

How many times each day do you tell someone in your family that you love him or her? Some families say those words regularly and some do not. Even if the words aren't spoken, God says families are bound together by love. In the same way, He loves us and tells us every day when we read His Word. Just like the way love keeps families together, so does love also bind us to our Lord. Today, why don't you see how many times you can tell a family member you love him or her? And while you're at it, don't forget to tell God, too!

•••

Family Dinnertime Tip

Create a wonderful enhancement for your meals. Soften a stick
of real butter to room temperature. Mince ¼ cup of a fresh herb of
your choice (basil, chive, oregano, rosemary, thyme). Blend the butter
and herb, and store in an airtight container. Enjoy with breads
and vegetables for up to three weeks.

Creamy Orange Drink

6 cups orange juice, divided
1 teaspoon vanilla

1 (3.4 ounce) package instant
vanilla pudding mix
1 envelope whipped topping mix

In large mixing bowl, combine half of orange juice with vanilla, pudding mix, and whipped topping mix. Beat until smooth; then mix in remaining juice. Chill thoroughly.

Yield: 6 to 8 servings

Fishers of Men

But Peter and John replied, "Which is right in God's eyes: to listen to you, or to him? You be the judges! As for us, we cannot help speaking about what we have seen and heard."
ACTS 4:19–20 NIV

Peter and John lived in dangerous times. Merely speaking the truth about who Jesus was and what He was doing was cause for not only arrest but possible death. And yet, neither man could be kept quiet even with such great penalties facing him. What can we learn from these two men, especially in regard to talking about Jesus with those who do not know Him? Peter tells us to speak out, even if you're frightened. Do it anyway. Step out when you're called. It's practice for next time. Eventually all followers become fishers. What can you do today to learn how to be a better fisher of men?

Brown Sugar Cutouts

1 cup butter or margarine,
   softened
½ cup sugar
1 cup brown sugar, packed
1 large egg, lightly beaten
½ cup sour cream

1 teaspoon vanilla
4½ cups flour
½ teaspoon baking powder
½ teaspoon baking soda
½ teaspoon salt

In large mixing bowl, cream butter and sugars. Add egg; beat until well blended. Stir in sour cream and vanilla. Combine dry ingredients; add slowly to creamed mixture. Mix well. Refrigerate dough for 1 hour. On lightly floured surface, roll out half of chilled dough to ¼-inch thickness. Cut with desired cookie cutters and place on lightly greased cookie sheets. Repeat with remaining chilled dough. Bake at 350 degrees for 10 to 12 minutes.

Yield: 3 to 4 dozen cookies

A Divided Mind

"No one can serve two masters. Either you will hate the one and love the other, or you will be devoted to the one and despise the other. You cannot serve both God and money."
MATTHEW 6:24 NIV

A divided mind cannot settle on one thing or another. Jesus warns us about being so concerned about the things of the world, especially those things that money can buy, that we forget about the eternal things we should be considering. When you are tempted to fret about money or perhaps to spend it freely without consulting the Lord, ask yourself where your allegiance lies. Is it with God or money? Jesus says you cannot serve both.

Tuna Cheese Spread

1 (8 ounce) package cream
   cheese, softened
1 (6 ounce) can tuna, drained
   and flaked
½ cup green onion, finely
   chopped

¼ cup mayonnaise
1 tablespoon lemon juice
¾ teaspoon curry powder
Dash salt

Combine all ingredients. Spread onto bread slices for quick, tasty sandwiches.

Yield: 2 cups

Forgiveness Is Hard

*Who is a God like you, who pardons sin and forgives the
transgression of the remnant of his inheritance? You do not
stay angry forever but delight to show mercy. You will again
have compassion on us; you will tread our sins underfoot
and hurl all our iniquities into the depths of the sea.*
MICAH 7:18–19 NIV

Do you have a hard time forgiving someone who has wronged you?
Maybe it's not the forgiving that gives you trouble but rather the
forgetting. You may think you've got the situation under control and
that you have put everything in the past. Then you see the person with
whom you were once upset, and all those old hurts
rise to the surface again. That's human nature
and something that can only be remedied with
time, practice, and prayer. Aren't you glad God
doesn't look at our transgressions that way?
What a compassionate God we serve!

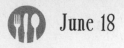

Ham with Apple Relish

1 teaspoon ground cloves
1 (3 to 4 pound) fully cooked
  boneless ham
4 medium tart apples, peeled
  and chopped
2 cups sugar

1 cup chopped dried apricots
½ cup dried cranberries
½ cup golden raisins
¼ cup white vinegar
2 tablespoons grated orange rind
½ teaspoon ground ginger

Rub cloves over ham. Wrap ham tightly in foil and bake at 325 degrees for 1 to 1½ hours or until internal temperature reaches 140 degrees. Meanwhile, combine remaining ingredients in saucepan for relish. Stirring constantly, bring mixture to boil. Reduce heat and simmer for 25 to 30 minutes or until thickened. Serve relish over ham slices.

Yield: 8 to 10 servings

Mind the Gap

Now a man named Ananias, together with his wife Sapphira, also sold a piece of property. With his wife's full knowledge he kept back part of the money for himself, but brought the rest and put it at the apostles' feet.
ACTS 5:1–2 NIV

If you have read the story of Sapphira and Ananias, you know it does not end well. Suffice it to say that this Ananias had one foot in the church and one foot in the world. What lesson can you and I take from this? Above all, beware the gap between who we are and who we want to be. Pursue Jesus, and the gap closes. Fake it, and the gap increases. In all things, mind the gap!

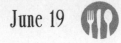

Fruity Cranberry Salad

2 cups fresh or frozen cranberries
1 medium unpeeled orange,
    quartered and seeded
¾ cup sugar
1 (3 ounce) package cherry
    gelatin

1 cup boiling water
1 cup seedless red grapes, halved
1 cup crushed pineapple,
    well drained
½ cup chopped celery
¼ cup finely chopped pecans

In food processor, combine first three ingredients. Cover and process until fruit is coarsely chopped. Set aside for 30 minutes. Meanwhile, dissolve gelatin in boiling water. Chill until gelatin begins to thicken. Stir in cranberry mixture, grapes, pineapple, celery, and pecans. Pour into serving bowl and refrigerate overnight.

Yield: 12 servings

A Different Standard

Therefore, I urge you, brothers and sisters, in view of God's mercy,
to offer your bodies as a living sacrifice, holy and pleasing
to God—this is your true and proper worship.
ROMANS 12:1 NIV

As Christians, we live by a different standard and answer to God, not man. There is never an excuse to sin, ever. Of course, we are human, and as such sin is an ongoing struggle. When you fall, get right back up, confess, repent, and then turn away. Setting yourself back onto the right path is a spiritual act of worship. Taste God's mercy! There's nothing better!

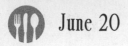

Shrimp Dip

6 ounces cream cheese
4 tablespoons mayonnaise
2 tablespoons ketchup

1 tablespoon onion, chopped
1 tablespoon celery, chopped
2 (4.5 ounce) cans shrimp

Mix all ingredients except shrimp together in bowl. Serve with shrimp.

Yield: 4 to 6 servings

The Thorny Issue

Three times I pleaded with the Lord to take it away from me.
2 CORINTHIANS 12:8 NIV

The apostle Paul was given a thorn in his flesh that plagued him throughout his days. What exactly that thorn might have been—whether it was an actual thorn or a figurative one—is left up to the speculations of scholars. However, the lesson for us is clear. Satan uses thorns like Paul's to try and take the focus off God. God uses these very same thorns as a tool to make us humble and reliant on Him. What is it in your life that God is using to make you reliant on Him? Difficult as it might be, thank Him for it!

. . . .

Family Dinnertime Tip

Counter space is often a precious commodity in a busy kitchen.
For a quick and handy extra countertop, set up your ironing
board and cover it with a plastic tablecloth.

Chive Mashed Potatoes

2½ pounds potatoes, about 8
   medium, peeled and cut into
   1-inch cubes
1 (8 ounce) package cream
   cheese, cubed and softened

¾ to 1 cup milk
½ cup snipped fresh chives
1¼ teaspoons salt
¼ teaspoon black pepper

Boil potatoes, covered, in medium saucepan in 2 inches water for 10 to 12 minutes or until tender; drain. Return to pan and mash with electric mixer or potato masher, gradually stirring in cream cheese until blended. Blend in milk, chives, salt, and pepper. Stir gently over medium heat until heated through. Serve immediately.

Yield: 8 servings

Beating the Bullies

Therefore he is able to save completely those who come to God through him, because he always lives to intercede for them.
HEBREWS 7:25 NIV

Don't you love movies where the bully gets his just desserts when someone finally stands up for the underdog? Perhaps you are the type of person who easily steps in between someone helpless and someone determined to take advantage of him. Or maybe that type of bold behavior isn't something you feel you can manage. But we serve a loving God who does exactly that for us. And with His help, we, too, can do that for others. Just ask Him and He will equip you.

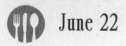

Candied Drop Cookies

2 cups flour
2 teaspoons baking powder
½ teaspoon salt
½ cup butter, softened
2 cups brown sugar, packed

2 large eggs
2 tablespoons heavy cream
2 cups chopped pecans
1 cup golden raisins, chopped
1 cup candied cherries, chopped

In small bowl, combine flour, baking powder, and salt. Set aside. In large bowl, cream butter and brown sugar. Beat in eggs and cream. Gradually add dry ingredients. Stir until well blended. Fold in pecans, raisins, and cherries. Drop by teaspoonfuls 1½ inches apart on lightly greased cookie sheets. Bake at 325 degrees for 15 to 20 minutes, until cookies begin to color lightly. Transfer to cooling racks to cool completely.

Yield: 3 to 4 dozen cookies

Great News

For I am convinced that neither death nor life, neither angels nor demons, neither the present nor the future, nor any powers, neither height nor depth, nor anything else in all creation, will be able to separate us from the love of God that is in Christ Jesus our Lord.
ROMANS 8:38–39 NIV

Have you ever lost a loved one or been lost yourself in a crowded place? It's a heart-stopping and helpless feeling to search for a loved one knowing it's possible you may never be successful. Thankfully, we never have to worry that we will lose sight of God and be separated from Him. Why is that? Because He has declared it so. Nothing and no one will ever come between you and God! Isn't that great news!

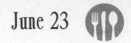

Egg Salad with a Twist Sandwich Spread

6 hard-boiled eggs, chopped
¼ cup carrots, shredded
2 tablespoons celery, finely
    chopped
1 tablespoon green onion, finely
    chopped
¼ cup cream cheese, softened

2 tablespoons mayonnaise
¼ teaspoon seasoned salt
¼ teaspoon dill weed
Pinch dry mustard
Pinch salt
Pinch pepper

Combine eggs, carrots, celery, and green onion in bowl; set aside. Mix cream cheese, mayonnaise, and seasonings until thoroughly blended. Combine cream cheese mixture and egg mixture. Cover and refrigerate until ready to use.

Yield: 6 servings

Test the Waters

The Spirit and the bride say, "Come!" And let him who hears say, "Come!" Let the one who is thirsty come; and let the one who wishes take the free gift of the water of life.
REVELATION 22:17 NIV

There is nothing better than an ice-cold glass of water on a hot day. It slides down a parched throat and instantly all is well again, isn't it? As great as that feeling of having a raging thirst quenched may be, even better is the knowledge that God offers living water that will give so much more. Come and drink, He implores. Test the waters, they are fine. Come to Jesus. He will quench your thirst!

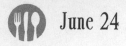

Home-Style Roast Beef

1 (10 to 12 pound) bottom round beef roast
1 (14½ ounce) can chicken broth
1 (10¼ ounce) can beef gravy
1 (10¾ ounce) can condensed cream of celery soup
¼ cup water
¼ cup Worcestershire sauce
¼ cup soy sauce

3 tablespoons dried parsley flakes
3 tablespoons dill weed
2 tablespoons dried thyme
4½ teaspoons garlic powder
1 teaspoon celery salt
1 teaspoon black pepper
1 large onion, sliced into rings

Place roast in large roasting pan, fat side up. Prick meat with meat fork. In bowl, combine broth, gravy, soup, water, Worcestershire sauce, and soy sauce. Pour mixture evenly over roast, then sprinkle with seasonings. Place onion rings over roast. Bake uncovered at 325 degrees for 2½ to 3½ hours or until meat reaches desired doneness. Meat thermometer should read 140 degrees for rare roast, 160 degrees for medium roast, and 170 degrees for well-done roast. Let stand for 15 to 20 minutes before slicing.

Yield: 25 to 30 servings

A Child of the King

And having disarmed the powers and authorities, he made a public spectacle of them, triumphing over them by the cross.
Colossians 2:15 NIV

The enemy loves to make us feel as though he has authority to wreak havoc, but the reality is he has no authority in the world of a follower of Christ. Jesus conquered the devil, and we no longer have to fear the dark forces of the underworld. All the devil can do is bluff by lying, tempting, and accusing. Watch out for the voices that tell you God is not sovereign or make you believe that He cannot save you from any temptation. You are a child of the King! The next time you are tempted to think otherwise, say that out loud and just see what happens!

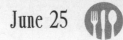

Hot Fruit Salad

1 (29 ounce) can sliced peaches, partially drained
1 (20 ounce) can pineapple chunks, partially drained
1 cup fresh cranberries

¾ cup brown sugar, packed
2 tablespoons minute tapioca
Butter
Cinnamon

Mix together peaches, pineapple chunks, cranberries, brown sugar, and tapioca. Spoon into greased casserole. Dot with butter and sprinkle with cinnamon. Bake covered at 350 degrees for 30 minutes. Stir; bake uncovered for 15 minutes longer. Serve warm.

Yield: 6 servings

Listen, Forgive, and Act

"Lord, listen! Lord, forgive! Lord, hear and act!"
DANIEL 9:19 NIV

Daniel and his buddies were in quite a fix when he stopped to utter this simple and direct prayer. Not only were they far from home, they were facing a decision to either give up their God or declare Him sovereign and give up their lives. Faced with such a dire situation, what does he ask of the Lord? To listen, to forgive their sins, and to do something fast! Though it is unlikely you will face the same situation Daniel did, his prayer still remains relevant today. Listen, forgive, and act—a great formula for prayer!

Bruschetta

4 cups Roma tomatoes, chopped and seeded

1 medium onion, chopped

6 to 8 basil leaves, chopped

2 to 3 tablespoons fresh oregano, chopped

3 to 5 garlic cloves, minced

½ teaspoon black pepper

2 tablespoons olive oil

1 (16 ounce) loaf French bread, cut into 24 slices

Olive oil cooking spray

In medium mixing bowl, combine tomatoes, onion, basil, oregano, garlic, pepper, and olive oil. Cover and chill for 2 to 3 hours to blend flavors. When ready to serve, spray each bread slice with cooking spray and broil until lightly browned. Spoon mixture onto bread slices and serve.

Yield: 24 slices

Slow to Anger

*Do not be quickly provoked in your spirit,
for anger resides in the lap of fools.*
ECCLESIASTES 7:9 NIV

Do you wear your emotions on your sleeve? Can you be easily provoked to react to gentle prodding or perhaps good-natured ribbing? Are you the one in the group who keeps hearing that you cannot take a joke? If so, then God is speaking to you with this verse. Do not be easily provoked. Be slow to anger. Why? Because the Lord calls those who do not heed this advice fools. And who among us wants the sovereign God of the universe to think we are a fool?

Creamy Corn Casserole

3 tablespoons butter or
   margarine, divided
1 cup finely chopped celery
¼ cup finely chopped onion
¼ cup finely chopped red pepper
1 (10¾ ounce) can condensed
   cream of chicken soup

3 cups fresh, frozen, or canned
   corn, drained
1 (8 ounce) can sliced water
   chestnuts, drained
½ cup soft bread crumbs

Melt 2 tablespoons butter in medium skillet. Add celery, onion, and red pepper and sauté until vegetables are tender, about 2 minutes. Remove from heat and stir in soup, corn, and water chestnuts. Spoon into greased 2-quart casserole dish. Toss bread crumbs with remaining 1 tablespoon melted butter. Sprinkle on top of casserole and bake uncovered at 350 degrees for 25 to 30 minutes.

Yield: 8 servings

Humble in Heart

At that time Jesus said, "I praise you, Father, Lord of heaven and earth, because you have hidden these things from the wise and learned, and revealed them to little children."
MATTHEW 11:25 NIV

God reveals Himself to the humble in heart. Like the little children who have no artifice or defense, our weakness makes room for the Lord to act on our behalf. And who among us wishes to go our own way and handle our own affairs when the God of the universe will do that for us if we allow Him to?

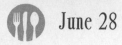

Candy Bar Cookies

1 cup butter or margarine,
   softened
1 cup creamy peanut butter
1 cup sugar
1 cup brown sugar, packed
2 large eggs, lightly beaten
2 teaspoons vanilla
3 cups flour
1 teaspoon baking powder

1 teaspoon baking soda
1 (16 ounce) milk chocolate
   candy bar, chopped into
   ½-inch squares

Chocolate Glaze:
1 cup powdered sugar
2 tablespoons cocoa
1 tablespoon milk, plus extra

In large bowl, beat together butter, peanut butter, sugar, and brown sugar until light and fluffy. Add eggs and vanilla and beat well. In another bowl, combine flour, baking powder, and baking soda. Stir into creamed mixture. Form teaspoonful of dough around each piece of chopped chocolate and bake at 350 degrees on ungreased cookie sheets for 10 to 12 minutes. Cool completely.

For chocolate glaze, combine powdered sugar, cocoa, and milk until smooth. Add additional milk slowly to reach desired drizzling consistency. Drizzle cooled cookies with glaze.

Yield: 5 dozen cookies

Use the Tools

"I tell you, use worldly wealth to gain friends for yourselves, so that when it is gone, you will be welcomed into eternal dwellings."
LUKE 16:9 NIV

Jesus certainly gives some interesting advice, doesn't He? Upon first look, it almost seems as if He is telling us to go out and buy friends. But look closely. What He's really saying here is to use your worldly wealth as a tool to impact others for Christ. We have so little time here on this earth and so many opportunities to affect others. Use what God gives you for the good of the kingdom and see what happens!

Buttermilk Biscuits

½ cup cold butter
2 cups flour
3 teaspoons baking powder

¼ teaspoon salt
¾ cup buttermilk

In mixing bowl, use pastry blender to cut butter into blend of flour, baking powder, and salt. Stir in buttermilk with fork until batter is just moistened. Turn dough out onto lightly floured board and knead lightly 4 to 5 times. Pat dough by hand out into a circle ¾ inch thick. Cut with round biscuit cutter. Place biscuits on greased baking pan. Bake at 450 degrees for 8 to 10 minutes.

Yield: 10 biscuits

The Attitude of a Servant

*"Very truly I tell you, no servant is greater than his master,
nor is a messenger greater than the one who sent him."*
JOHN 13:16 NIV

Jesus calls us to take on the attitude of a servant, but do we really understand what that means? A servant does not care about status, and he is always willing to take on menial tasks that are assigned to him. A servant does not think he is better than others, and he is always willing to grab the heavy end of the log. Above all, a servant is focused on the happiness of others and not on his own happiness. When you consider the role of a servant in these terms, can you see how God is calling us to that job? Will you take it on? God certainly hopes so!

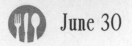

Seafood Bake

1 cup chopped onion
1 cup chopped celery
4 tablespoons butter
½ pound crabmeat and/or
   lobster meat
¼ pound medium shrimp
¼ pound scallops
½ teaspoon garlic powder
½ teaspoon salt

½ teaspoon black pepper
¼ cup flour
2 cups milk
2 cups shredded mild cheddar
   cheese
1 to 2 cups buttered bread
   crumbs or cracker crumbs
   (optional)

In large skillet, sauté onion and celery in butter until they start to soften; add crabmeat, shrimp, and scallops, tossing in butter. Season with garlic powder, salt, and pepper. Sprinkle meat with flour, allowing butter to absorb. Slowly add milk, stirring constantly over low heat until well blended and some thickening is apparent. Mix in cheese, then place in greased casserole. Sprinkle with bread or cracker crumbs if desired. Bake uncovered at 350 degrees for 25 to 30 minutes.

Yield: 4 servings

Firm Footing

Therefore we will not fear, though the earth give way and the mountains fall into the heart of the sea, though its waters roar and foam and the mountains quake with their surging.
PSALM 46:2–3 NIV

Have you ever stood on ground that was shaking from an earthquake? It's a helpless feeling knowing even the earth beneath your feet is not a safe place to stand. No wonder so many fear earthquakes! And yet the Lord tells us He is bigger than any fear, more reliable than any bank account. He will make a way where there seems to be no way. With God, there is no shifting sand, only firm footing and a future free of fear!

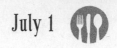

Layered Broccoli-Cauliflower Salad

6 slices bacon
1 cup broccoli florets
1 cup cauliflower florets
3 hard-boiled eggs, chopped
½ cup chopped red onion

1 cup mayonnaise
½ cup sugar
2 tablespoons white wine vinegar
1 cup shredded cheddar cheese

In large skillet, cook bacon over medium-high heat until crispy. Crumble and set aside. In medium glass salad bowl, layer in order broccoli, cauliflower, eggs, and onion. Prepare dressing by whisking together mayonnaise, sugar, and vinegar. Drizzle dressing over top. Sprinkle crumbled bacon and cheese over dressing. Chill completely to blend flavors.

Yield: 8 servings

Money in the Bank

"'Their silver and gold will not be able to deliver them in the day of the Lord's wrath. It will not satisfy their hunger or fill their stomachs, for it has caused them to stumble into sin.'"
EZEKIEL 7:19 NIV

Are you a shopper? Many of us love to spend the day wandering through shops displaying all sorts of wares. There's certainly nothing wrong with that kind of fun, at least when enjoyed within reason and with an eye to watching the budget. Even if you're someone with an unlimited budget, however, there will come a day when the amount of money you have in the bank will become inconsequential. On that day, only Jesus will matter. Why not live that way today?

Cheese and Chicken Empanadas

½ cup shredded Monterey Jack
cheese
½ cup shredded mild cheddar
cheese
1 cup shredded cooked chicken
1 jalapeño pepper, diced
½ tablespoon minced red onion

½ teaspoon ground cumin
½ teaspoon salt
2 frozen pie shells, thawed
3 egg yolks, lightly beaten
2 tablespoons coarse kosher salt
1 tablespoon chili powder

In bowl, mix together cheeses, chicken, jalapeño, onion, cumin, and salt.
Refrigerate until ready to assemble empanadas. On floured surface, roll
out pie shells and cut into eight 4-inch circles. Use all dough by rerolling
scraps. Place approximately 2 tablespoons of cheese and chicken mixture
in center of each dough circle. Fold each circle in half and crimp edges
with fork. Place on greased baking pan or cookie sheet and brush top
of each empanada with egg yolk. Sprinkle top with kosher salt and chili
powder. Bake at 400 degrees for 12 to 13 minutes. Serve warm or at room
temperature.

Yield: 8 servings

Love and Faithfulness

*Let love and faithfulness never leave you; bind them around your
neck, write them on the tablet of your heart. Then you will win
favor and a good name in the sight of God and man.*
PROVERBS 3:3–4 NIV

Love. It's so easy to say, "I love that car" or "that color" or "that movie."
We use the word *love* so frequently that it has almost come to mean
something commonplace. God's version of love is anything but
commonplace. Next time you're tempted to say you love something,
consider the true meaning of the word from our Lord's point of view.
Perhaps love isn't the word you're looking for.

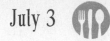
Cinnamon-Glazed Almonds

1 egg white
1 teaspoon cold water
4 cups whole almonds

½ cup sugar
¼ teaspoon salt
½ teaspoon cinnamon

Lightly grease 10x15-inch jelly roll pan. Lightly beat egg white; add water, and beat until frothy but not stiff. Place almonds in large bowl. Drizzle egg mixture over nuts and stir until well coated. In small bowl, combine sugar, salt, and cinnamon; sprinkle over nuts. Toss to coat, and spread evenly in prepared pan. Bake at 250 degrees for 45 minutes to 1 hour, stirring occasionally, until golden. Allow to cool completely. Store almonds in airtight container.

Yield: 4 cups

Superheroes

*But the L*ORD *is with me like a mighty warrior.*
JEREMIAH 20:11 NIV

When you think of a warrior, what comes to mind? Perhaps you think of someone strong and brave, someone who will stand up for those who cannot stand up for themselves? Maybe your idea of a warrior comes from knowing or reading about soldiers or police officers who do brave things to keep our cities and country safe. Did you realize that the mightiest of all warriors is the Lord Himself? King David was head of an army of warriors mightier than any other that lived. Even so, he knew his mighty men were no match for the Lord. See, unlike human warriors, God can defeat any enemy. Aren't you glad He is protecting you?

Easy Cinnamon Apples

8 tart apples, cored and sliced   1 teaspoon lemon juice
2 tablespoons sugar   ¼ cup red cinnamon candies

Place all ingredients in microwave-safe bowl. Heat on high power for 15 minutes, stirring every 5 minutes. May be served warm or cool.

Yield: 8 servings

Free Indeed

Now the Lord is the Spirit,
and where the Spirit of the Lord is, there is freedom.
2 CORINTHIANS 3:17 NIV

A little over two centuries ago in the United States, a handful of men came together with an idea to gain freedom for themselves and the country they wished to form. These men hoped for freedom. Eventually they fought for that same freedom and changed the course of history. Imagine, then, a freedom that comes without any effort on your part beyond turning your life over to the Lord. God says that freedom is within your power. Rest in Him, and you will be free.

· ·

Family Dinnertime Tip

Use three-ring binders to create family cookbooks. Include recipes for all the family favorites with a brief bio and photo of the creator of each dish. These gifts will be cherished for years to come.

Chocolate-Filled Pinwheels

2 cups flour
1 teaspoon baking powder
½ teaspoon salt
¾ cup vegetable shortening
1 cup sugar
1 large egg
1 tablespoon vanilla

Filling:
1 cup (6 ounces) semisweet
 chocolate chips
2 tablespoons butter
½ tablespoon vanilla

Combine flour, baking powder, and salt. Set aside. Cream shortening and sugar. Beat in egg and vanilla. Gradually blend in dry ingredients. Remove ⅔ cup dough and set aside. Cover and chill remaining dough for 2 hours. To prepare filling, melt chocolate chips and butter in double boiler over low heat, stirring constantly until smooth. Remove from heat and stir in vanilla. Blend in reserved dough. To assemble cookies, roll out chilled dough into 12x16-inch rectangle on lightly floured surface. Spread chocolate mixture over dough to within ¼ inch of edges. Beginning on long side, roll up dough jelly-roll fashion. Pinch seam to seal. Cut roll in half to create two 8-inch logs. Wrap well in waxed paper and chill for 8 hours or overnight. To bake, heat oven to 350 degrees. Slice logs into ¼-inch-thick slices and place 2 inches apart on ungreased cookie sheets. Bake for 10 to 12 minutes, until lightly golden. Cool on wire racks.

Yield: 4 to 5 dozen cookies

Obeying the Lord

The LORD then said to Noah, "Go into the ark, you and your whole family, because I have found you righteous in this generation."
GENESIS 7:1 NIV

God told Noah to build an ark large enough to hold his family and a giant menagerie of animals. Can you imagine Noah explaining that to his wife? But the fact the instructions came from God was enough, and soon an ark was built. In obeying the Lord, Noah saved not only of the world's animals, but he also saved his own family. Do you think he expected *that* result when he started? Do we ever really know what God is up to?

Salmon with Pecans

2 pounds fresh salmon
½ small bottle balsamic vinegar
   salad dressing
1 teaspoon fresh parsley,
   chopped

1 teaspoon fresh basil, chopped
Salt and pepper to taste
Pecans

Place salmon on foil. Pour dressing over fish. Add parsley, basil, salt, and pepper. Broil for 20 to 30 minutes. Fish is done when light pink and flaky. Garnish with pecans.

Yield: 4 to 6 servings

God's Creative Abundance

She went away and did as Elijah had told her. So there was food every day for Elijah and for the woman and her family.
1 KINGS 17:15 NIV

Do you know the story of the woman who had so little that she was certain she and her son would starve? She was wrong, of course, because God had a plan that only required plenty of jars and even more trust. When the holy man Elijah told this woman to go and fetch as many jars as she could find, do you think she considered he'd misunderstood? How many times have we been convinced that God has misunderstood our prayers? Surely He would do something different if He just understood. And yet just like in this story, there is no misunderstanding, only God's creative abundance at work.

Family Dinnertime Tip

When you need to test the doneness of a cake or bread, and you don't have a cake-testing tool, use an uncooked piece of spaghetti. It is long enough to test the doneness of your deepest baked goods.

Mandarin Orange Salad

2 cups boiling water
1 (6 ounce) package orange
   gelatin
1 pint orange sherbet

1 (11 ounce) can mandarin
   oranges, drained
1 (8½ ounce) can crushed
   pineapple, undrained

In mixing bowl, pour boiling water over gelatin. Stir until dissolved. Spoon orange sherbet into gelatin and stir until well combined. Fold in remaining ingredients. Pour into gelatin mold and refrigerate until firm.

Yield: 8 servings

The Power of Love

Then King David went in and sat before the LORD, and he said: "Who am I, LORD God, and what is my family, that you have brought me this far?"
1 CHRONICLES 17:16 NIV

David was king, and yet he was humbled when he considered a power much greater than his own, the power of God's love for him and his family. Have you stopped to think that the same God who humbled the king of Israel with His love is the same God who watches over your loved ones? It's true. And it's humbling, isn't it? King David thought so, too.

Pineapple Cream Cheese Ball

2 (8 ounce) packages cream
  cheese
1 small can crushed pineapple,
  drained

1 (3 ounce) box instant vanilla
  pudding
Walnuts or pecans
Cinnamon graham crackers

In large bowl, mix together first three ingredients and form into a ball.
Roll in walnuts or pecans. Serve with cinnamon graham crackers.

Yield: 20 servings

For Such a Time as This

*"For if you remain silent at this time, relief and deliverance for
the Jews will arise from another place, but you and your father's
family will perish. And who knows but that you have come
to your royal position for such a time as this?"*
ESTHER 4:14 NIV

Do you know the story of Esther? She was a young Jewish woman who
rose to the rank of queen, a position that allowed her to save the Jewish
people. God placed Esther where He wanted her and then gave her the
ability to do what He needed done. In the same way, He places us where
we are most useful to Him. When we are willing, we are used. Ask God
how He can use you "for such a time as this."

Family Dinnertime Tip

Fill a canning jar with colorful candies. Tie a ribbon and tag around
the neck of the jar, and you have an instant gift. Add a note tag
that says, "You are a real sweetie" or "I appreciate your sweet
friendship." You could also fill a jar with small cookie cutters
and attach your favorite sugar cookie recipe.

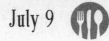

Cranberry Salsa

1 cup water
1 cup sugar
1 (12 ounce) package fresh or
    frozen cranberries
2 tablespoons canned
    jalapeño peppers, chopped

1 teaspoon dried cilantro
¼ teaspoon ground cumin
1 green onion, thinly sliced
1 teaspoon lime juice

In saucepan, bring water and sugar to boil over medium heat. Add cranberries; return to boil. Gently boil cranberries for 10 minutes without stirring. Pour into glass mixing bowl. Gently stir in remaining ingredients. Place piece of plastic wrap directly on salsa. Cool to room temperature, then refrigerate. Serve with tortilla chips.

Yield: 6 servings

The Wandering Mind

*Finally, brothers and sisters, whatever is true, whatever is noble,
whatever is right, whatever is pure, whatever is lovely,
whatever is admirable—if anything is excellent or
praiseworthy—think about such things.*
PHILIPPIANS 4:8 NIV

Does your mind wander? Do you tend to allow yourself to imagine scenarios that might happen, maybe even things that could be disastrous? God says to fix your mind on other things, things that are good, things that are worthy of praise. When you're thinking of these things, you cannot be worrying about other things, can you? Perhaps that is exactly what God had in mind.

English Pea Casserole

½ cup chopped onion

1 small sweet red pepper, chopped

¼ cup butter or margarine, melted

1 (5 ounce) package medium egg noodles

1 (8 ounce) package cream cheese, softened

2 cups (8 ounces) shredded sharp cheddar cheese

1 (10 ounce) package frozen English peas, thawed and drained

1 (2½ ounce) jar mushroom stems and pieces, undrained

½ teaspoon black pepper

10 butter-flavored crackers, crushed

In small skillet, sauté onion and red pepper in butter until tender. Set aside. Cook noodles according to package directions; drain. Add cream cheese and cheddar cheese to hot noodles; stir until cheeses melt. Stir in onion mixture, peas, mushrooms, and pepper. Spoon into greased baking dish and top with cracker crumbs. Cover and bake at 325 degrees for 25 to 30 minutes.

Yield: 8 servings

Slave or Son?

*"Now a slave has no permanent place in the family,
but a son belongs to it forever."*
JOHN 8:35 NIV

In biblical times, a slave was bound to his master and forced to do his will for a specific period of time. Sometimes slaves were treated well, but oftentimes they were not. Depending on the terms of the slave's service to the master, the slave might be released and allowed to go free. Unlike the slaves, the sons and daughters of the master were cherished throughout their lifetimes. Their ties with the master were never cut. God tells us in His Word that we are not slaves to Him but rather sons and daughters. We are cherished and He will never release us. Isn't that something!

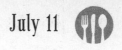

Parmesan Cheese Dip

2 cups milk
16 ounces cream cheese
¾ cup grated Parmesan cheese

½ teaspoon garlic powder
French bread

Cook milk and cream cheese slowly on low heat until creamy; do not boil. Remove from heat and add Parmesan cheese, whipping mixture with wire whisk to melt cheese. Add garlic powder. Add more milk if dip is too thick. Serve with French bread.

Yield: 20 servings

His People's Provision

He defends the cause of the fatherless and the widow, and loves the foreigner residing among you, giving them food and clothing.
DEUTERONOMY 10:18 NIV

God never fails to provide for all of His people, but sometimes He calls on His people to provide for one another in His name. Can you think of anyone who might fit the description in this verse? Perhaps you know older men or women at church who have no spouses or families at home. If you live in a college town, no doubt you can easily identify many students from out of state or out of the country in your midst. And sadly, it is far too easy to find single parents in our communities. Read that verse again, this time aloud and asking God for direction. Now consider what you will do for the people God brought to mind.

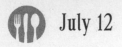

Taco Bake

1 pound ground beef
1 (10¾ ounce) can condensed
   tomato soup
1 cup salsa
½ cup milk

6 medium flour tortillas, cut into
   1-inch strips
1 cup Colby/Monterey Jack
   cheese, divided

Brown ground beef; drain. Add soup, salsa, milk, tortilla strips, and half of cheese. Pour mixture into 2-quart casserole dish and cover. Bake at 400 degrees for 30 minutes. Remove from oven and sprinkle with remaining cheese before serving.

Yield: 4 servings

Trust God, Not Logic

Trust in the LORD with all your heart and lean not on your own understanding; in all your ways submit to him, and he will make your paths straight.
PROVERBS 3:5–6 NIV

Do you ever try to figure out what God's doing? If you say yes, you're in good company. It is fundamental to our human nature to use our logic to discern the Lord's actions just as we try to figure out human actions. But God isn't human nor are His actions subject to human understanding. He is God, and He wouldn't be much of a God if we could figure Him out! Instead, trust Him, not logic.

Marinated Vegetable Salad

¾ cup white vinegar
½ cup oil
1 cup sugar
1 teaspoon salt
½ teaspoon black pepper
2 (11 ounce) cans white corn
1 (15 ounce) can small sweet peas

1 (15 ounce) can French-style
 green beans
1 cup diced green pepper
1 cup diced celery
1 cup diced onion
1 (2 ounce) jar diced pimiento

In small saucepan, bring vinegar, oil, sugar, salt, and pepper to boil; stir until sugar dissolves. Cool. Combine remaining ingredients in bowl. Stir in vinegar mixture. Chill for 8 hours or overnight. Drain before serving.

Yield: 10 to 12 servings

Listen!

"Listen! A farmer went out to sow his seed. As he was scattering the seed, some fell along the path."
MARK 4:3–4 NIV

Have you read the parable of the sower? If not, refer to Mark 4 to see how Jesus' story about sowing seeds on different types of ground is actually a lesson in faith for His people. In the parable, the seed (God's Word) and the sower (Jesus) are good; it is the ground (the receiver) that makes the difference. Did you notice how Jesus begins this scripture by telling those gathered to listen? Of course, they were already listening—this was Jesus!—so why the emphasis? Because hearing the Word and taking it to heart are the first steps to giving our lives to Him. It is the beginning, and this parable is a lesson in how to begin well. Read it and see.

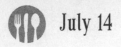

Creamy Cinnamon Fruit Dip

1 (8 ounce) carton sour cream
1½ teaspoons cinnamon

1 (13 ounce) jar marshmallow
cream

Blend all ingredients together until creamy. Chill. Serve with fresh fruit.

Yield: 3 cups

The Need for Bathing

*Jesus answered, "Those who have had a bath
need only to wash their feet."*
JOHN 13:10 NIV

What an interesting statement! Before any of your family members claim this as their life verse and refuse to bathe, let's see what He actually meant. Jesus loved to tell stories to teach deep truths, and this statement is no exception. When you give your life to Jesus, you are born again—clean and pure. However, the place where you dwell, this imperfect earth, is anything but clean and pure. Sin abounds and can attach itself to us like mud after a rainstorm. Jesus is telling us that as long as our feet touch this impure earth, they need to be bathed. How do we do that? We don't, but Jesus does. He washes away our sins when we go to Him and confess them. Have you had your feet washed today? Jesus is waiting.

• •

Family Dinnertime Tip

To keep your dips chilled at a long party, choose two complementary glass bowls—one larger than the other. Fill the larger bowl with ice chips. Fill the smaller bowl with your dip and set the bowl down into the ice.

Baked Squash

3 small yellow squash, cubed
1 small onion, chopped
2 eggs, beaten
¼ cup milk
Dash salt

Dash pepper
¼ cup shredded cheddar cheese
4 tablespoons butter or
    margarine

Mash squash; add onion and cook over low heat. Add beaten eggs, milk, salt, pepper, and cheese. Place all in greased casserole dish; dot with butter. Bake at 325 degrees until firm, approximately 30 to 40 minutes.

Yield: 8 servings

R-E-S-P-E-C-T

*Show proper respect to everyone, love the family
of believers, fear God, honor the emperor.*
1 PETER 2:17 NIV

How many times have you sat through a television commercial where one political candidate is slamming another and shook your head? Perhaps you offered a few choice words to the screen or changed the channel. Watching people aiming for a place of power disrespecting one another is unpleasant to say the least, especially when God tells us to do exactly the opposite. We are to find a way to love all of His people, no matter whether they are lovable or not. Why? Because that's exactly how God treats us!

Pecan Cookies

½ cup shortening
1 cup brown sugar
1 egg
¼ teaspoon salt

1 teaspoon vanilla
1¼ cups flour
1 teaspoon baking powder
½ cup chopped pecans

Mix ingredients in order given. Drop by teaspoonfuls onto cookie sheet. Bake at 350 degrees for 10 to 12 minutes.

Yield: 2 dozen cookies

In Honor of Your Elders

"'Stand up in the presence of the aged, show respect for the elderly and revere your God. I am the Lord.'"
LEVITICUS 19:32 NIV

If you're among those who would identify themselves as aged, don't you love this verse? Maybe you're not quite ready to admit you're in that category. Can you at least agree that respect for our elders is not only virtuous but essential? God insists we respect those in our lives who have lived more years than we have. He will honor you if you honor them.

Family Dinnertime Tip

Keep brown sugar soft by placing 2 to 3 large marshmallows in the canister with the brown sugar.

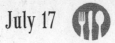

Hawaiian Burgers

2 pounds ground beef
½ cup honey
¼ teaspoon cinnamon
¼ teaspoon curry powder
⅛ teaspoon nutmeg
⅛ teaspoon ground ginger
¼ cup soy sauce

1 (23 ounce) can pineapple slices,
   drained
8 hamburger buns
8 lettuce leaves
8 tomato slices
Mayonnaise

In mixing bowl, combine beef, honey, cinnamon, curry, nutmeg, and ginger. Shape into 8 patties. Grill burgers over medium heat for 3 minutes on each side. Baste with soy sauce. Grill 4 to 6 minutes longer, until juices run clear. Place pineapple slices on grill during end of burgers' cooking time; turn once. Serve burgers on buns with pineapple, lettuce, tomato, and mayonnaise.

Yield: 8 servings

Hearts and Ears

*Apply your heart to instruction
and your ears to words of knowledge.*
PROVERBS 23:12 NIV

Your hearts and your ears. . .isn't it interesting that the Lord doesn't tell you to do something or to say something or even to learn something? He first says to apply your heart, to desire to hear from Him. How do we do this? By getting quiet before God. No speaking, no actions, just being. Then what? Do exactly what God says. We listen.

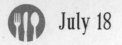

Merry Vegetable Salad

1 (16 ounce) can whole-kernel
   corn, drained
1 large tomato, seeded and
   chopped
1 cup frozen peas

½ cup chopped celery
⅓ cup chopped green pepper
¼ cup chopped red pepper
¼ cup finely chopped onion

Dressing:
¼ cup sour cream
2 tablespoons mayonnaise

2 teaspoons white vinegar
¼ teaspoon salt
⅛ teaspoon black pepper

Combine vegetables. In small bowl, whisk together dressing ingredients.
Just before serving, add dressing to vegetables and toss to coat.

Yield: 6 to 8 servings

Be Prepared

*But in your hearts revere Christ as Lord. Always be prepared to
give an answer to everyone who asks you to give the reason for the
hope that you have. But do this with gentleness and respect.*
1 PETER 3:15 NIV

Why do you believe what you believe about Jesus? Can you tell
someone in very simple terms what it is that led you to call Christ your
Savior? Some of us are very good at sharing our faith. Others of us
find it more difficult to put what we know about God and salvation into
understandable terms. God says to be prepared, to plan for the time when
you are called upon to give such an answer. How? By deciding now what
you will say before you are asked. There are so many good resources for
teaching people how to share the Gospel. Find one that works for you and
be prepared.

Pepperoni Cheese Ball

2 (8 ounce) packages cream
    cheese
¼ cup mayonnaise

⅓ cup grated Parmesan cheese
6 ounces pepperoni, grated

Soften cream cheese at room temperature. Mix all ingredients together
and shape into ball. Refrigerate. Allow to soften at room temperature
before serving.

Yield: 20 servings

Keeping Up with the Joneses

*Am I now trying to win the approval of human beings, or of God?
Or am I trying to please people? If I were still trying to
please people, I would not be a servant of Christ.*
GALATIANS 1:10 NIV

Does seeing a brand-new car or bike in the driveway next door cause
you to wish you could have one, too? When your best friend's family
takes a trip, do you start daydreaming about where you can take yours?
Or maybe there's a book or toy or something else that has captured your
attention, and you must have it. There is absolutely nothing wrong with
new cars and trips and other nice things as long as your desire for them
is kept in its proper place. Never allow any of these things to take the
place of God. When He comes first, everything else comes after. That is
the antidote for keeping up with the Joneses!

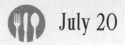

Italian Cream Cake

1 cup butter or margarine,
2 cups sugar
5 eggs, separated
2½ cups flour
1 teaspoon baking soda
1 cup milk
⅔ cup finely chopped pecans
1 (3½ ounce) can sweetened,
   flaked coconut
2 teaspoons vanilla

½ teaspoon cream of tartar

Cream Cheese Frosting:
1 (8 ounce) package cream
   cheese, softened
½ cup butter, softened
1 (16 ounce) package powdered
   sugar, sifted
1 cup chopped pecans
2 teaspoons vanilla

Grease and flour three 9-inch round cake pans. Line with waxed paper; grease paper. Cream butter; add sugar and beat well. Add egg yolks one at time, beating after each addition. Combine flour and baking soda. Add to creamed mixture alternately with milk, beginning and ending with flour mixture. Stir in pecans, coconut, and vanilla. In glass or metal mixing bowl, beat egg whites until foamy. Add cream of tartar; beat until stiff peaks form. Gently fold beaten egg whites into batter. Pour batter into prepared pans. Bake at 350 degrees for 25 to 30 minutes or until wooden pick inserted in center comes out clean. Let cool in pans for 10 minutes. Remove from pans; peel off waxed paper and let cool completely on wire racks. For frosting, combine cream cheese and butter, beating until smooth. Gradually add powdered sugar and beat until light and fluffy. Stir in pecans and vanilla. Frost cooled cake.

Yield: 12 to 16 servings

At the Scent of Bread

"Along with their fellowship offering of thanksgiving they are to present an offering with thick loaves of bread made with yeast."
LEVITICUS 7:13 NIV

It's hard to resist the scent that rises from a crusty loaf of yeasty goodness. Next time you're enjoying a slice, take a moment to consider that bread was once part of an offering of thanksgiving to God.

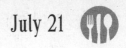
Home-Style Macaroni 'n' Cheese

1½ cups elbow macaroni
1 (10¾ ounce) can condensed
   cheddar cheese soup
½ cup milk

¼ teaspoon pepper
1 tablespoon dry bread crumbs
2 teaspoons butter, melted

Cook macaroni according to package directions. Mix soup, milk, pepper, and macaroni in 1-quart casserole dish. Stir together bread crumbs and melted butter; sprinkle over macaroni mixture. Bake at 400 degrees for 20 minutes.

Yield: 4 servings

A Firm Foundation

With praise and thanksgiving they sang to the LORD: "He is good; his love toward Israel endures forever." And all the people gave a great shout of praise to the LORD, because the foundation of the house of the LORD was laid.
EZRA 3:11 NIV

Have you ever watched a house being built? First comes the preparation of the building site. Trees and undergrowth are removed, and the land is made level. Only then can the foundation be measured and staked out, and then finally the concrete is poured. Great care goes into each step because if the foundation is not straight and level then the house will not stand. In the same way, the house of the Lord stands forever because it stands on a firm and unchanging foundation.

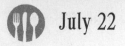

Boiled Spice Cake

2 cups sugar
2 cups raisins
1 teaspoon ground ginger
2 teaspoons cinnamon
2 cups water

1 cup shortening or oil
1 teaspoon salt
3 cups flour
2 teaspoons baking soda

Boil sugar, raisins, spices, water, and shortening until sugar is dissolved. Add salt, flour, and baking soda; mix. Pour into 2 ungreased loaf pans or one 9x13-inch pan. Bake at 350 degrees for 45 minutes.

Yield: 24 servings

He Is Worthy

I will give thanks to you, LORD, with all my heart;
I will tell of all your wonderful deeds.
PSALM 9:1 NIV

When someone you know does something exceptional, you cannot wait to tell others, can you? A friend or loved one's success is something to be proud of. In the same way, shout God's success from the rooftops. Boast about Him. Thank Him for who He is and what He has done. He is worthy of all thanks and praise.

. . . .

Family Dinnertime Tip

When measuring dry ingredients, especially if your children are helping, chances are you'll wind up with a mess on your countertop. Do your measuring over a paper plate or a sheet of waxed paper. Spills can then be picked up easily and returned to the canister.

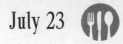
Easy Beef Skillet

1 cup potatoes, sliced
1 tablespoon canola oil
1 pound ground beef
1 (10¾ ounce) can condensed
    tomato soup
¼ cup water

1 tablespoon Worcestershire
    sauce
⅓ teaspoon pepper
1 (8 ounce) can cut green beans,
    drained

Fry potatoes in oil over medium heat until soft. Remove from heat. Brown ground beef in skillet over medium heat; drain. Add tomato soup, water, Worcestershire sauce, pepper, green beans, and cooked potatoes. Cook over low heat for 10 to 15 minutes or until heated through.

Yield: 4 servings

The Birds of the Air

*"Look at the birds of the air; they do not sow or reap or store away
in barns, and yet your heavenly Father feeds them.
Are you not much more valuable than they?"*
MATTHEW 6:26 NIV

Are you a worrier? Do you concern yourself with what will happen tomorrow, next week, or next month? Do you wonder sometimes why God seems not to care for your concerns? He does care. In fact, He cares enough to allow you to rest and not worry. Can you try that? Just for today, see if you can take to heart the words of this verse. Are you not much more valuable than the birds of the air? Of course you are. Believe it!

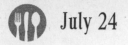

3-Bean Salad

1 (14½ ounce) can wax beans,
    drained
1 (14½ ounce) can green beans,
    drained
1 (15 ounce) can kidney beans,
    drained
1 small onion, minced
⅓ cup sugar

1 teaspoon salt
¼ teaspoon pepper
½ cup vinegar
½ cup oil
½ cup water
2 hard-boiled eggs, sliced
    (optional)

Combine beans and onion in large serving bowl. Thoroughly mix sugar, salt, pepper, vinegar, oil, and water; pour over beans. Garnish with egg slices. Allow to chill in refrigerator for a few hours before serving.

Yield: 10 servings

Action Words

*Do not merely listen to the word,
and so deceive yourselves. Do what it says.*
JAMES 1:22 NIV

How many verses of scripture can you recite from memory? A few? A lot? Maybe you're new to the Christian life and have not yet committed verses to memory. Don't worry. You'll soon find yourself recalling just the right scripture at just the right time. It's something the Lord does, and when you're immersed in the Word, He does it all the time. As valuable as it is to learn God's Word, if all you and your family do is memorize, you've missed the point. God wants you to take those words and put them into action. Don't just hear—do!

Sherry's Super-Easy Crab Dip

1 (12 ounce) jar cocktail sauce
1 (6 ounce) can crabmeat,
    drained

1 (8 ounce) package cream
    cheese

Mix together cocktail sauce and crabmeat; pour over cream cheese. Serve with crackers.

Yield: 10 servings

The Lord's Prayer

"This, then, is how you should pray: 'Our Father in heaven, hallowed be your name, your kingdom come, your will be done, on earth as it is in heaven. Give us today our daily bread. And forgive us our debts, as we also have forgiven our debtors. And lead us not into temptation, but deliver us from the evil one.'"
MATTHEW 6:9–13 NIV

Don't you love the Lord's Prayer? First, we worship by acknowledging the holiness of the name of the Lord, and then we indicate we are anxious for Him to return and claim us for His own, for His kingdom to come. Next, we ask Him for what we need for that day, just our daily bread and nothing more. Finally, we admit our need for His direction and forgiveness and our desire for Him to keep us from the schemes of the devil. The next time you and your family pray this prayer, try breaking it down into its parts and discussing each aspect of the prayer.

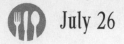

Cheesy Noodle Casserole

1 (16 ounce) package egg
   noodles
¼ cup butter
⅛ cup flour
½ teaspoon garlic salt

½ teaspoon onion salt
3 cups milk
1 pound processed cheese, cubed
¼ cup bread crumbs
· 1 tablespoon butter, melted

Cook noodles according to package directions. Melt butter in medium saucepan; add flour, garlic salt, and onion salt, stirring after each addition. Gradually add milk; stir thoroughly. Bring to boil. Cook and stir for 2 minutes or until mixture thickens. Add cheese and stir until melted. Add noodles. Pour into greased 2-quart baking dish. Toss bread crumbs in melted butter and sprinkle over top of casserole. Bake uncovered at 350 degrees for 25 minutes or until golden brown.

Yield: 6 to 8 servings

Giving Back

Whoever is kind to the poor lends to the Lord,
and he will reward them for what they have done.
PROVERBS 19:17 NIV

What is your favorite way of giving back to God? Do you tithe? Maybe you donate your time at a food pantry or volunteer with children at your church or a neighborhood school. Have you considered volunteering together as a family? What better way for your children to learn than to watch their parents being the hands and feet of Jesus?

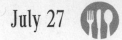
Devil's Food Cake with Fluffy Frosting

2¼ cups flour
⅔ cup cocoa
1¼ teaspoons baking soda
¼ teaspoon baking powder
1 teaspoon salt
¾ cup vegetable shortening
1⅔ cups sugar
2 large eggs
1 teaspoon vanilla

1½ cups water

Frosting:
¼ cup flour
1 cup milk
1 cup butter or margarine,
    softened
1 cup sugar
1 teaspoon vanilla

Grease and flour 9x13-inch baking pan. Combine flour, cocoa, baking soda, baking powder, and salt. Set aside. In large mixing bowl, cream shortening and sugar. Beat in eggs and vanilla. Gradually add dry ingredients alternately with water. Beat on low speed for 30 seconds, then on high speed for 3 minutes, scraping bowl occasionally. Pour batter into prepared pan. Bake at 350 degrees for 40 to 45 minutes or until wooden pick inserted in center comes out clean. Cool on wire rack.

For frosting, whisk together flour and milk in saucepan; cook until thick, stirring constantly. Remove from heat, cover. Let cool, stirring frequently to keep mixture smooth. In bowl, cream together butter, sugar, and vanilla; add flour and milk mixture. Beat until light and fluffy. Frost cooled cake.

Yield: 12 to 16 servings

The Buffet

"Everything that lives and moves about will be food for you. Just as I gave you the green plants, I now give you everything."
GENESIS 9:3 NIV

Don't you love how God has provided for His people? He gave us so many choices! Do you prefer dining at a buffet? Filling your plate with a plethora of tastes is what you love best. The Lord has given us a full buffet of food from which to choose. Enjoy His bounty!

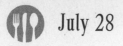

BBQ Hamburger Muffins

1 pound ground beef
½ cup onion, finely chopped
½ cup barbecue sauce
Garlic powder

1 (10 count) tube refrigerated
  biscuits
½ cup shredded cheddar or swiss
  cheese

Brown ground beef and onion; drain. Add barbecue sauce and garlic powder. Pull apart biscuits and place individual biscuits in muffin pan. Place meat mixture on top of biscuits. Bake at 375 degrees for 15 to 20 minutes. Remove from oven and cover each hamburger muffin with cheese; bake additional 5 minutes or until cheese is completely melted.

Yield: 10 servings

Keeping a Promise

The one who calls you is faithful, and he will do it.
1 THESSALONIANS 5:24 NIV

What does your family say about promises? In my family, we learned at a very young age not to make a promise we couldn't keep. Even our best efforts, however, sometimes result in promises that just cannot be kept. Aren't you glad our heavenly Father is not bound by human frailties? He always keeps His promise. Every time!

Caramel Apple Salad

1 (4 serving size) package instant
butterscotch pudding mix
1 (8 ounce) tub whipped topping
1 (10 ounce) can crushed
pineapple, including juice

1 cup miniature marshmallows
3 cups apples, pared and cut into
small chunks

Mix all ingredients together; refrigerate for 1 hour before serving.

Yield: 12 to 14 servings

Praise His Name

LORD, our Lord, how majestic is your name in all the earth!
PSALM 8:9 NIV

I'll bet you and your family are proud of your name, aren't you? You
might even have your name worked into some sort of art, or maybe your
monogram is out on display. Your name is what identifies you as a family
and sets you apart from others who are not related to you. As great as your
name might be to you, however, there is a name that is above all other
names, and that belongs to the Lord. Praise His mighty name!

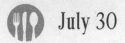

Curry Dip

1 cup real mayonnaise
¼ teaspoon curry powder
  (or ½ teaspoon onion powder)

½ teaspoon tarragon vinegar
Dash salt
½ medium onion, finely chopped

Combine all ingredients and chill for 2 hours. Serve with fresh vegetables.

Yield: 6 servings

The Gathering Place

I will be fully satisfied as with the richest of foods;
with singing lips my mouth will praise you.
PSALM 63:5 NIV

The family table is the gathering place of the home, isn't it? The table is where homework is done, where family and friends enjoy each other's company, and where coffee is lingered over in quiet moments of the day. There's not much better than time spent together at the table, especially when good food and God are the focus!

Family Dinnertime Tip

If you're overworked and overstressed, take a time-out and spend some family "quiet time" together. Savor this time and let the Lord speak to your hearts.

Lolita's Summer Zucchini Casserole

⅓ cup olive oil
2 tablespoons white wine vinegar
2 tablespoons parsley
3 teaspoons salt
¾ teaspoon pepper
1 teaspoon hot sauce
1 medium zucchini, chopped
2 white potatoes, chopped
2 small green bell peppers,
    chopped

2 carrots, chopped
1 celery stalk, chopped
Olive oil cooking spray
3 to 4 medium tomatoes, thinly
    sliced, divided
⅓ to ½ cup raw rice (not instant)
1¾ cups cheddar cheese,
    shredded

Blend oil, vinegar, parsley, salt, pepper, and hot sauce; set aside. In large bowl, combine zucchini, potatoes, green peppers, carrots, and celery. Spray large casserole dish with oil. Cover bottom with sliced tomatoes (saving some for top layers). Cover with half of vegetables. Add another layer of tomatoes. Sprinkle with rice. Add remaining vegetables and top with final layer of tomatoes. Stir oil mixture and pour over all. Cover with foil and bake at 350 degrees for 1 hour and 25 minutes. Remove foil and sprinkle casserole with cheese. Bake for additional 15 minutes.

Yield: 8 servings

Listening and Watching

Their mouths lay claim to heaven,
and their tongues take possession of the earth.
PSALM 73:9 NIV

Have you ever met someone who professes the Lord with words but does not exactly show those same beliefs with actions? The Lord tells us we are to carry ourselves at all times as children of God, always expecting that we are being watched by those who may not yet know Jesus. Do you want to push someone away who might otherwise be searching for the Lord? Of course not!

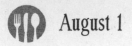

Honey-Nut Latte

1 ounce hazelnut syrup	Steamed milk
1 ounce honey	Whipped topping
1 to 2 shots espresso	Honey to taste
(approximately 1 to 2 ounces)	Nuts, finely ground

In large mug, mix hazelnut syrup and honey with espresso; stir until honey dissolves. Fill mug with steamed milk. Garnish with whipped topping, honey, and nuts.

Yield: 1 serving

The Principle of Giving

John answered, "Anyone who has two shirts should share with the one who has none, and anyone who has food should do the same."
LUKE 3:11 NIV

One of the first things children are taught is to share. The lesson may be learned with toys or treats, but those children who understand giving have created a lifetime habit that will serve them into adulthood. Did your parents insist you take the principle of giving to heart as a child? If so, then how can you make sure you pass it on to your family? If not, it is never too late to learn and never too late to pass that treasure on to those you love.

Fruit Cocktail Cake

2 cups fruit cocktail
2 eggs, well beaten
1½ cups sugar
2 cups flour
2 teaspoons baking soda
¼ teaspoon salt
½ cup brown sugar, packed
½ cup chopped pecans

Icing:
½ cup butter or margarine,
  softened
¾ cup sugar
1 cup sweetened, flaked coconut
½ cup evaporated milk
1 teaspoon vanilla

In mixing bowl, combine fruit cocktail, eggs, and sugar. Mix well. In small bowl, combine flour, baking soda, and salt. Blend dry ingredients with fruit mixture. Pour into buttered 9-inch square pan; sprinkle with brown sugar and pecans. Bake at 300 degrees for 30 minutes or until cake tests done. Cool completely.

To prepare icing, cream butter with sugar. Add remaining ingredients and blend well. Frost cooled cake.

Yield: 9 to 12 servings

God's Kindness

*"I am unworthy of all the kindness and faithfulness you have shown
your servant. I had only my staff when I crossed this Jordan,
but now I have become two camps."*
GENESIS 32:10 NIV

"I am unworthy." Have you ever taken a moment to consider what God has given you? From the home and family where your life and love is centered to the friends He has allowed into your life, God has blessed you. From the meal you're cooking for dinner to the friends and family who sit at your table, He has given you so very much. Whether you are blessed with material treasure or your treasure is only waiting in heaven, the Lord has shown you great kindness and faithfulness. Thank Him today.

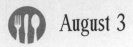

No-Peek Steak

4 pounds round steak, cut into squares

1 (10¾ ounce) can condensed cream of mushroom soup

1 (10¾ ounce) can condensed cream of celery soup

1 (10¾ ounce) can condensed cream of onion soup

1 (6 ounce) jar sliced mushrooms

Place steak in casserole dish. Combine soups and pour over top of steak. Spread mushrooms over all. Bake at 225 degrees for 4 hours. Don't peek!

Yield: 6 servings

A Lasting Legacy

Know therefore that the LORD your God is God; he is the faithful God, keeping his covenant of love to a thousand generations of those who love him and keep his commandments.
DEUTERONOMY 7:9 NIV

God promises us love through a thousand generations. Can you even fathom how many years that is? If each generation comprises thirty years, that is thirty thousand years! Of course, His love and faithfulness are unconditional and without beginning or end, and His promises will be true forever. What a lasting legacy He offers. If your family loves the Lord, consider what kind of legacy you will leave to the generations who follow. What can you do now to create a legacy worthy of passing forward? Start today.

Summer Chicken Salad

1 cup mayonnaise
1 tablespoon Dijon mustard
1½ tablespoons vinegar
1 teaspoon garlic powder
½ teaspoon salt
2 to 3 chicken breasts, cooked, cubed, and chilled

8 ounces corkscrew pasta, cooked and rinsed in cold water
1 green bell pepper, chopped
½ small onion, chopped
2 cups grapes, sliced in half
½ cup sliced almonds

Blend mayonnaise, mustard, vinegar, garlic powder, and salt. Place chicken, pasta, bell pepper, onion, and grapes in large bowl. Coat with dressing and chill for at least 1 hour. Add almonds when ready to serve.

Yield: 4 to 6 servings

Habits Are Hard to Break

"Now fear the LORD and serve him with all faithfulness. Throw away the gods your ancestors worshiped beyond the Euphrates River and in Egypt, and serve the LORD."
JOSHUA 24:14 NIV

Habits can be hard to break. Often we don't even know why we do certain things until we realize we are simply repeating behaviors we learned from our parents—who learned the same behaviors from their parents. God is calling you to a higher standard than mindless repetition. He wants the best for you and your family. What things in your life need changing? What habits can you throw away or perhaps learn that will lead you and those you love to a closer relationship with God? Ask Him and He will tell you.

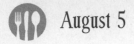

Oyster Corn Bread Dressing

2 (8 ounce) packages corn bread mix
4 tablespoons butter
¾ cup chopped onion
3 stalks celery, chopped
2 garlic cloves, minced
2 (8 ounce) cans oysters, liquid reserved and oysters chopped
(less is acceptable, or substitute ½ to 1 cup turkey giblets, cooked and chopped)
2 eggs, beaten
½ teaspoon black pepper
1½ teaspoons ground sage
3 teaspoons poultry seasoning
1 (14 ounce) can chicken stock

Prepare corn bread as instructed on package; allow to cool before crumbling corn bread into large mixing bowl. In large saucepan, melt butter over low heat and sauté onion, celery, garlic, and oysters until onion is glassy and tender. Stir oyster mixture into corn bread crumbs. In separate bowl, beat eggs, then season with pepper, sage, and poultry seasoning. Mix in chicken stock and reserved oyster liquid. Blend egg mixture into corn bread mixture. Place in oiled 2-quart casserole. Bake uncovered at 350 degrees for 45 minutes.

Yield: 8 servings

He Is Waiting

"But when you pray, go into your room, close the door and pray to your Father, who is unseen. Then your Father, who sees what is done in secret, will reward you."
MATTHEW 6:6 NIV

We live in a world where very few things are private anymore. Social media allows almost instant broadcast of almost anything, whether good or bad. While there are many good reasons to go public to proclaim the glory of the Lord and take His salvation message to the masses, God also says He wants time with only you. Have you and your family made time to be alone with the Lord today? He's waiting.

Hot Artichoke Dip

1 (8 ounce) package cream
    cheese, softened
1 (14 ounce) can artichoke hearts,
    drained and chopped
½ cup real mayonnaise
½ cup grated Parmesan cheese

2 tablespoons fresh basil, finely
    chopped (or 1 teaspoon dried
    basil leaves)
2 tablespoons red onion, finely
chopped
1 clove garlic, minced
½ cup tomato, chopped

Mix all ingredients except tomato with mixer on medium speed until well blended. Spoon into 9-inch pie pan. Bake at 350 degrees for 25 minutes. Sprinkle with tomatoes. Serve with assorted vegetables or toasted pita wedges.

Yield: 10 servings

Not Forgotten

*Remember me for this, my God, and do not blot out what I have
so faithfully done for the house of my God and its services.*
NEHEMIAH 13:14 NIV

Do you ever feel like the good things you did yesterday—whether for your family or at work or in some other area of your life—are forgotten today? Maybe it sometimes feels like no one notices what you've done for others. God says that He notices. In fact, He says in His Word that He sees everything and never forgets. While we will never be perfect like God, we can try to be like Him to the best of our abilities. Tomorrow, why don't you bless someone by telling them that you have noticed something nice they've done? After you've told them, you can tell your family the story at dinner tomorrow. Sound like fun? Great! Just wait and see, though. You will be as blessed as the person you're blessing.

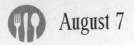

Café Mocha

1 ounce chocolate syrup
1 shot espresso (approximately 1 ounce)

Steamed milk
Whipped topping
Chocolate sprinkles

Place chocolate syrup and espresso in coffee mug. Fill remainder of coffee mug with steamed milk. Garnish with whipped topping and chocolate sprinkles.

Yield: 1 serving

Because He Loves You

*Know that the L*ORD *has set apart his faithful servant*
*for himself; the L*ORD *hears when I call to him.*
PSALM 4:3 NIV

Have you ever been in a noisy room where all the voices blended together. . .until you heard your loved one? That one voice, so very familiar to your ears and your heart, is somehow the one that reaches your ears. In the same way, when you call on God, He always hears, not because your voice is louder than others but because He loves you. And when He loves you, your voice always reaches His ears.

Family Dinnertime Tip

Do you find that you spend too much time worrying about what you just have to get done? Intentionally redirect your thoughts toward gratitude. What are you most thankful for? Your health? A loving family? A great career? You'll quickly forget about your worries when you see how richly the Lord has blessed you.

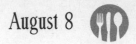

Grasshopper Cake

1 package white cake mix
½ cup crème de menthe, divided
1 (16 ounce) jar fudge topping

1 (12 ounce) carton whipped
 topping, thawed

Prepare cake mix according to package directions. Stir in ¼ cup crème de menthe. Spread into prepared 9x13-inch cake pan. Bake at 350 degrees according to package directions, until cake tests done. Cool completely. Spread cooled cake with fudge topping. Fold ¼ cup crème de menthe into thawed whipped topping. Spread evenly over fudge topping. Chill until ready to serve.

Yield: 12 to 16 servings

Practice Forgiveness

A person's wisdom yields patience;
it is to one's glory to overlook an offense.
PROVERBS 19:11 NIV

Do you practice forgiveness in your family? When someone you love says or does something hurtful, how do you respond? God says with wisdom comes patience. Are you patient with those who try your patience? Have you found a way to look past the wrongs? God says with His help and by following His lead, you and your family can create an environment of forgiveness. What step can you take today toward that goal?

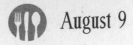

Pepper Steak

1½ pounds round steak
2 tablespoons cooking oil
2 medium green bell peppers, cut
   into short strips
1 small onion, sliced
2 medium tomatoes, peeled
   and chopped
1 cup water

¼ cup soy sauce
½ teaspoon pepper
¼ teaspoon salt
¼ teaspoon ground ginger
2 tablespoons cornstarch
2 tablespoons water
4 cups rice, cooked

With meat mallet, pound steak to ¼ inch thick, then cut steak across grain into thin strips. In large skillet, heat oil and brown steak on both sides; drain. Add green peppers, onion, and tomatoes. Pour in water and soy sauce, then season with pepper, salt, and ginger. Cover skillet and simmer over low heat for 1 hour. Blend cornstarch into 2 tablespoons water; pour over steak mixture. Cook for 2 minutes until thick, stirring constantly. Serve over hot rice.

Yield: 4 servings

Complete Trust

Into your hands I commit my spirit;
deliver me, LORD, my faithful God.
PSALM 31:5 NIV

When David penned those words, he was in dire circumstances. His enemies were closing in, and his life was in jeopardy. In the verses leading up to this one, David asks God to save him. Then comes this part of his prayer, possibly the most important words he says to the Lord: no matter what the result, he commits his spirit to God. Like David, we all come to a point in our lives and in our prayers where we must tell God that no matter the result, we leave our lives in His capable hands. That, friends, is complete trust. God calls us to trust Him, even with our lives. Can you honestly say that you have turned over whatever situation is bothering you today to Him? If not, then why?

45-Minute Casserole

1 pound ground beef
1 large onion, chopped
1 (10¾ ounce) can condensed
    cream of celery soup

1 (14½ ounce) can sauerkraut
1 (38 ounce) bag frozen Tater
    Tots

Brown ground beef and onion; drain. Place in casserole dish. Top with soup. Drain and rinse sauerkraut; spread over casserole mixture. Place Tater Tots over all. Bake at 350 degrees for 45 minutes.

Yield: 4 servings

Stubborn

They would not be like their ancestors—a stubborn and rebellious
generation, whose hearts were not loyal to God,
whose spirits were not faithful to him.
PSALM 78:8 NIV

Would you say you come from stubborn people? Would people call you stubborn? God says we are not to be like those whose stubborn nature caused them to be rebellious and disloyal to God. There's nothing wrong with taking a strong stand on an issue or standing firm for things you believe in. Be mindful, however, of being stubborn when it comes to the things of God. He never blesses the rebellious, and a disloyal heart will never please Him. Next time you're tempted to stubbornness, ask yourself if you're obeying God with that behavior. Ouch!

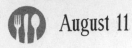

Beefy Noodle Casserole

1 pound ground beef
1 (16 ounce) package egg
   noodles
1 (10¾ ounce) can condensed
   cream of mushroom soup

½ cup milk
5 tablespoons butter
Salt and pepper to taste

Brown ground beef; drain. Cook noodles according to package directions; drain. Combine all ingredients in large casserole dish. Bake at 350 degrees for 30 minutes.

Yield: 4 servings

Beneath the Starry Skies

For great is your love, higher than the heavens;
your faithfulness reaches to the skies.
PSALM 108:4 NIV

Have you ever stood beneath a starry sky on a clear night and looked up at the vastness of the universe our Lord created? The same Creator who made you, the same Creator who spins the planets in orbit and guides your steps on earth, lovingly and purposefully made each of those tiny pinpoints of light. After dinner tonight, take your family out to see the majesty of the heavens above and know that as vast as those skies are, so much more is the vastness of God's love for us.

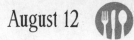

Ham and Swiss Dip

1 (8 ounce) package cream
   cheese, softened
⅔ cup real mayonnaise
1½ cups fully cooked ham, diced
1 cup (4 ounces) swiss cheese,
   shredded

1 tablespoon spicy brown
   mustard
¾ cup rye cracker crumbs
2 tablespoons butter, melted
Rye crackers

In small mixing bowl, beat cream cheese and mayonnaise until smooth.
Stir in ham, cheese, and mustard. Spread in ungreased 9-inch pie plate.
Toss cracker crumbs in butter; sprinkle over cream cheese mixture. Bake
uncovered at 400 degrees for 12 to 15 minutes or until heated through.
Serve with rye crackers.

Yield: 10 servings

In Him Is Life

In him was life, and that life was the light of all mankind.
JOHN 1:4 NIV

Do you know the difference between happiness and life? God says life
is found in Him. Does He mean that once you and your family become
believers, you will find the just-right formula that will keep all troubles
away? Unfortunately, no believer will find complete happiness this side
of heaven. That's just how God designed things. The next time you're
tempted to complain about unhappy circumstances,
think about God's promise: in Him is life.

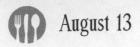

White Chocolate Coffee

3 ounces white chocolate, grated   2 cups hot brewed coffee
2 cups whole milk   Whipped topping (optional)

Place white chocolate and milk in microwave-safe bowl and heat for 2 minutes; stir until mixture is smooth and chocolate is melted completely. Stir in coffee. Serve in large mugs and top with whipped topping if desired.

Yield: 4 servings

Keep Your Eyes on Jesus

Immediately Jesus reached out his hand and caught him.
"You of little faith," he said, "why did you doubt?"
MATTHEW 14:31 NIV

Have you ever played a game where you followed a map to find a buried treasure? How did you find that treasure? By reading the map, of course! What would have happened if you'd stopped reading that map halfway through the search? Or what if you'd closed your eyes and tried to find the treasure? How likely do you think it would have been that you would find that treasure? Not likely, right? In the same way, Jesus tells us He is the treasure we are seeking. How do you find Him? Easy! You keep your eyes on Him and have faith that, just like that treasure map in your game, He will guide you to where you will find exactly what you're looking for: Him!

Hummingbird Cake

3 cups flour
2 cups sugar
1 teaspoon salt
1 teaspoon baking soda
1 teaspoon cinnamon
3 eggs, beaten
1½ cups vegetable oil
2 teaspoons vanilla
1 (8 ounce) can crushed
   pineapple, undrained
2 cups chopped bananas
   (about 4 medium)

2 cups chopped pecans, divided

Cream Cheese Frosting:
2 (8 ounce) packages cream
   cheese, softened
1 cup butter or margarine
1 (2 pound) package powdered
   sugar
2 teaspoons vanilla
1 dash salt

Grease and flour three 9-inch round cake pans. In large mixing bowl, combine dry ingredients. Add eggs and oil and stir until moistened. Stir in vanilla, pineapple, bananas, and 1 cup pecans. Divide batter evenly between pans. Bake at 350 degrees for 25 minutes or until toothpick inserted in center comes out clean. Cool for 10 minutes in pans; then transfer to wire cooling racks. Cool completely.

For frosting, beat cream cheese and butter until smooth. Add powdered sugar and beat until light and fluffy. Beat in vanilla and salt. Spread between cooled cake layers and on sides and top of cake. Garnish with remaining pecans.

Yield: 8 to 12 servings

Will They Know You?

As water reflects the face, so one's life reflects the heart.
PROVERBS 27:19 NIV

As you look around your table at mealtime, it is likely that you know each person there very well. Each face, each life, is as familiar to you. You know them, and they know you. What about people outside your family? When strangers listen to you talk or watch how you live, do they know who you are and what you believe? Can they recognize you as a Christian?

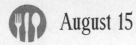

Chicken 'n' Pasta Skillet

1 tablespoon vegetable oil
1 pound boneless, skinless
   chicken breasts, cut into strips
1 (10¾ ounce) can condensed
   cream of mushroom soup
2¼ cups water

2 cups frozen vegetable
   combination of your choice
2 cups corkscrew pasta,
   uncooked
Grated Parmesan cheese

Heat oil in skillet. Add chicken; cook until browned. Remove chicken from skillet and set aside. To skillet, add soup, water, vegetables, and pasta. Heat until boiling, then reduce heat to medium. Cook for 10 minutes, stirring frequently. Add chicken. Cook for an additional 5 minutes. Sprinkle with Parmesan cheese.

Yield: 4 to 6 servings

What Is Your Question?

"Have faith in God," Jesus answered.
MARK 11:22 NIV

I love that this scripture is an answer to a question, don't you? I also love that this answer fits a plethora of questions. Do you have questions about what God is doing in your current circumstances? Have faith in God! Are you concerned about how your children will turn out? Have faith in God! Maybe you're just prone to worry about a hundred little things every day until you reach the point where your mind is constantly spinning. Have faith in God! Do you see how Jesus has given you the answer? Tell me, what is your question?

Ham 'n' Potato Casserole

3 (16 ounce) packages frozen
   hash browns
3 (8 ounce) packages cheddar
   cheese, shredded
2 pounds ham, diced

2 (10¾ ounce) cans condensed
   cheddar cheese soup
2 onions, diced
1 quart milk

Mix all ingredients in large roaster pan. Bake at 400 degrees for 1 hour. Stir occasionally while baking.

Yield: 8 to 10 servings

The Obedient Child

*As obedient children, do not conform to the evil
desires you had when you lived in ignorance.*
1 PETER 1:14 NIV

Were you an obedient child? Perhaps you were one of those children that might be termed difficult. Perhaps you're a parent of one of those children. There is definitely a difference in the two types, just as there is a difference in a person prior to becoming a Christian and after. As followers of Jesus, you and your family are now walking a different path than you all once walked. God says to continue to be obedient because you are His child. He is greatly pleased when you do obey.

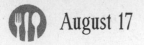

Slush Punch

4 cups sugar
Water
3 (3 ounce) packages peach gelatin
 (or flavor of your choice)

2 (46 ounce) cans unsweetened
 pineapple juice
1 tablespoon lemon juice
2 liters lemon-lime soda, at room
 temperature

In saucepan, mix sugar and 4 cups water; bring to boil. Let cool. Dissolve gelatin in 3 cups boiling water then add 6 cups cold water. Add sugar and gelatin mixtures together with juices. Freeze until solid (approximately 2 days). Remove from freezer 2 to 3 hours before serving and pour warm lemon-lime soda over top. Mix until slushy.

Yield: 16 to 20 servings

The Limits of Fun

Jesus said to his disciples: "Things that cause people to stumble are bound to come, but woe to anyone through whom they come."
LUKE 17:1 NIV

Does your family like playing practical jokes? Perhaps you've made good use of a whoopee cushion or plastic spider, all in good fun, of course. These pranks are, for the most part, harmless expressions of fun. But what about when something someone thinks is fun goes beyond the limits God has set up for His people? God says temptations will happen as long as we are on this side of heaven. His warning is stern, however, against being the person who is the cause of someone else straying from God's path. That, He says, is cause for great woe. It's no joke!

Family Dinnertime Tip

Did you know lemons and limes can be frozen whole? Then when you're in need of fruit juice, you can simply thaw the lemon or lime in the microwave and squeeze out fresh-tasting juice any time of the year.

Cheesy Baked Spaghetti

8 ounces thin spaghetti noodles
1 pound ground beef
1 (45 ounce) jar spaghetti sauce
½ small white onion, finely
　chopped

1 green bell pepper, chopped
1 cup shredded mozzarella
　cheese

Cook spaghetti noodles according to package directions; drain. Brown ground beef; drain. Place noodles and beef in buttered square baking dish. Cover with spaghetti sauce; stir in onion and green pepper. Top with cheese. Bake at 300 degrees for 25 minutes.

Yield: 4 to 6 servings

Always!

No temptation has overtaken you except what is common to mankind. And God is faithful; he will not let you be tempted beyond what you can bear. But when you are tempted, he will also provide a way out so that you can endure it.
1 CORINTHIANS 10:13 NIV

"I'm not perfect!" How many times have you said that or heard it from a family member? Well, of course you're not. Despite our good intentions, God says in His Word that there has never been a perfect person other than Jesus. Because we are imperfectly human, we will be tempted to stray from the path He has placed us on. That's the bad news. The good news is that He promises always to provide a way back to the path. Always. Don't you love that? Not sometimes. Always!

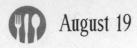

Fiesta Casserole

1½ pounds ground beef
1 envelope taco seasoning
1 (15 ounce) can tomato sauce
1 (11 ounce) can whole-kernel
    corn, drained
1 cup shredded cheddar cheese

1 cup tortilla chips, coarsely
    crushed
Sour cream
1 tomato, chopped
½ head lettuce, chopped

Brown ground beef in large skillet; drain. Stir in taco seasoning, tomato sauce, and corn. Simmer for 5 minutes. Spoon mixture into 2-quart baking dish. Top with cheese and crushed tortilla chips. Bake at 250 degrees until cheese is melted, approximately 6 to 10 minutes. Garnish with sour cream and top with tomato and lettuce.

Yield: 4 to 6 servings

A Worthy Tradition

Impress them on your children. Talk about them when
you sit at home and when you walk along the road,
when you lie down and when you get up.
DEUTERONOMY 6:7 NIV

Parents, do you have a tradition of reading to your children? Or perhaps you tell them stories that you once heard from your parents or grandparents. Handing down stories from parent to child is a tradition as old as time. God says to do the same thing with His Word, His stories. A parent who impresses the rich tradition of Christianity on his or her children is a parent with whom God is well pleased.

Jewel Cakes

2 cups pecan pieces
1¾ cups walnut pieces
1¼ cups golden raisins
½ pound pitted dates, chopped
¾ cup red candied cherries,
    coarsely chopped

¾ cup green candied cherries,
    coarsely chopped
1½ cups candied pineapple,
    coarsely chopped
1 (14 ounce) can sweetened
    condensed milk

In large mixing bowl, combine all ingredients and mix well with large spoon. Pack tightly into well-greased mini muffin cups. Bake at 275 degrees for 25 to 30 minutes.

Yield: 24 cakes

The Family of God

*If you belong to Christ, then you are Abraham's seed,
and heirs according to the promise.*
GALATIANS 3:29 NIV

There are all sorts of families. Some are made up of siblings born to the same set of parents, while others are composed of children who are adopted. God tells us in this verse that we are never to think of ourselves as anything but God's family. If we belong to Christ, we belong to the family of God. Just as it does not matter whether the children in your family were born into it, it also does not matter to God where you began. He only cares that you're His now. Welcome to the family of God!

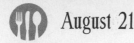

Mexican Stuffed Shells

24 jumbo pasta shells
1 pound ground beef
2 cups salsa
1 (8 ounce) can tomato sauce
1 cup whole-kernel corn, drained
1 (16 ounce) can refried beans

½ cup shredded cheddar cheese
½ cup sour cream
½ cup salsa
¼ cup black olives, sliced
¼ cup green onions, sliced

Cook pasta shells according to package directions; drain. In large skillet, brown ground beef; drain. Stir 2 cups salsa, tomato sauce, corn, and beans into beef. Carefully spoon mixture into cooked pasta shells. Place shells in lightly greased 9x13-inch baking dish. Sprinkle each shell with cheese. Cover dish with aluminum foil and bake at 350 degrees for 25 to 30 minutes. Serve shells topped with sour cream, ½ cup salsa, olives, and onions.

Yield: 6 to 8 servings

Traveling Man

"So on that day Moses swore to me, 'The land on which your feet have walked will be your inheritance and that of your children forever, because you have followed the LORD my God wholeheartedly.'"
JOSHUA 14:9 NIV

Moses did a lot of traveling during his life, from a basket in the rushes to Egypt and finally to the edge of the Promised Land. His feet did a lot of walking! Moses never saw the land of milk and honey promised by God, but his children and grandchildren did. Are you willing to do all the work, just as Moses did, to benefit your children and grandchildren even if it means you will never see the blessing this side of heaven?

Yellow Tomato Preserves

8 pounds pear-shaped yellow
   tomatoes
2 lemons, thinly sliced with seeds
   removed

1½ quarts water
6 pounds sugar
4 to 6 pieces gingerroot

Wash tomatoes and leave skins on; or, if desired, scald and remove skins.
Cook lemons for approximately 20 minutes in 1 pint water. Boil remaining
water and sugar to make a syrup; add tomatoes, gingerroot, and cooked
lemon liquid. Boil until tomatoes are somewhat clear and the syrup thick.
Remove the filmy covering and pour the preserves into hot sterilized
glass jars.
Seal and store in a cool, dry place.

Yield: 9 cups of preserves

A Clean Slate

Because of the LORD's great love we are not consumed,
for his compassions never fail. They are new
every morning; great is your faithfulness.
LAMENTATIONS 3:22–23 NIV

Don't you love fresh starts? There's nothing quite like turning the page
and beginning again. Did you have a bad day? Perhaps you said things
you wish you could take back or missed out on a good night's sleep thanks
to something out of your control. Tomorrow is a new day!
Tomorrow you can make those misspoken words
right again. You can get a good night's sleep
and awaken fresh and ready to see what God
has for you. Just believe that He's capable of
giving you a clean slate daily, because He is!

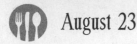

Oatmeal–Chocolate Chip Cake

1¾ cups boiling water
1 cup quick or old-fashioned oats
1 cup brown sugar, packed
1 cup sugar
3 tablespoons milk
½ cup butter or margarine,
    softened
3 eggs, beaten

1¾ cups flour
1 teaspoon baking soda
½ teaspoon salt
2 tablespoons cocoa
1 (12 ounce) package mini
    chocolate chips, divided
1 cup chopped walnuts

Pour boiling water over oatmeal; let stand at room temperature for 15 minutes. Add sugars, milk, butter, and eggs; beat well. In small bowl, combine flour, baking soda, salt, and cocoa. Gradually stir into oatmeal mixture. Stir in 1 cup chocolate chips. Pour into greased 9x13-inch pan. Sprinkle remaining chocolate chips and walnuts on top. Bake at 350 degrees for 40 minutes.

Yield: 12 to 16 servings

Amazing Grace

*For it is by grace you have been saved, through faith—
and this is not from yourselves, it is the gift of God.*
EPHESIANS 2:8 NIV

Amazing grace, how sweet the sound! How many times have you sung those words without actually considering what they mean to you personally? Indeed we all were lost, every one of us on this earth, but those who have given their lives to the Lord have the blessing of being saved thanks to the grace of God. We do nothing to earn this salvation beyond accepting what the Lord offers. It is His grace, His loving-kindness, that allows us entry into the family of God. How sweet indeed is the sound of that!

Macaroni-Sausage Bake

1 cup elbow macaroni
1 pound bulk pork sausage
½ cup green bell pepper,
    chopped
½ cup red bell pepper, chopped
⅛ cup onion, chopped

½ teaspoon dried oregano
¼ teaspoon pepper
2 (8 ounce) cans tomato sauce
1 cup water
⅛ cup grated Parmesan cheese,
    divided

Cook macaroni according to package directions; drain and set aside. Cook sausage in skillet over medium heat until no longer pink; drain. Add green pepper, red pepper, onion, oregano, and pepper. Stir in tomato sauce and water. Boil. Reduce heat and simmer for 5 minutes. Stir in macaroni and half of Parmesan cheese. Pour mixture into ungreased 2-quart baking dish. Sprinkle remaining cheese on top. Bake uncovered at 350 degrees for 25 minutes or until bubbly.

Yield: 4 servings

A Valuable Inheritance

"As for me, this is my covenant with them," says the LORD. "My Spirit, who is on you, will not depart from you, and my words that I have put in your mouth will always be on your lips, on the lips of your children and on the lips of their descendants— from this time on and forever," says the LORD.
ISAIAH 59:21 NIV

Don't you love how God has set us all into families of His own design? He entrusts each of us with a circle of family and friends to love and care for, and in the same way, He loves and cares for us. Tell those you love about the Lord. It is His plan for them to hear what has been so kindly done for you. Keep praises for the Lord on your lips, especially in the presence of others. In that way, you will pass on an inheritance far more valuable than any earthly treasure.

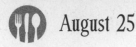

Corn Casserole

1 (15 ounce) can whole-kernel corn

1 (15 ounce) can cream-style corn

1 (8 ounce) container sour cream

1 egg, beaten

3 tablespoons onion, chopped

1 (8½ ounce) box corn muffin mix

½ stick margarine, softened

⅓ teaspoon parsley

½ teaspoon salt

½ teaspoon pepper

Combine all ingredients in greased 2½-quart casserole dish. Bake at 350 degrees for 45 minutes.

Yield: 8 to 10 servings

Wear Love and Faithfulness

Let love and faithfulness never leave you; bind them around your neck, write them on the tablet of your heart.
PROVERBS 3:3 NIV

Do you or any of your family members wear a cross necklace? It's a lovely expression of faith and a reminder of what our Savior went through to take away our sins. It is also a sign to others that the wearer is a believer in Christ. Even more than wearing a cross around our necks, how we think and behave is a sign of our faith. God says to let love and faithfulness never leave us. Like you wear your cross, also wear those habits proudly. They mark you as a child of the King.

Old-Fashioned Gingerbread Cake

2 (10¾ ounce) cans condensed
    tomato soup
3 eggs, lightly beaten
2 (14 ounce) packages
    gingerbread mix

1 cup raisins
1 cup chopped walnuts
Powdered sugar

In large mixing bowl, blend soup and eggs. Stir in gingerbread mix. Blend at low speed until thoroughly moistened, then beat 2 minutes on medium speed. Fold in raisins and nuts. Pour into well-greased 9-inch tube pan. Bake at 325 degrees for 1 hour and 15 minutes or until cake tests done. Cool in pan for 10 minutes; remove from pan. Sprinkle top with powdered sugar. Serve warm or at room temperature.

Yield: 12 servings

The Eternal Promise

"I will establish my covenant as an everlasting covenant between me and you and your descendants after you for the generations to come, to be your God and the God of your descendants after you."
GENESIS 17:7 NIV

What is a covenant? One dictionary defines it as a legal and binding agreement that remains in effect as long as the persons who made the covenant are alive. In the same way, God has made a covenant with us that will last until we reach heaven. He has offered His Holy Spirit and His Word to be our guide until the day our journey toward Him ends. When we are long departed from this earth, our families and their families will share the same covenant with God that we have. His words and His promises are eternal. What a blessing!

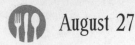
One-Dish Lasagna

2 (45 ounce) jars spaghetti sauce, divided
1 (12 ounce) box lasagna noodles, uncooked, divided
1 pound ground beef, uncooked, divided
¼ cup onion, finely chopped
1 (8 ounce) container small-curd cottage cheese
4 cups shedded mozzarella cheese, divided
1½ cups hot water
Grated Parmesan cheese

Cover bottom of 9x13-inch baking dish with ⅓ of spaghetti sauce. Layer in following order: half of lasagna noodles, half of ground beef, onion, cottage cheese, ⅓ of sauce, remaining noodles, half of mozzarella cheese, remaining ground beef, remaining sauce, and remaining mozzarella cheese. Press down with spoon, then add hot water. Press mixture down with spoon again, then sprinkle with Parmesan cheese. Cover with aluminum foil and bake at 375 degrees for 1 hour. Remove from oven and uncover; bake for additional 45 minutes. Let stand for 10 minutes before serving.

Yield: 6 to 8 servings

The Undivided Heart

Teach me your way, LORD, that I may rely on your faithfulness; give me an undivided heart, that I may fear your name.
PSALM 86:11 NIV

God promises that if we ask, He will teach us. Unlike a class where you don't understand the topic and thus make less than stellar grades, He never gives us more to learn than what we can manage. All He asks in return is for us to love Him with all our heart. Is there any part of your heart that hasn't been given over to God? If so, ask Him to show you how you can have an undivided heart. Ask. He will answer.

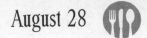

Harvard Beets

1 (15 ounce) can beets, diced
1 teaspoon butter
1 tablespoon sugar

1 tablespoon vinegar
2 teaspoons cornstarch

Place beets in saucepan and cover with enough liquid from can to nearly cover beets. Heat through and add butter. Blend sugar, vinegar, and cornstarch; add to beets and liquid. Stir rapidly over medium heat until thickened. If mixture is too thick, add a few drops of water.

Yield: 4 servings

Be Fully Committed

*"May your hearts be fully committed to the LORD our God,
to live by his decrees and obey his commands, as at this time."*
1 KINGS 8:61 NIV

How many commitments do you have in any given day? Perhaps you work at an office or attend school, and then after you've spent eight hours at your desk, you're heading home to care for your family or do homework. Maybe you've got soccer, baseball, or children who are involved in other after-school activities. All these things are good and pleasant—well, mostly—but none of them should be the most important part of your day. The most important thing in your heart, in your mind, and on your calendar should be God. Love Him and keep His commands, but also find time for Him in your day. Be fully committed to Him. How can you take steps to do that today?

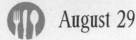

Pineapple Upside-Down Cake

½ cup butter or margarine
1 cup brown sugar, packed
3 (8¼ ounce) cans pineapple
   rings in juice, undrained
10 pecan halves
11 maraschino cherries, halved
2 eggs, separated
1 egg yolk

1 cup sugar
1 cup flour
1 teaspoon baking powder
½ teaspoon cinnamon
¼ teaspoon salt
1 teaspoon vanilla
¼ teaspoon cream of tartar

Melt butter in 10-inch cast-iron skillet over low heat. Sprinkle brown sugar in skillet and remove from heat. Drain pineapple, reserving ¼ cup juice. Set juice aside. Cut pineapple rings in half, reserving 1 whole ring. Place whole pineapple ring in center of skillet. Arrange 10 pineapple pieces in spoke fashion around whole ring in center of skillet. Place pecan half and maraschino cherry half between each piece of pineapple. Place cherry half in center of whole pineapple ring. Arrange remaining pineapple pieces, cut side up, around sides of skillet. Place cherry half in center of each piece of pineapple around sides of skillet. Beat 3 egg yolks until thick and lemon colored. Gradually add sugar, beating well. Combine flour, baking powder, cinnamon, and salt; stir well. Add to egg mixture alternately with reserved pineapple juice. Stir in vanilla. Beat egg whites and cream of tartar at high speed until stiff peaks form; fold beaten egg whites into batter. Spoon batter evenly over pineapple in skillet. Bake at 350 degrees for 45 to 50 minutes or until cake is set. Invert cake onto serving plate immediately. Cut into wedges to serve.

Yield: 8 servings

Equals before the Lord

The LORD is the Maker of them all.
PROVERBS 22:2 NIV

Each of us is God's chosen child. None of us are more important than the others. What can you do as a family to remember this important principle? Ask God and He will show you.

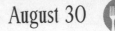
Creamy Ham 'n' Broccoli Bake

1½ pounds fresh broccoli, cooked
   until tender
½ cup ham, cooked and cubed
1 (10¾ ounce) can condensed
   cream of mushroom soup

¼ cup milk
½ cup shredded cheddar cheese
1 cup all-purpose baking mix
¼ cup margarine

Place broccoli and ham in 1½-quart baking dish. Beat soup and milk until smooth; pour over broccoli and ham. Sprinkle with cheese. Combine baking mix with margarine and mix until crumbly; sprinkle over top. Bake at 400 degrees for 20 minutes.

Yield: 4 servings

Missions Work

*Then he said to his disciples, "The harvest is plentiful but the
workers are few. Ask the Lord of the harvest, therefore,
to send out workers into his harvest field."*
MATTHEW 9:37–38 NIV

Have you ever felt the call to missions work? God says there are many who wish to hear the good news of the Gospel, and yet there are not nearly enough who are willing to take the Word to them. Perhaps you do not feel called? What are you then to do? The best thing you and your family can do is to regularly pray for those who are called. Perhaps your church sponsors missionaries. Great! Find out who they are and pray for them by name. Perhaps you can even write to them as a family and let them know you are calling out to God on their behalf.

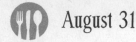

Classic Green Bean Bake

1 (10¾ ounce) can condensed
    cream of mushroom soup
½ cup milk
1 teaspoon soy sauce
Dash pepper

4 cups fresh green beans, cooked
    (or 2 cans cut green beans,
    drained)
1 (2.8 ounce) can french-fried
    onions, divided

Combine soup, milk, soy sauce, and pepper in 1½-quart casserole dish. Stir in beans and half of onions. Bake at 350 degrees for 25 minutes or until heated through. Remove from oven and stir; top with remaining onions. Bake for additional 5 minutes.

Yield: 6 servings

The Past Is Gone

"The man who formerly persecuted us is now preaching the faith he once tried to destroy." And they praised God because of me.
GALATIANS 1:23–24 NIV

It is doubtful that you or anyone you know has done as much to eradicate the spread of Christianity as the apostle Paul. Before his experience on the Damascus Road, Paul, known as Saul at the time, actively searched out believers and took their lives. Using the logic of this world, Paul's murderous past would make him most unfit for God's purposes. And yet, our Lord defies the logic of this world, doesn't He? Look at how He used Paul! In the same way, He can use you, too. Give Him your past, and He will offer a future!

Sweet Potato Casserole

2 cups sweet potatoes, mashed
  (1 large can, drained)
½ teaspoon salt
3 tablespoons butter
½ cup milk
1 cup sugar
2 eggs, beaten

1 teaspoon vanilla

Topping:
1 cup brown sugar, packed
⅓ cup flour
½ cup butter, melted
1 cup pecans, chopped

Mix first seven ingredients and place in greased 8x8-inch baking dish. Combine topping ingredients and spread over sweet potato mixture. Bake at 350 degrees for 35 minutes.

Yield: 4 servings

Restoring the Joy

*Restore to me the joy of your salvation
and grant me a willing spirit, to sustain me.*
PSALM 51:12 NIV

Are you new to the faith or have you known Christ for quite some time? In either case, you probably know that there are days when trusting in God seems a little more difficult than others. It is specifically for those days that the Lord gives us this promise: He will restore our joy and keep us moving forward on the path He has put us on. What a great promise!

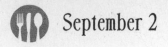

Toffee Coffee Cake

2 cups brown sugar, packed
2 cups flour, sifted
1 cup butter or margarine
1 large egg, beaten
1 cup buttermilk

1 teaspoon vanilla
1 teaspoon baking soda
⅛ teaspoon salt
8 ounces toffee candy, crushed
½ cup chopped pecans

In medium bowl, combine brown sugar, flour, and butter to form crumbly mixture. Reserve 1 cup for topping. In another bowl, combine egg, buttermilk, vanilla, baking soda, and salt. Add to first mixture; blend well with electric mixer. Spoon into greased 9x13-inch cake pan. Sprinkle with reserved topping, candy, and pecans. Bake at 350 degrees for 50 to 55 minutes.

Yield: 16 servings

What He Says Goes

God said to Moses, "I AM WHO I AM. This is what you are to say to the Israelites: 'I AM has sent me to you.'"
EXODUS 3:14 NIV

When God gave His instructions to Moses on how to lead His people out of Egypt, the words were simple but powerful. His is the ultimate authority, and what He says will happen. When God told Moses what to say, He was not just giving instructions to Pharaoh. He was telling the world who He was. Who He is. What He says goes.

Chickenetti

8 ounces spaghetti noodles,
  broken into 2-inch pieces
3 cups chicken, cooked and
  cubed
¼ cup green bell pepper,
  chopped
2 (10¾ ounce) cans condensed
  cream of mushroom soup

1 cup chicken broth
¼ teaspoon salt
¼ teaspoon pepper
1 onion, grated
2 cups shredded processed
  cheese, divided

Place ingredients in 9x13-inch baking dish, reserving 1 cup cheese to sprinkle on top of mixture. Bake at 350 degrees for 1 hour.

Yield: 6 servings

God Loves Pets

The righteous care for the needs of their animals.
PROVERBS 12:10 NIV

Do you have a dog or a cat? Maybe your preference in pets runs toward birds or fish, or perhaps you are the proud owner of a snake or hamster. Whatever the pet, aren't you glad the Lord mentions them in His Word? As pet owners, we are called by God to care for the needs of our furry, feathered, or scale-covered friends. The next time you pet your dog or watch your goldfish swim by, remember that our Lord is greatly pleased with your gentle care of His creatures.

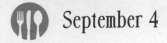

Make-Ahead Mashed Potato Casserole

12 large potatoes, peeled, cooked, and drained

1 (8 ounce) container sour cream

1 (8 ounce) package cream cheese, softened

1 teaspoon onion powder

¼ cup butter, melted

Salt and pepper to taste

Combine all ingredients except butter, salt, and pepper. Mash until fluffy (add milk if too stiff). Spread in buttered 9x13-inch baking dish; top with melted butter and salt and pepper. Bake at 350 degrees for 1 hour.

Yield: 10 servings

Leading the Children

*I have no greater joy than to hear that
my children are walking in the truth.*
3 JOHN 1:4 NIV

If you are a parent, you no doubt have had plans and hopes for your children ever since the moment the doctor placed each of them into your arms. God says there is no greater hope for any child of yours—who are also children of His—than for them to live their lives as believers in Christ. Perhaps you are not a parent. God says you are also responsible for seeing that His children know and love Him. Perhaps that means helping in the church nursery. Perhaps it means that you look at the more broad definition of a child of God to minister to any of the persons He brings into your life. Above all, it means that God is greatly pleased when He sees His children leading others to Him.

Family Dinnertime Tip

Before peeling new potatoes, soak them in cold salted water for 30 minutes. They will peel more easily and won't stain your hands.

Tres Leches

1½ cups sugar
¾ cup butter, softened
9 eggs, separated, room
    temperature
2 cups flour
1½ teaspoons baking powder
1 cup milk
1 teaspoon vanilla
1 teaspoon cream of tartar

Three Milks:
2 cups heavy cream
1 (5 ounce) can evaporated milk,
    room temperature
1 (14 ounce) can sweetened
    condensed milk, room
    temperature

Cream Icing:
2 cups heavy cream
⅓ cup sugar
Sweetened, flaked coconut
    (optional)

In large mixing bowl, cream sugar and butter together until light and fluffy. Add egg yolks and beat until fluffy again, 2 to 3 minutes on medium-high speed. In small bowl, combine flour and baking powder. In third bowl, mix milk and vanilla. Alternately add flour mixture and milk mixture to butter mixture until all are combined. Beat egg whites with cream of tartar until soft peaks form; gently fold into flour and butter mixture. Pour batter into greased 9x13-inch cake pan; bake at 350 degrees for approximately 25 minutes, until golden brown. Poke holes in cake with fork or wooden skewer. Cool. Gently stir milks together until thoroughly combined. Carefully pour over cooled cake. Refrigerate. When ready to serve, beat together cream and sugar until stiff. Frost refrigerated cake and sprinkle with coconut if desired. Keep refrigerated.

Yield: 12 servings

God Understands Doubt

Be merciful to those who doubt.
JUDE 1:22 NIV

God says He understands your doubts. In the same way, be merciful with those who are going through a season of doubt. How can you help someone in your life through a time of questioning? Ask and God will show you.

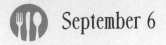

Country-Style Scalloped Potatoes 'n' Ham

8 red potatoes, thinly sliced
   (skin on)
1½ pounds ham, cubed
¼ cup flour

Whole milk
4 tablespoons butter
Pepper

Place potatoes and ham in deep baking dish; mix well. Pour in flour and enough milk to cover mixture; stir. Place butter over top. Sprinkle with pepper. Bake at 350 degrees for 1½ hours or until potatoes reach desired tenderness.

Yield: 4 servings

He Is All

"I am the Alpha and the Omega," says the Lord God,
"who is, and who was, and who is to come, the Almighty."
REVELATION 1:8 NIV

Unlike humans, God is not bound by the ties of time. He tells us in the book of Revelation that He was here before there was an earth or people on it, and He will be here long after any life is left. He is the beginning, and He is the end. There is no way to speak of the majesty of the Lord in human terms. Words do not do justice to Him. Our thoughts cannot comprehend Him. Take a moment and thank Him for all He is. He is all.

Grilled Hobo Potatoes

6 large red potatoes, chopped
1 large green bell pepper, finely
   chopped
1 large red bell pepper, finely
   chopped

1 small white onion, chopped
4 tablespoons butter, divided
Salt and pepper to taste

Divide potatoes and vegetables into four even portions on top of four sheets of aluminum foil. Top each portion with 1 tablespoon butter. Season with salt and pepper as desired. Wrap foil tightly, being sure to cover potatoes completely. Place on hot grill (or in coals at outer edges of campfire). Cook for 30 minutes or until potatoes are tender. Be careful about turning or moving the foil pouches, as hot juices will escape.

Yield: 4 servings

Listen Up!

To answer before listening—that is folly and shame.
PROVERBS 18:13 NIV

Don't you hate it when people cut you off before you've finished speaking? Perhaps you're working with one of your children—or several of them—to stop this behavior before it becomes a habit. Or maybe the offender is a friend or colleague. In any case, it is frustrating to feel as if you are not being heard. Worse, perhaps this describes you. Thankfully, we serve a God who hears us fully, who listens without interrupting and always knows what we need. The next time you're tempted to believe that you can jump in and answer before a colleague, a child, or even God is done speaking, remember this verse. God calls this folly.

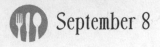

Almond Pie

½ cup butter, melted
1 cup sugar
3 eggs, beaten
¾ cup light corn syrup

¼ teaspoon salt
1 teaspoon vanilla
2 cups chopped almonds
1 (9 inch) pie shell, unbaked

In medium mixing bowl, combine butter, sugar, eggs, corn syrup, salt, and vanilla. Beat until well blended. Fold in almonds and pour into unbaked pie shell. Bake at 375 degrees for 40 to 50 minutes or until set. Cool completely on wire rack.

Yield: 8 servings

Your Royal Heritage

*"'I will give them a heart to know me, that I am the LORD.
They will be my people, and I will be their God,
for they will return to me with all their heart.'"*
JEREMIAH 24:7 NIV

Don't you love it that before you knew God, He had already prepared your heart to know Him? His presence filled your world even before you were aware of Him. That same God keeps in step with you as you walk through every single day of your life. Why? Because you belong to the Lord. You are sons and daughters of the King! Celebrate your royal heritage and pass it on!

Family Dinnertime Tip

To protect the edges of your piecrust from overbrowning,
grab a disposable aluminum pie pan. Cut out the bottom
of the pan. The ring is perfect for setting down over
your pie during the last fourth of baking time.

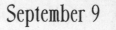

Spicy Beef Stew

2 pounds beef stew meat
1 (11 ounce) can whole-kernel
  corn, undrained
1 (11 ounce) can cut green beans,
  undrained
1 (11 ounce) can stewed tomatoes,
  undrained

5 medium potatoes, cubed
1 small onion, sliced
2 tablespoons minced garlic
1 tablespoon crushed red pepper
½ teaspoon onion salt
Dash hot sauce
Pepper to taste

Place all ingredients in slow cooker. Cook on medium heat for approximately 8 to 10 hours.

Yield: 4 to 6 servings

The Widow's Mite

*"They all gave out of their wealth; but she, out of her poverty,
put in everything—all she had to live on."*
MARK 12:44 NIV

Do you know the story of the widow's mite? The widow in this tale lived in very meager circumstances. She had very little, and what little she did have was not nearly enough to provide for her welfare. And yet when it came time to give, she offered up the tiny amount she had rather than hold anything back from God. While the sum of her donation was small, the amount she gave—really all she had—was enormous in comparison to those around her. Jesus calls us to be like that widow, to give out of the abundance of our heart and not out of the abundance of our wealth. He sees and He loves it when we trust Him with what is ours.

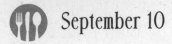

Spanish Rice (Wanda's Style)

½ pound ground beef
1 small onion, chopped
½ medium green bell pepper,
   chopped
2 cups tomato juice

1 cup rice, uncooked
1 teaspoon chili powder
1 teaspoon salt
½ teaspoon pepper

In large skillet, brown beef with onion and green pepper; drain. Add tomato juice, rice, chili powder, salt, and pepper. Bring to boil; cover skillet and turn heat to low. Let cook for 20 minutes, stirring occasionally to keep from sticking. It is done when rice is tender.

Yield: 4 servings

God Never Loses

"This is what the LORD says to you: 'Do not be afraid or discouraged because of this vast army. For the battle is not yours, but God's.'"
2 CHRONICLES 20:15 NIV

Can you imagine standing in the shoes of this warrior as he looked out over the vast plain and saw the imposing army heading his way? Outnumbered, with little to arm themselves, the ragtag army had but one defense: God. Though the odds could be calculated using human logic, the result defied those odds. Why? Because God never loses. Perhaps you're fighting a battle right now. Know that with God by your side, the odds do not matter. Do not be discouraged! The battle belongs not to you but to God.

Ida's Hobo Stew

1 (15 ounce) can baked beans
1 (15 ounce) can black beans,
    drained
1 (15 ounce) can kidney beans,
    drained
2 pounds lean ground beef or
    venison
1 large green bell pepper, diced

1 medium sweet onion, diced
2 tablespoons garlic, chopped
1½ to 2 tablespoons steak
    seasoning
2 tablespoons brown sugar,
    packed
1 (15 ounce) can diced tomatoes

Place beans in slow cooker on high heat. In skillet, brown beef; drain. Add green pepper, onion, garlic, steak seasoning, and brown sugar; cook over low heat until onion is transparent. Stir in tomatoes until warmed. Add meat mixture to beans in slow cooker. Turn heat to low and let simmer for 2 hours.

Yield: 4 to 6 servings

Pleasing God

*To do what is right and just is more
acceptable to the LORD than sacrifice.*
PROVERBS 21:3 NIV

God's ways are not our ways. You've heard this over and over, haven't you? And perhaps you've taken this statement to heart, but do you really understand what it means? We humans believe that if we sacrifice enough, if we work hard enough, anything is possible. In our logic, achievement is gained through our efforts. However, that is not how it works in God's economy. All the striving and hard work and good deeds in the world will not get you into heaven. No sacrifice on our part will ever be sufficient. So how do we please the Lord? We follow His commands and give our hearts to Him. That's it.

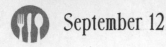

Apple Crumble Pie

5 cups peeled, thinly sliced
    apples (about 5 medium)
1 (9 inch) deep-dish pie shell,
    unbaked
½ cup sugar

¾ teaspoon cinnamon
⅓ cup sugar
¾ cup flour
6 tablespoons butter

Arrange apple slices in unbaked pie shell. Mix ½ cup sugar with cinnamon; sprinkle over apples. Mix ⅓ cup sugar with flour; cut in butter until crumbly. Spoon mixture over apples. Bake at 400 degrees for 35 to 40 minutes or until apples are soft and top is lightly browned.

Yield: 8 servings

Seeing by Faith

Then he touched their eyes and said, "According to your faith
let it be done to you"; and their sight was restored.
MATTHEW 9:29–30 NIV

When Jesus opened the eyes of the blind men, all He had to do was touch the eyes that did not work and they were healed. Of course, He could have healed the men's eyes without touching them, but He chose to place His fingers on those closed lids and make His proclamation. Why do you think that was? Because sometimes we need a touch from Jesus before we can take in the miracle He is about to bestow on us. Look what Jesus tells the men: "According to your faith let it be done to you." Could Jesus have healed those men without any participation from them? Of course! Did He? No, He didn't, and I have to wonder if that's because Jesus was more concerned about the condition of those men's hearts that He was about the condition of their eyes. What do you think?

Snowy Cinnamon Cocoa

4 cups milk
1 cup chocolate syrup
1 teaspoon cinnamon

Whipped topping
¼ cup semisweet chocolate chips

Place milk and chocolate syrup in microwave-safe bowl and stir. Cook on high for 3 to 4 minutes or until hot. Stir in cinnamon. Pour into four large mugs and garnish with whipped topping and chocolate chips.

Yield: 4 servings

His Sheep

"You are my sheep, the sheep of my pasture,
and I am your God, declares the Sovereign Lord.'"
EZEKIEL 34:31 NIV

Have you spent much time around sheep? They can be loud and somewhat smelly, can't they? They also tend to wander off and can sometimes be caught alone and taken away by predators. How like these animals are we humans! God says we are His sheep, His people who, though we tend to wander, are still much loved. We might be messy and smelly and prone to predators, but we have a Shepherd who is there to see that each and every one of His sheep is safe. Aren't you glad?

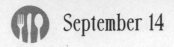

Creamy Noodles

1 (12 ounce) package egg noodles
⅓ cup butter, softened
½ cup evaporated milk

¼ cup grated Parmesan cheese
2¼ teaspoons dry Italian
    dressing mix

Cook noodles according to package directions; drain. Toss noodles and butter together in bowl. Add remaining ingredients and mix thoroughly. Serve immediately.

Yield: 6 servings

Share Boldly

"Now, Lord, consider their threats and enable your servants to speak your word with great boldness."
ACTS 4:29 NIV

Often the apostles were faced with threats from the ruling government regarding speaking out about Jesus. Those in power did not appreciate hearing about the Messiah and often went to great lengths to silence converts. Today in certain parts of the world, believers still face an uncertain future if they proclaim the Gospel. It is easy to speak of the goodness of God when we are doing so from our comfortable homes or welcoming churches. Won't you pray today for those who do not have such an easy path to Jesus? Ask God how you can support these saints as they carry the light into a dark world.

Applescotch Pie

5 cups peeled, thinly sliced tart
   apples (about 5 medium)
1 cup brown sugar, packed
¼ cup water
1 tablespoon lemon juice
¼ cup flour
2 tablespoons sugar

¼ teaspoon salt
1 teaspoon vanilla
3 tablespoons butter or
   margarine
Pastry for (9 inch) double-crust
   pie, unbaked.

Combine apples, brown sugar, water, and lemon juice in medium saucepan. Cover and cook over medium heat until apples are tender, 5 to 10
minutes. Blend flour, sugar, and salt. Stir into apple mixture. Cook, stirring
constantly until syrup thickens, about 2 minutes. Remove from heat; stir
in vanilla and butter. Pour into pastry-lined pie plate and cover with top
crust; slit to vent. Bake at 425 degrees for 40 to 45 minutes.

Yield: 8 servings

Give God Your Guilt

Then David said to God, "I have sinned greatly by doing this.
Now, I beg you, take away the guilt of your servant.
I have done a very foolish thing."
1 CHRONICLES 21:8 NIV

When David spoke these words, he had done more than just a foolish
thing. His actions had cost an innocent man's life.
David knew he had done wrong, and he offers
God no excuses for his actions nor does he say
they are anything but wrong. Instead, he places
himself at the feet of God and begs for mercy.
Are you carrying guilt around? Lay that guilt at
God's feet. He already knows and is waiting for
you to come to Him.

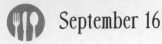

BBQ Stew

2½ tablespoons vegetable oil
2 pounds beef stew meat
¾ cup onion, sliced
½ cup green bell pepper,
    chopped
1 large clove garlic, minced
½ teaspoon salt

⅛ teaspoon pepper
2 cups beef stock
1 (14½ ounce) can tomatoes
⅓ cup barbecue sauce
3 tablespoons cornstarch
¼ cup cold water

Heat oil in skillet over medium heat. Brown meat lightly on all sides; remove from oil and place in slow cooker. Sauté onion, green pepper, and garlic in hot vegetable oil. Add to slow cooker. Blend in salt, pepper, beef stock, tomatoes, and barbecue sauce. Cover and cook on low heat for 8 to 10 hours. Mix cornstarch with cold water and stir into stew approximately 20 minutes before done. Serve with hot cooked noodles or rice.

Yield: 6 servings

Peace like a River

"If only you had paid attention to my commands, your peace would have been like a river, your well-being like the waves of the sea."
Isaiah 48:18 niv

"When peace like a river attendeth my soul. . ." What a beautiful song about the peace that only God can give. Can you see it now, a river of peace filled to the brim and lapping over with a feeling of well-being that can only come from the Lord? Do you or someone you know need to find that sort of peace? Maybe there's someone in your family who needs to hear the good news that there's no need to worry and fret. Head toward the river. Jump in. The water's fine!

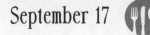

Orange Slush

2 cups cold water
2 cups sugar

1 (6 ounce) can frozen orange
juice concentrate
Ginger ale

In saucepan, mix water and sugar. Bring to boil for 2 minutes. Remove from heat and add orange juice concentrate; freeze. Spoon into glasses to serve and pour ginger ale over slush mixture.

Yield: 4 to 6 servings

How Many Rooms?

"My Father's house has many rooms; if that were not so, would I have told you that I am going there to prepare a place for you?"
JOHN 14:2 NIV

How many rooms does your house have? Five? Ten? More than that? No matter how big your home is, you will never have as many rooms as God has. Are they actual rooms with doors and ceilings and floors? We can never know for sure this side of heaven, but we can know that they exist and that God is preparing one for each of us. What do you think your room will look like? It's fun to guess, isn't it?

. . . .

Family Dinnertime Tip

When measuring corn syrup, first spray your measuring cup with cooking oil. The syrup will come out easily, and cleanup will be quicker. This also works well for peanut butter, marshmallow cream, honey, and molasses.

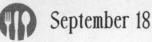

Beefy Pasta 'n' Salsa Soup

1 pound ground beef, cooked and
   drained
2 (14 ounce) cans beef broth
1 (14½ ounce) can diced
   tomatoes with juice
1½ cups medium salsa

1 cup small-shell pasta, uncooked
½ cup onion, chopped
2 cloves garlic, chopped
2 teaspoons chili powder
¼ cup shredded cheddar cheese

Combine all ingredients except cheese in medium saucepan; bring to boil.
Reduce heat to low; cook for 15 minutes or until pasta is tender. Garnish
with cheese.

Yield: 8 servings

Making Memories

*"Prepare me the kind of tasty food I like and bring it
to me to eat, so that I may give you my blessing."*
Genesis 27:4 niv

Prepare a tasty food. This is what Isaac asked of the son he thought was
his firstborn. He wanted a nice meal and a full belly so that when the time
came to bestow his blessing, he would be prepared. Does your family have
a tradition of sharing meals together? I hope that you do. If not, why not
begin that tradition right now? You may not have a birthright to bestow,
but you will be making memories that will last a lifetime.

Home-Style Baked Beans

1 (16 ounce) can pork and beans
¼ cup ketchup
¼ cup onion

2 tablespoons brown sugar, packed
½ teaspoon mustard
4 slices bacon, cooked

Place all ingredients in baking dish and bake, covered, at 325 degrees for 1½ hours.

Yield: 4 servings

More Than Able

*"Indeed, the very hairs of your head are all numbered.
Don't be afraid; you are worth more than many sparrows."*
LUKE 12:7 NIV

How many hairs are on your head? Unless you're bald, you probably have no idea. However, God knows. He numbered each of those hairs. The same God who knows you that well also knows how to care for you and keep you safe. The next time you're tempted to worry or to feel as though God does not hear you, consider this: the Creator of the universe knows you and loves you. He is more than able to care for you.

Family Dinnertime Tip

Keep your cutting board from sliding around the countertop when you apply pressure by cutting a piece of nonskid shelf liner to fit under the board.

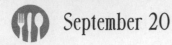

Butterscotch Pie

1½ cups brown sugar, packed
¼ teaspoon salt
2 tablespoons flour
3 tablespoons cornstarch
1½ cups hot water
2 egg yolks
1 tablespoon butter
1 teaspoon vanilla

1 (9 inch) pie shell, baked

Meringue:
2 egg whites
¼ teaspoon cream of tartar
½ teaspoon vanilla
4 tablespoons sugar

In medium saucepan, mix together brown sugar, salt, flour, and corn-starch. Stir in hot water, blending well. Cook until thick and clear. Beat egg yolks. Add small amount of hot mixture to egg yolks and mix well. Slowly blend egg yolks into hot sugar mixture, stirring constantly. Cook, stirring constantly, over low heat for 1 minute. Remove from heat and stir in butter and vanilla. Cool slightly, then pour into baked pie shell.

Prepare meringue: Beat egg whites with cream of tartar and vanilla until soft peaks form. Add in sugar one tablespoon at a time, beating until stiff peaks form and sugar dissolves. Spread meringue evenly over pie, sealing at pastry edges. Bake at 350 degrees for 12 to 15 minutes or until meringue is golden. Let cool before serving.

Yield: 8 servings

Are You a Giver?

"Bring the whole tithe into the storehouse, that there may be food in my house. Test me in this," says the Lord Almighty, " and see if I will not throw open the floodgates of heaven."
MALACHI 3:10 NIV

Are you a giver? That's good news to God. Why? Because there are few places in the Bible where God invites you to test Him. Generally, He does the opposite and warns us not to defy Him. But in the matter of giving alone, He is clear: test Him. Do as He says and see what happens. Not a giver yet? Perhaps you and your family could decide on a plan of giving together. What a legacy to pass down to future generations!

Spicy Orange-Apple Punch

1½ quarts orange juice
1 quart apple juice
⅓ cup light corn syrup

24 whole cloves
6 cinnamon sticks
12 thin lemon slices

Combine orange and apple juices, corn syrup, cloves, and cinnamon sticks in large saucepan. Gradually bring to boil. Reduce heat and simmer at least 5 to 10 minutes to blend flavors. Strain out cloves and cinnamon sticks. Serve hot with lemon slice.

Yield: 12 servings

Better Than a Night-Light

"No one will be able to stand against you all the days of your life. As I was with Moses, so I will be with you; I will never leave you nor forsake you."
JOSHUA 1:5 NIV

When you were a child, did you have a problem sleeping without a night-light? Was a darkened room an invitation to fear? That feeling of being left alone to face whatever is hiding in the dark is one that can persist all the way into adulthood. For someone who is fearful, there is nothing more comforting than to hear someone say he or she will never leave. We serve a God who makes you that promise. He will never leave. Ever. Better yet, no one and nothing will stand against you. Better than a night-light and far more effective against what hides in the dark is our God.

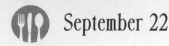

Caramel Apple Pie

6 cups peeled, thinly sliced tart
    apples (about 6 medium)
¾ cup sugar
¼ cup flour
¼ teaspoon salt

Pastry for double-crust pie,
    unbaked
2 tablespoons butter or
    margarine
⅓ cup caramel ice cream topping
4 tablespoons chopped pecans

In large bowl, combine apples, sugar, flour, and salt. Spoon apple mixture into pastry-lined pie pan. Dot with butter. Top with second pastry. Flute edges and cut slits in several places to let steam escape. Bake at 425 degrees for 35 to 45 minutes or until apples are tender. Cover edge of piecrust with strip of foil during last 10 to 15 minutes of baking to prevent excessive browning. Remove pie from oven and immediately drizzle with caramel topping and sprinkle with pecans.

Yield: 8 servings

Rules!

How can a...person stay on the path of purity?
By living according to your word.
PSALM 119:9 NIV

Do you have rules in your family? It's very likely you do. Maybe you have to take turns washing the dishes or you have to go to bed at a certain time. Or perhaps there are rules about cleaning rooms and making beds. Guess what? Parents have rules they must follow each day, too. We all do. Have you thought of why those rules exist? Rules protect us from bad consequences. For example, if the dishes aren't washed, there will soon be no plates on which to serve dinner. If a parent drives too fast, he or she could get a speeding ticket. In the same way, God gives us rules to follow. When we follow His rules, we stay on the right path. Where do we find these rules? In the Bible, of course!

Cowboy Stew

1 pound ground beef
¾ cup onion, chopped
1 green bell pepper, chopped
1 (15 ounce) can dark red kidney
  beans

1 (15 ounce) can pork and beans
1 (15 ounce) can whole-kernel
  corn, drained
2 (10¾ ounce) cans condensed
  tomato soup

In skillet, brown beef, onion, and green pepper; drain. Combine all ingredients in slow cooker; cover and cook on low heat for 6 to 8 hours.

Yield: 4 servings

Love like God

"My command is this: Love each other as I have loved you."
JOHN 15:12 NIV

Unconditional love is a rare thing in today's society. To be completely and totally loved and accepted by another person is an amazing thing. God says we are to continue to try and love everyone in the way He loves us, with an open heart. Is there someone in your world who needs unconditional love? Ask God to show you how to be His hands and feet today. He will.

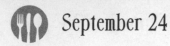

Baked Corn

1 (15 ounce) can cream-style corn
1 (15 ounce) can whole-kernel
   corn
1 (8½ ounce) box corn muffin mix

2 eggs
1 cup sour cream
½ cup margarine

Mix together all ingredients except margarine; place in baking dish. Melt margarine and pour over corn mixture. Bake at 350 degrees for 30 to 40 minutes.

Completing the Work

*"I have brought you glory on earth
by finishing the work you gave me to do."*
JOHN 17:4 NIV

Have you ever felt as though you are so insignificant that God could not possibly use you to achieve His mission here on earth? Perhaps you've come from a background where you did not always proclaim Jesus as your Savior. Maybe you have sins in your past that you'd rather not recall. Perhaps your family has not yet determined to give their hearts to Jesus. Whatever the reason, know that your worthiness before God is not determined by whether you feel as though you have something to offer Him. Rather, God uses those as He sees fit, and He only asks one thing: finish the task you are given. Don't know what your task is? Ask the Lord. He will tell you.

Caramel Pie

2 (14 ounce) cans sweetened
  condensed milk
1 (9 inch) prepared shortbread
  piecrust

1 (12 ounce) carton frozen
  whipped topping, thawed

Remove labels from condensed milk cans. Place in large pot and cover completely with water. Bring water to boil over high heat; reduce heat to medium-high for 4 hours, adding water to keep cans covered. Remove cans from pot and cool slightly. Very carefully open cans and pour cooked milk into shortbread crust. Chill. Prior to serving, spread whipped topping evenly over pie.

Yield: 8 to 12 servings

Wise Choices

The wise store up choice food and olive oil,
but fools gulp theirs down.
PROVERBS 21:20 NIV

Does your family like to cook together? Are you one of those families who likes nothing better than finding a new recipe and making it for dinner and then enjoying it together? Perhaps you have been blessed with a big family but not a big budget. Likely you have learned how to make the most of every penny and have found recipes that are not only tasty but budget conscious. And of course you have learned to make a little go a long way, haven't you? According to God's Word, you are wise indeed!

Beef Barley Vegetable Soup

1½ pounds beef shank
2 tablespoons onion, chopped
½ teaspoon garlic, minced
2 tablespoons vegetable oil
1 (14 ounce) can beef broth
1½ cups strong-brewed coffee
1½ cups water
1 tablespoon Worcestershire
    sauce
1 bay leaf

1 (16 ounce) package frozen
    mixed vegetables, cooked in ½
    cup water until heated through
1 stalk celery, chopped
1 tablespoon sugar
2 pints stewed tomatoes
Dash thyme
2 teaspoons salt
⅛ teaspoon pepper
½ cup barley
1 cup cabbage, chopped

Brown beef, onion, and garlic in oil. Move to slow cooker; add broth, coffee, water, Worcestershire sauce, and bay leaf. Cook covered on low heat for at least 1 hour. Remove meat and cut into small pieces. Return meat to slow cooker; turn heat to high and add mixed vegetables, celery, sugar, tomatoes, thyme, salt, and pepper. Cover and cook for 1 to 2 hours. Add barley and cabbage in last hour of cooking. Discard bay leaf. Total cooking time: 4 hours.

Yield: 6 servings

Coming to the Aid of Jesus

*Jesus commanded Peter, "Put your sword away!
Shall I not drink the cup the Father has given me?"*
JOHN 18:11 NIV

Have you ever come to the rescue of someone you love? Perhaps you have defended a friend or family member in an unjust situation. This is exactly what is on Peter's mind as he comes to Jesus' aid. See how Jesus responds. Though He understands His friend's motives, He cannot allow Peter to intervene. I'm sure Peter hoped to right a wrong, but in retrospect can you see how Jesus had to allow the situation to continue? Had Jesus not gone to the cross, the resurrection could not have occurred. The next time you're tempted to rush to someone's aid, first consider what God might have in mind. Allow Him to prompt your actions.

Aunt Diane's Broccoli Cheese Casserole

1 medium onion
½ cup margarine
1 (10¾ ounce) can condensed
    cream of chicken soup
¾ cup milk

½ pound processed cheese, diced
1 cup minute rice, uncooked
2 (12 ounce) packages frozen
    chopped broccoli

Sauté onion in margarine. Add soup, milk, and cheese; stir until cheese is melted. Add rice and broccoli. Pour mixture into baking dish and bake uncovered at 325 degrees for 45 to 50 minutes.

Yield: 6 to 8 servings

The Light Has Risen

Early on the first day of the week, while it was still dark,
Mary Magdalene went to the tomb.
JOHN 20:1 NIV

Early while it was still dark, Mary Magdalene slipped out and headed for a destination she hoped she would never have to face. The tomb where her Savior was buried was a place of grief and sorrow, and not a place she would likely seek out. And yet go she did, hurrying toward this sad place well before the sun was in the sky. Have you ever felt the kind of hopelessness that this woman must have felt? Has your world seemed to have ended—perhaps something you felt was certain is no longer certain? Take heart in what happens next in this story. Mary Magdalene arrives to find the tomb empty. And we all know what that means. Her world is not at an end, but rather it has just begun. Take heart in this woman's journey and know that your darkest hour is not the end. The light has risen just as the morning sun rose on that empty tomb.

Chocolate Pecan Pie

1½ cups coarsely chopped
  pecans
1 cup semisweet chocolate chips
1 (8 inch) pie shell, partially
  baked

½ cup light corn syrup
½ cup sugar
2 eggs, lightly beaten
¼ cup butter, melted

Sprinkle pecans and chocolate chips into pie shell. In mixing bowl, combine corn syrup, sugar, eggs, and butter. Mix well. Slowly pour mixture over pecans and chocolate. Bake at 325 degrees for 1 hour.

Yield: 8 to 12 servings

Try to Imagine

Jesus did many other things as well. If every one of them were written down, I suppose that even the whole world would not have room for the books that would be written.
JOHN 21:25 NIV

Are you a reader? Do you and your family love books? Have you ever stood inside a very large bookstore and tried to count all the volumes on the shelves? Can you imagine enough books to fill the entire world? Probably not, and yet the apostles are speaking about that very thing. Don't you love that the writers of the ultimate book—the Bible—took a moment to let us know that even they could not record all the amazing things Jesus did during His short time on this earth? If you're a reader, this is probably the most vivid example of Jesus and His abilities in the entire Bible. Savor it and try to imagine!

Family Dinnertime Tip

Make the conscious choice to be joyful. You'll be delighted at what a change this simple but powerful choice will make in your life!

Split Pea Soup

1 (16 ounce) package dried
   split peas
2 cups ham, diced
1 cup carrots, diced
1 medium onion, chopped
2 cloves garlic, minced

2 bay leaves
½ teaspoon salt
½ teaspoon pepper
5 cups boiling water
Milk

Layer all ingredients except milk in slow cooker. Cover and cook on high heat for 4 to 5 hours. Stir in milk until soup reaches desired consistency; discard bay leaves.

Yield: 4 servings

Something to Ponder

*He said to them: "It is not for you to know the times
or dates the Father has set by his own authority."*
ACTS 1:7 NIV

Do you like guessing games? Perhaps you and your family like to clear off the dining room table and play board games that involve skills like anticipating what the other players will do. Often we treat God like a player in one of our games, an equal whose moves can be anticipated and countered. But God is neither defined by human logic nor limited by it. The next time you hear someone tell you what the Lord will do or explain a timetable for something He will cause to occur, remember this verse. It is not for us to know the times or dates the Father has set. Indeed, this is something to ponder, isn't it?

Joanne's Brown Rice Casserole

1¼ cups natural long-grain
brown rice
1 (10¾ ounce) can French onion
condensed soup

1 (14 ounce) can beef broth
bouillon
2 (4 ounce) cans mushrooms,
drained
½ cup margarine

Mix all ingredients except margarine in casserole dish. Slice margarine into squares and place over top of casserole mixture. Cover; bake at 350 degrees for 1 hour.

Yield: 4 to 6 servings

Building a Lasting Legacy

*They devoted themselves to the apostles' teaching
and to fellowship, to the breaking of bread and to prayer.*
ACTS 2:42 NIV

Teaching and fellowship, breaking bread and prayer. Don't you love how these four things just seem to fit together? As far back as the early church, believers met to enjoy a meal and to talk about God. In this modern world, people are often too busy to pause and pray together or share a time of fellowship and feasting. Make it a priority in your family to do as the apostles did and meet regularly at the table. Consider creating a tradition of doing these four things as a family. What a lasting legacy you will be building!

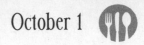

Classic Chess Pie

2 eggs, beaten
1½ cups sugar
1 tablespoon flour
1 tablespoon white cornmeal
¼ cup milk

½ cup butter, melted
½ teaspoon vanilla
½ teaspoon white vinegar
1 (9 inch) pie shell, unbaked

In mixing bowl, combine eggs with sugar, flour, and cornmeal. Add in milk, butter, vanilla, and vinegar. Pour into unbaked pie shell. Bake at 325 degrees for 45 minutes. Decrease oven temperature to 300 degrees and bake for additional 10 minutes.

Yield: 8 servings

Asking for Just Enough

Keep falsehood and lies far from me; give me neither poverty nor riches, but give me only my daily bread.
PROVERBS 30:8 NIV

Make me not too rich and not too poor, this is what King Solomon asks of God. Why? It seems easy to understand why a man would not wish to be poor. Among other hardships, he might be tempted to steal to provide for his family, and that is a sin he wishes not to commit. But wouldn't it be easier to ask for vast wealth? Solomon says that a wealthy man is tempted to trust in his bank account rather than God, and thus he wants just enough to keep him fed but not so much that he forgets where the food comes from. Consider this the next time you pray. Are you asking God for just enough?

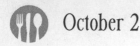
Easy Beef and Veggie Soup

1 family-sized package beef
    stew meat
2 (45 ounce) jars plain spaghetti
    sauce
Water
Potatoes

Celery
Corn
Peas
Carrots
Other vegetables if desired

Cook meat in slow cooker, shred meat, then prepare soup. Empty spaghetti sauce into large stockpot. Fill empty jars with water and add to sauce. Add vegetables as desired. Heat over medium heat, then return to slow cooker on low for 3 to 4 hours or until vegetables are tender.

Yield: 6 servings

The Early Church

*Those who had been scattered preached
the word wherever they went.*
ACTS 8:4 NIV

Back in the early days of the church, those who spoke out about their faith in Jesus were often treated horribly. They were persecuted, imprisoned, and punished in the worst way. Many were expelled from their homelands and sent into hiding. The result of this persecution was that believers left the places where they were not welcome and went to new lands, bringing the Gospel with them. Can you see how God used what they thought was a tragedy in the loss of their homes to bring glory to His name and to gain believers? The next time you're tempted to believe that God couldn't possibly turn something around, consider the plight of the early church. Perhaps He can!

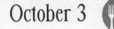

Sweet Potatoes

8 tablespoons margarine, divided
5 (40 ounce) cans sweet potatoes
Flour

Brown sugar to taste
4 (8 ounce) cartons whipping cream

Melt 4 tablespoons margarine in skillet. Roll potatoes in flour, then brown in margarine. Place potatoes in two baking pans and dot with margarine. Sprinkle brown sugar on top to taste, then pour juice from skillet over top. Pour whipping cream over potatoes. Bake covered at 350 degrees for 30 minutes.

Yield: 35 servings

Spreading the News

But the word of God continued to spread and flourish.
ACTS 12:24 NIV

Throughout the book of Acts, God tells us of the persecution of the church and the apostles who were spreading the Gospel. Though chased by enemies of Jesus and often beaten and imprisoned, these carriers of the good news never failed to tell others about the risen Savior. How like God it is to use what others meant for evil—the chasing of apostles into foreign lands—to show His glory and hasten the spreading of the church! The good news continues even now for you and your family. See how God uses current circumstances to further His cause? Ask Him today what the people who live under your roof can do, and be sure to ask for an extra measure of boldness like the apostles of old had. If you ask, He will answer. He always does.

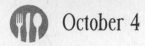

Coconut Cream Pie

⅔ cup sugar
¼ cup cornstarch
½ teaspoon salt
3 cups milk
4 egg yolks, lightly beaten
2 tablespoons butter
2 teaspoons vanilla
¾ cup sweetened, flaked coconut

1 (9 inch) pie shell, baked

Whipped Cream Topping:
1 cup heavy cream, chilled
1 teaspoon powdered sugar
¼ cup sweetened, flaked coconut,
    toasted

In saucepan, mix sugar, cornstarch, and salt. Blend together milk and egg yolks and gradually stir into sugar mixture. Cook over medium heat, stirring constantly until mixture is thickened and bubbly. Cook for 1 minute, stirring constantly; remove from heat. Stir in butter, vanilla, and coconut. Let cool slightly. Pour into baked pie shell and cover with plastic wrap. Chill pie thoroughly for at least 2 hours.

For topping, whip cream together with powdered sugar until stiff peaks form. Spread evenly over pie and sprinkle with toasted coconut.

Yield: 8 servings

Getting What You Ask For

But they soon forgot what he had done and did not wait for his plan to unfold. In the desert they gave in to their craving; in the wilderness they put God to the test. So he gave them what they asked for.
Psalm 106:13–15 NIV

This is one of the most frightening passages in scripture. God's people forgot, gave in to cravings, and put Him to the test, so He gave them what they asked for. Read the verses again. He gave them what they *asked for*, not what *He wanted them to have*. If you continue to read the remainder of the psalm, you will see that once this happened, things did not go well. The next time you are tempted to repeatedly demand your way from God, consider this passage of scripture and realize it is possible you could get what you ask for. Just be prepared to receive it knowing it is not what God wanted you to have.

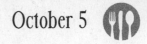

Cranberry-Raisin Pie

1 cup brown sugar, packed
2 tablespoons cornstarch
2 cups raisins
½ teaspoon grated orange rind
½ cup orange juice
½ teaspoon grated lemon rind

2 tablespoons lemon juice
1⅓ cups cold water
1 cup cranberries
1 (9 inch) pie shell, unbaked, with
    pastry for lattice crust

Combine brown sugar and cornstarch in saucepan. Stir in raisins, orange rind and juice, lemon rind and juice, and cold water. Cook and stir over medium heat until thick and bubbly. Cook for 1 minute, stirring constantly. Remove from heat and stir in cranberries. Let cool slightly; pour into unbaked pie shell. Top with lattice crust. Bake at 375 degrees for 40 minutes.

Yield: 8 servings

God Speaks

"Do not be afraid, Daniel. Since the first day that you set your mind to gain understanding and to humble yourself before your God, your words were heard, and I have come in response to them."
DANIEL 10:12 NIV

If you and your family know the story of Daniel, you know that although he loved God with all his heart, he faced serious and potentially fatal trials because of his faith. God knew he would need strength to endure what was ahead, so He sent His messenger with good news. God heard his words! Better yet, He had been hearing Daniel ever since the day that Daniel first set his mind on learning more about God. Don't you wish the Lord would send a message back to you every time you cry out to Him? How much simpler things would be! Unlike Daniel, we have a book of God's responses, the Bible, and it is filled with messages for you. Open the book and read. I promise God will speak.

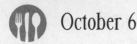

Slow 'n' Savory Fish Chowder

1 pound white fish (use any one or combination of cod, flounder, haddock, halibut, ocean perch, pike, or rainbow trout)
1 teaspoon dried rosemary
1 (14 ounce) can diced tomatoes
½ cup chicken broth
1 teaspoon salt
½ cup onion, chopped
½ cup celery, chopped
½ cup carrot, chopped
¼ cup fresh parsley, snipped (or 1 tablespoon parsley flakes)
1 cup clam juice
2 tablespoons butter (no substitutions), melted
3 tablespoons flour
⅓ cup half-and-half

Cut cleaned fish into small chunks. Combine all ingredients except butter, flour, and half-and-half in 2-quart slow cooker; stir well. Cover and cook on low heat for 7 to 8 hours (or on high heat for 3 to 4 hours). One hour before serving, combine butter, flour, and half-and-half and stir into fish mixture. Continue to cook for 1 hour as mixture thickens slightly.

Yield: 4 to 6 servings (approximately 2 quarts)

God Is Good

Through whom we have gained access by faith into this grace in which we now stand. And we boast in the hope of the glory of God.
ROMANS 5:2 NIV

Do you like to brag about your family? Perhaps you have the smartest spouse, children, or other family members ever. It's great to think highly of those you love. But bragging on God is the best. He loves it when you tell others how great He is. What can you say about God today?

Nutty Sweet Potato Casserole

4 eggs, slightly beaten
1 cup butter, melted
2 cups sugar
1 cup flaked coconut
1 cup evaporated milk
2 teaspoons baking powder
1 teaspoon vanilla
4 cups mashed sweet potatoes
  (canned or fresh)

Topping:
1 cup brown sugar, packed
½ cup flour
1 cup pecans, chopped
½ teaspoon salt
½ teaspoon baking powder
¼ cup butter

Mix ingredients in order given. Pour into large, greased deep-dish casserole pan.

For topping, mix first five ingredients; spread onto sweet potato mixture. Dot with butter. Bake at 350 degrees uncovered for 1 hour. Top should be firm and crusty, and inserted knife will come out clean when casserole is done.

Yield 8 to 10 servings

We All Fall Down

Though I have fallen, I will rise.
Though I sit in darkness, the LORD will be my light.
MICAH 7:8 NIV

We all fall down, don't we? Some of us get up faster than others. Some of us just sit down where we landed and have a pity party. What do you do in your family when one of you is having troubles? Do you just let your family member stew in his or her bad attitude or do you offer help? Next time, it might be a good idea to remind him or her of this verse. When you have the Lord, it is impossible to remain in the dark.

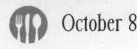

Double-Layer Pumpkin Pie

4 ounces cream cheese, softened
1 tablespoon cold milk
1 tablespoon sugar
1 (8 ounce) carton frozen
   whipped topping, thawed and
   divided
1 prepared graham cracker
   crumb piecrust

1 (16 ounce) can pumpkin
2 (4 serving size) packages
   instant vanilla pudding mix
1 teaspoon cinnamon
½ teaspoon ground ginger
¼ teaspoon ground cloves
1 cup cold milk

In large bowl, beat cream cheese, 1 tablespoon milk, and sugar until smooth. Gently stir in 1½ cups whipped topping. Spread on bottom of piecrust. In another bowl, whisk together pumpkin, pudding mix, spices, and 1 cup milk until well blended. Spread evenly over cream cheese layer. Refrigerate for at least 4 hours before serving. Serve with remaining whipped topping.

Yield: 8 servings

Opinionated?

*A person may think their own ways are right,
but the LORD weighs the heart.*
PROVERBS 21:2 NIV

Is your family made up of people with strong opinions? Probably. What do you do when those opinions clash? Taking the topic of discussion, whatever it might be, back to the Bible to see what God says in the matter is always the best way to solve an issue. We all have opinions and beliefs, but only those that line up with the Lord's teachings are correct. Is your heart seeking truth, or are you choosing your own truth and ignoring God?

Delicious Slow-Cooked Beef Sandwiches

2 pounds beef stew meat
1 (10¾ ounce) can condensed
   cream of celery soup

1 (10¾ ounce) can condensed
   cream of mushroom soup
½ envelope dry onion soup mix
Buns or bread

Rinse stew meat and place in slow cooker. Add soups and onion soup mix; stir. Turn heat to low and let cook overnight. Beef will become shredded as it cooks. Enjoy on buns or other bread of your choice.

Yield: 6 to 8 servings

Watch for Opportunities

"If your enemy is hungry, feed him; if he is thirsty, give him something to drink. In doing this, you will heap burning coals on his head."
ROMANS 12:20 NIV

God's wisdom is sometimes in direct opposition to what we feel like doing, isn't it? If we consider someone an enemy, we certainly don't want to seat him at our table like a family member and treat him like an honored guest. And yet that is exactly what the Lord calls us to do. Today, we rarely have true enemies bent on killing us as they did back in the early days of the church, but we do have people in our lives who irritate us, don't we? Paying back rudeness with kindness, greediness with generosity, and hate with love is exactly what God calls us to do. Watch for opportunities to be the hands and feet of God this week. He will give them to you if you ask.

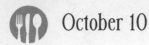

Pork Ribs 'n' Kraut

8 pork spareribs   1 (30 ounce) can sauerkraut
Seasoned salt to taste

Brown pork spareribs in frying pan over medium heat; season and place in slow cooker. Add sauerkraut. Set heat on low and cook for 6 to 8 hours.

Yield: 2 servings

Joining the Family

*This is the genealogy of Jesus the Messiah
the son of David, the son of Abraham.*
MATTHEW 1:1 NIV

Take a moment to read through the genealogy of Jesus that is listed in the first sixteen verses of the book of Matthew. Throughout that list are names of men and women like Tamar, Rahab, and David, who contributed to the lineage of the Savior. If you aren't familiar with the stories of these three and others in that illustrious list, take time to learn their stories. Each of these men and women chose not to live in their sinful pasts but rather to submit themselves to a cleansing God. The result is nothing short of miraculous. In the same way, you can offer your heart to Jesus and become new. Not only that, but you will then be grafted into quite an illustrious family tree.

....

Family Dinnertime Tip

After you've cleaned up the kitchen and everything is back in order (or even if it's not!), take a walk through the neighborhood with your family. Or if the weather isn't cooperating, stay indoors and play a board game. Savor this extra special time together.

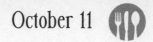

Pot Roast with Carrots

1 (10¾ ounce) can condensed
   cream of mushroom soup
1 envelope dry onion soup mix

1 small package baby carrots
1 (4 pound) boneless chuck pot
   roast

Mix soup, onion soup mix, and carrots in slow cooker. Add roast; turn to coat. Cover. Cook on low heat for approximately 8 hours.

Yield: 8 servings

God's Greatest Treasure

In him we have redemption through his blood, the forgiveness of sins, in accordance with the riches of God's grace.
EPHESIANS 1:7 NIV

Don't you love how when the God of the universe refers to His riches—and truly everything is His, so His riches are vast and uncountable—He is not referring to material things? Instead, the most precious item of value He describes is His grace. Amazing grace! How sweet the sound! And oh, how precious a treasure He offers to us completely free of any cost on our end. His cost, however, was the blood of His Son. Consider this and realize how very much God loves you and your family. Not only did He create you, but He also saved you and continues to forgive your sins. What a God we serve!

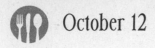

Clam Chowder

¼ cup celery, chopped
2 tablespoons onion, chopped
2 tablespoons butter

1 cup potatoes, cubed
1 cup milk
2 cups minced clams with juice

In large saucepan, sauté celery and onion in butter until brown. Add potatoes and cook until tender. Add milk and clams; heat thoroughly.

Yield: 4 servings

Teaching Fishermen to Fish

Simon answered, "Master, we've worked hard all night and haven't caught anything. But because you say so, I will let down the nets."
LUKE 5:5 NIV

In every family there is at least one practical person. This family member always has a logical explanation for everything. Perhaps that person is you. These very logical fishermen were no rookies. They had been at this for many years. What Jesus suggested defied everything they knew to be true about fishing, and yet Simon obeyed because he trusted Jesus. If you read on, you will learn that, indeed, Jesus knew what He was talking about, and the nets were soon overflowing. The next time you're tempted to apply human logic to God's instructions, remember those fishermen. Drop the net where Jesus tells you and wait and see what's coming!

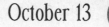

Slow-Cooker Burritos

1 pound ground beef or ground
    pork
2 tablespoons onion, chopped
1 (14½ ounce) can diced and
    spiced tomatoes

1 (16 ounce) can refried beans
1 (12 ounce) bag corn tortilla
    chips
1½ cups shredded cheese

In skillet, cook meat and onion; drain. In bowl, combine tomatoes and beans; blend well. Spray inside of large slow cooker with oil. Divide ingredients in thirds and start layering. Cover bottom of slow cooker with chips, cover with ⅓ of meat, spread on ⅓ of beans, and sprinkle with ⅓ of cheese. Repeat layers, ending with cheese on top. Cover and cook on low heat for 4 hours or on high heat for 2 hours.

Yield: 4 to 6 servings

Salt and Grace

*Let your conversation be always full of grace, seasoned with salt,
so that you may know how to answer everyone.*
Colossians 4:6 niv

A little salt in the pot makes the stew taste better, doesn't it? Too much salt and the whole meal is ruined. In the same way, God calls on us to season our conversation not only with salt but also with grace so as not to ruin things. How do we do that? We listen and pray before we speak. Too often the words come out before the prayer goes up. Try it and see what a difference this practice makes in your conversations!

. . . .

Family Dinnertime Tip

Don't throw away your leftovers! Use leftover chicken, chili, beans, and more to create tasty burritos. Your family will love this tasty new twist, and you won't need to throw out your leftovers anymore.

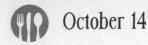

Sour Cream 'n' Bean Chicken

4 boneless, skinless chicken
   breasts, frozen
1 (15½ ounce) can black beans,
   drained

1 (15 ounce) jar salsa
1 (8 ounce) package cream
   cheese

Place frozen chicken breasts in slow cooker. Add black beans and salsa. Cook on high heat for approximately 5 hours. Toss block of cream cheese on top and let stand for 30 minutes.

Yield: 4 servings

Just Ask

I thank Christ Jesus our Lord, who has given me strength,
that he considered me trustworthy, appointing me to his service.
1 TIMOTHY 1:12 NIV

Managing a home and family is a big job. If you are also working outside the home, that is one more responsibility to add to all the others. Or perhaps you are a student taking a load of classes that are bearing down on you. Whatever your day looks like, are there days when you feel like God has given you more than you can handle? He probably has, but only if you are trying to handle these responsibilities alone. When the burden on your shoulders feels too heavy to bear, remember God considered you trustworthy to take this on, and He will give you strength to complete the task. Just ask, and He will help!

Double Pecan Pie

Pecan Pastry:
1 cup flour
¼ cup ground pecans
¼ teaspoon salt
¼ cup plus 2 tablespoons butter
   or margarine
1 to 2 tablespoons cold water

Pie Filling:
1 cup light corn syrup

¾ cup sugar
3 eggs, beaten
3 tablespoons butter or
   margarine, melted
2 teaspoons vanilla
¼ teaspoon salt
1 cup pecan pieces
1 cup pecan halves

Prepare pecan pastry by combining flour, pecans, and salt in medium bowl; cut in butter with pastry blender until mixture resembles coarse meal. Sprinkle water over mixture, stirring until just moistened. Shape pastry into ball and chill for 30 minutes. On floured surface, roll pastry to ⅛-inch thickness. Place in 9-inch pie pan and flute edges. Set aside.

For pie filling, combine corn syrup, sugar, eggs, butter, vanilla, and salt in medium mixing bowl. Beat at medium speed just until blended. Stir in pecan pieces. Pour mixture into pastry. Top with pecan halves. Bake at 350 degrees for 50 to 60 minutes or until set. If edges begin to brown excessively, cover edges with aluminum foil.

Yield: 8 to 12 servings

Approaching the Throne

Let us then approach God's throne of grace with confidence, so that we may receive mercy and find grace to help us in our time of need.
Hebrews 4:16 NIV

In some cultures, daring to approach the king's throne without an invitation meant certain doom. Consider the story of Esther and her risky choice to enter the King's presence in order to save the Jewish people as an example. Aren't you glad that the Ruler of the universe, beckons you to His presence without any fear of harm? Unlike Esther who faced fear in going for help in her time of need, all we will face is our Savior's loving arms!

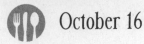

Finger Pecan Tarts

Pastry:
3 ounces cream cheese
½ cup butter (no substitutions)
1 cup flour

Filling:
1½ cups brown sugar, packed
2 tablespoons butter, melted
1 pinch salt
1 teaspoon vanilla
2 eggs, slightly beaten
1 cup chopped pecans

Mix cream cheese, butter, and flour together with pastry blender. Roll into 24 balls (the size of large marbles) and press into mini muffin tins.

To prepare filling: in pitcher, blend together sugar, butter, salt, vanilla, and eggs; pour into pastry shells and top with pecans. Bake at 350 degrees for 20 minutes or until crusts turn golden and centers are firm.

Yield: 24 tarts

The Best News

But whoever lives by the truth comes into the light,
so that it may be seen plainly that what they have
done has been done in the sight of God.
JOHN 3:21 NIV

Is there someone among your friends or family who always likes to report on the doings of others? If you ever wonder what's going on, you know you can go to that person and find out the latest news. Even those people, however, do not have perfect knowledge. In fact, while they may know some, God knows all. Nothing is hidden from the Lord. As much as we might like to, we cannot deny or change anything we have already done. But Jesus knows and loves us anyway. There may be consequences from the past, but the one who determines our future wants only the best for us. Isn't that the best news you've heard all day?

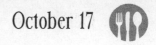

French Silk Pie

1 cup sugar
¾ cup butter (no substitutions)
3 squares (1 ounce each)
   unsweetened chocolate,
   melted and cooled

1½ teaspoons vanilla
¾ cup egg substitute
1 (9 inch) pie shell, baked

In mixing bowl, cream together sugar and butter until light and fluffy. Blend in chocolate and vanilla. Slowly add egg substitute, ¼ cup at time, beating for 2 to 3 minutes after each addition and scraping sides of bowl frequently. Pour into baked pie shell and chill thoroughly.

Yield: 6 to 8 servings

Stay on the Path

*Give careful thought to the paths for your feet
and be steadfast in all your ways.*
PROVERBS 4:26 NIV

Have you ever gone hiking? If so, then you know that staying on the path is by far the safest way to hike. In the same way, God marks out a path for us that is straight and safe. Once that path has been marked out, it is our job to stay on it. Never forget there is safety in staying where God put us!

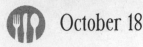

Baked Cheesy Potatoes

1 (2 pound) package frozen hash browns
1 (10¾ ounce) can condensed cream of potato soup
1 (10¾ ounce) can condensed cream of celery soup
Handful of chopped onion
1½ cups sour cream
Salt
Pepper
1 cup shredded cheddar cheese, divided

Place hash browns in large baking dish. Mix potato soup, celery soup, onion, sour cream, salt and pepper (to taste), and ½ cup cheese. Pour mixture over hash browns, then sprinkle ½ cup cheese over top. Bake at 350 degrees for 1 hour.

Yield: 16 to 20 servings

Guard Your Heart

Above all else, guard your heart,
for everything you do flows from it.
PROVERBS 4:23 NIV

Are you careful what you allow in your heart? Do you sit through television shows that make you uncomfortable or participate in conversations where others are behaving in a less than godly manner? It can be difficult to be the one who changes the channel when everyone else is enjoying the show. Your friends may not like you for walking away from conversations or situations where you know you shouldn't stay. God never said the Christian life was easy, but He does promise it is the best life. Guard your heart. It's worth it. I promise.

Creamy Mushroom Pork Chops

3 potatoes, peeled and sliced
4 pork chops
Salt and pepper to taste

2 (10¾ ounce) cans condensed
cream of mushroom soup

Slice potatoes and place in bottom of slow cooker. Season pork chops with salt and pepper and place on top of potatoes. Cover chops with mushroom soup and cook on low for 8 hours.

Yield: 4 servings

She Laughs

She is clothed with strength and dignity;
she can laugh at the days to come.
PROVERBS 31:25 NIV

Don't you love the image of the Proverbs 31 woman laughing at the days to come? When others are worrying about how to feed their families or manage their households, she laughs at those worries. Laughs! Why do you think that is? She laughs not because of her own success or efforts but because she knows the one who holds the future. She laughs because she can rest assured that the future is in good hands because it is in God's hands. He holds your future in His hands, too.

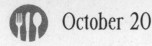

Fudge Brownie Nut Pie

1 (14 ounce) can sweetened
   condensed milk
½ cup cocoa
¼ cup butter or margarine
1 cup flour

3 large eggs, beaten
1 teaspoon vanilla
1¾ cups chopped pecans
1 (9 inch) pie shell, unbaked

In medium saucepan over low heat, stir together milk, cocoa, and butter. When butter melts and mixture is heated through, remove from heat. Stir in flour, eggs, vanilla, and pecans; pour into pie shell. Bake at 350 degrees for 50 minutes or until center is set.

Yield: 8 servings

Waiting on God

Blessed are all who wait for him!
ISAIAH 30:18 NIV

Satan knows speed kills. If the devil can keep you frantic, he can keep you weak. The enemy of our souls loves nothing better than to tempt us into hurrying, into getting ahead of God and taking matters into our own hands. Logically we know that plunging forward rather than following God at His pace is a bad idea. In the moment when we are frantic, however, doing something—anything—feels better than doing nothing. Waiting on God is not doing nothing! It is doing something extremely valuable!

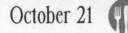

Slow 'n' Easy Spaghetti

1 pound lean ground beef
1 teaspoon Italian seasoning
2 cloves garlic, minced
½ cup onion, chopped
2 cups plain spaghetti sauce

1 (4 ounce) can sliced
   mushrooms, drained
1 quart tomato juice
8 ounces spaghetti noodles,
   uncooked and broken into
   3- to 4-inch pieces

Brown beef in skillet with Italian seasoning and garlic; drain and place in large slow cooker. Add remaining ingredients except noodles; stir well. Cover and cook on low heat for 6 to 7 hours or on high heat for 3 to 4 hours. For last hour of cooking, turn heat to high and stir in uncooked noodles.

Yield: 6 servings

God's Coworkers

As God's co-workers we urge you not to receive God's grace in vain.
2 CORINTHIANS 6:1 NIV

Have you ever thought of yourself as God's coworker? His subject, His servant, His child, of course. But His coworker? That concept is a little more difficult to accept, isn't it? Consider, however, the way God spread the message of Jesus. He used His people to speak of the good news to others who then went out and told their friends. Ultimately, the Gospel message traveled far and wide thanks to the people who told their stories to others. Could God spread His message without us? Of course! But how much more wonderful is it that He chooses to use us?

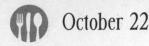

Lemon Chess Pie

4 eggs, lightly whisked
1½ cups sugar
2 tablespoons white cornmeal
¼ cup butter, melted

½ cup milk
Juice of 2 lemons
1 (9 inch) pie shell, unbaked

In large mixing bowl, combine eggs, sugar, cornmeal, melted butter, milk, and lemon juice. Stir to dissolve sugar completely. Pour filling into unbaked pie shell. Bake at 425 degrees for 10 minutes, then reduce temperature to 350 degrees and continue to bake until set, approximately 25 minutes. Serve at room temperature.

Yield: 8 servings

What's Your Rank?

For by the grace given me I say to every one of you: Do not think of yourself more highly than you ought, but rather think of yourself with sober judgment, in accordance with the faith God has distributed to each of you.
ROMANS 12:3 NIV

In a king's court, there is no doubt about the order of importance from the man on the throne to the beggar at the doorstep. On the battlefield, none of the soldiers have to question who is in command and in what order the soldiers are ranked below him. In God's kingdom, however, there is no such order of rank. None of us should consider ourselves more important than the other. Rather, we all should realize that without God we are equally nothing.

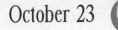

Melt-in-Your-Mouth Pie

1 (14 ounce) can sweetened
   condensed milk
⅓ cup lemon juice
⅓ cup sweetened, flaked coconut
⅓ cup chopped pecans

1 (8 ounce) can crushed
   pineapple, drained
1 (12 ounce) carton frozen
   whipped topping, thawed
1 (9 inch) prepared graham
   cracker crumb piecrust

In mixing bowl, combine sweetened condensed milk and lemon juice. Gently stir in coconut, pecans, and pineapple. Fold in whipped topping. Spoon into prepared piecrust. Refrigerate for several hours before serving.

Yield: 8 servings

Listen to Your Conscience

Now this is our boast: Our conscience testifies that we have conducted ourselves in the world, and especially in our relations with you, with integrity and godly sincerity. We have done so, relying not on worldly wisdom but on God's grace.
2 CORINTHIANS 1:12 NIV

Does your conscience bother you from time to time? Good! That means it is working as God designed it to work. The Lord calls us to a standard of integrity and sincerity, and when we fail to meet that standard, as we flawed humans sometimes do, then our conscience is there to remind us that adjustments are required.

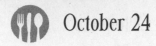

Slow-Cooker Mac 'n' Cheese

1 (16 ounce) box elbow macaroni
1 tablespoon vegetable oil
1 (13 ounce) can evaporated milk
1½ cups milk

4½ cups shredded cheddar cheese, divided
½ cup melted butter

Cook macaroni according to package directions; drain. Grease bottom and sides of slow cooker. Place hot macaroni and vegetable oil in slow cooker; add remaining ingredients, reserving ½ cup cheese. Stir gently to combine. Cover and cook on low heat for 3 to 4 hours, stirring occasionally. Just before serving, sprinkle with remaining cheese.

Yield: 6 servings

The Walls Fell

*By faith the walls of Jericho fell, after the army
had marched around them for seven days.*
HEBREWS 11:30 NIV

Any army worth its training goes into battle with a solid plan and plenty of ammunition to carry out the duties set forth for them by their commander. Imagine their surprise when the army commanded by Joshua got these orders: march around the walls of Jericho for seven days! What? The purpose of their battle was to break down those stone walls that surrounded the city of Jericho, and yet their commander told his men to put down their weapons and walk in circles for seven days. Surely these brave men had cause to wonder whether Joshua had lost his mind, don't you think? And yet, because their commander issued an order, they obeyed. If you're familiar with this story, you know what happened. Without a single weapon being used or a single man being lost, those walls fell! Don't we serve an imaginative God?

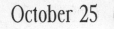

Peanut Butter Pie

1 (8 ounce) package cream
   cheese, softened
⅔ cup creamy peanut butter
1 (14 ounce) can sweetened
   condensed milk

1 (8 ounce) carton frozen
   whipped topping, thawed
1 prepared graham cracker
   crumb piecrust

Beat cream cheese, peanut butter, and sweetened condensed milk together until smooth. Fold in whipped topping. Spoon into graham cracker piecrust. Chill.

Yield: 8 servings

Help My Unbelief!

Immediately the boy's father exclaimed,
"I do believe; help me overcome my unbelief!"
MARK 9:24 NIV

At one time or another, all of us have come to a point where faith meets logic. We know God is able. We know He is capable of solving whatever dilemma is facing us. However, human logic tells us He might not come to our rescue. Or perhaps He will wait and not do things as we expect He will. Worse, He might even make us suffer. The next time you are tempted to give in to human logic and question your faith, do as this man did and call out to God: I believe; help my unbelief!

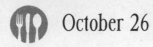

Quick Chocolate Bar Pie

1 (7 ounce) milk chocolate bar, divided
2 tablespoons milk

1 (8 ounce) carton frozen whipped topping, thawed and divided
1 (9 inch) pie shell, baked

Melt chocolate bar, minus 3 squares, in bowl placed over hot (not boiling) water. Gradually stir in milk. Cool slightly, then fold in whipped topping. Blend well; pour into prepared pie shell. Grate or shave remaining chocolate over pie. Chill.

Yield: 8 servings

The Great Equalizer

"Resentment kills a fool, and envy slays the simple."
JOB 5:2 NIV

Oh how tempting it is to peer into other people's lives and compare what they have to what you've got. How frustrating it feels to see someone who hasn't worked as long as you get the promotion. Worse, what of the player who isn't as good as you yet is chosen to start? Given the opportunity, you and your family could easily list a dozen instances of unfairness in just a few minutes' time. Well, look what God says about comparison and resentment. Do you want the Lord to think you are a fool? Then stop comparing, stop complaining about unfairness, and cry out to Him instead. He is the great equalizer!

Family Dinnertime Tip

If you're overextended, learn to say no! You'll be a happier person for it. . .and you'll find that you enjoy having the freedom to do something that isn't an obligation.

Sour Cream Pear Pie

4 cups peeled, sliced pears
⅓ cup sugar
2 tablespoons flour
1 (8 ounce) carton sour cream
1 teaspoon vanilla
½ teaspoon almond extract
1 (9 inch) pie shell, unbaked

Topping:
¼ cup flour
2 tablespoons butter or
  margarine, melted
2 tablespoons brown sugar,
  packed

In large mixing bowl, toss pears with sugar and flour. Mix in sour cream, vanilla, and almond extract. Blend well and pour into unbaked pie shell. In small bowl, mix flour, butter, and brown sugar until crumbly. Sprinkle mixture over pears. Bake at 400 degrees for 10 minutes, then reduce temperature to 350 degrees and bake for 45 minutes or until pears are tender.

Yield: 6 to 8 servings

Right Where You Are

"Build houses and settle down;
plant gardens and eat what they produce."
JEREMIAH 29:5 NIV

God is speaking to His people in exile when He tells them to settle down and plant gardens. These were people who were hoping to return to their homeland, and the Lord who led them to safety is now telling them to get comfortable right where you are. As you can imagine, this is not what they wanted to hear. In the same way, has God taken you from a place or situation and you miss home? Is He telling you to stop longing to return and get comfortable right where you are? Then listen! Plant a garden right where you are and watch it bloom! God says so!

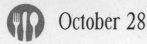

Cheesy Egg 'n' Mushroom Meal

8 eggs
¾ cup milk
8 ounces cheddar cheese,
    shredded

½ cup onion, chopped
1 cup fresh mushrooms, thinly
    sliced
Salt and pepper to taste

Beat eggs. Add milk and mix well. Pour mixture into greased slow cooker. Add cheese, onion, mushrooms, salt, and pepper. Cook on high heat for 1½ to 2 hours.

Yield: 4 to 6 servings

Sunday Is Coming

"A time is coming and in fact has come when you will be scattered, each to your own home. You will leave me all alone. Yet I am not alone, for my Father is with me."
JOHN 16:32 NIV

Jesus warned His disciples that the day would come when He would no longer be with them, and they would no longer be with one another. On that terrible Thursday when He was taken, that awful Friday when He was crucified, the apostles must have been terrified. Can you imagine what it was like? They had no hope of Sunday, no hope that Jesus would not be in the tomb three days later. Are you in a waiting period? Have you given up hope? Think of the apostles who stood at the cross on Friday with no idea that Sunday was coming.

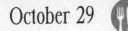

"Hot Vanilla"

4 cups milk
4 teaspoons honey

½ teaspoon vanilla
Cinnamon

In saucepan, heat milk until very hot (do not boil). Remove from heat and stir in honey and vanilla. Divide between four mugs and sprinkle with cinnamon.

Yield: 4 servings

The Noise of the World

How, then, can they call on the one they have not believed in?
And how can they believe in the one of whom they have not heard?
ROMANS 10:14 NIV

Billboards and television commercials proclaim the latest products everywhere you look. There are ads everywhere, including on social media and on the side of buses. Even football stadiums are covered in the logos of the products that advertisers hope you will purchase. Our modern world is so filled with messages telling us what we need, and yet at the same time, the greatest message of all seems to be crowded out by all the noise of the world. Ask God today what you can do to change this.

Family Dinnertime Tip

Feed the birds, too—don't forget the wild birds on those winter days. Spread peanut butter on a pinecone, then roll it in birdseed. Use a wire to hang it on a tree. You can also cut an orange in half, scoop out the fruit, and fill the rind cup with birdseed. It can be fashioned into a basket that will hang from a tree limb.

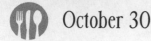

Tropical Peach Pie

1 cup brown sugar, packed
¼ cup butter or margarine,
   softened
½ cup flour
½ teaspoon cinnamon
⅛ teaspoon salt

1 (9 inch) pie shell, baked
1 (29 ounce) can sliced peaches,
   drained
1 cup crushed pineapple, drained
¼ cup whipping cream

Cream brown sugar and butter. Stir in flour, cinnamon, and salt. Sprinkle half of mixture in pie shell. Cover with peaches. Top with crushed pineapple. Pour cream over all. Sprinkle remaining sugar mixture on top. Bake at 400 degrees for 15 minutes. Reduce heat to 350 degrees and bake 40 to 45 minutes longer.

Yield: 8 servings

Turning a Deaf Ear

If anyone turns a deaf ear to my instruction,
even their prayers are detestable.
PROVERBS 28:9 NIV

It is extremely frustrating to say something important to someone only to find that person is not listening. What do you do when that happens? How likely are you to want to help if that same person came to you a few minutes later expecting you to listen to his or her every word? In much the same way, God tells us that when we ignore Him, He gives us the same response in return. Do you want the Lord to hear your prayers? Then listen before you speak and do as He says.

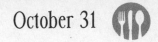

Pumpkin Nog

1 (15 ounce) can pumpkin puree
1 pint vanilla ice cream, softened
4 cups milk
1 teaspoon cinnamon, plus extra
    for topping

½ teaspoon nutmeg
¼ teaspoon ground ginger
1 cup whipped topping

Load blender with small portions of pumpkin, ice cream, milk, and spices; blend thoroughly. Pour blended ingredients in large pitcher and pour into mugs. Top with whipped topping and sprinkle of cinnamon if desired.

Yield: 10 servings

Deny, Immerse, Obey

Then Jesus said to his disciples, "Whoever wants to be my disciple must deny themselves and take up their cross and follow me."
MATTHEW 16:24 NIV

What is Jesus saying in this verse? First, He wants us to deny our self-centered nature and let God take control. Next, He wants us to take up our cross, that is, He wants us to immerse ourselves in His Word to the point of being willing to suffer as Jesus did rather than deny Him. Finally, He tells us to follow Him. To obey. That's it. Deny, immerse, and obey. So simple and yet so difficult, but oh so worth the effort.

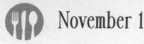

Chicken Fajitas

1 pound boneless, skinless
   chicken breasts, cut into strips
1 (14½ ounce) can diced
   tomatoes

1 (10 ounce) can diced green
   chilies
1 small onion, chopped
2 green bell peppers, sliced
1 envelope fajita seasoning

Layer ingredients in large slow cooker. Cook on high heat until juices boil. Set heat on low for 4 hours until chicken is tender. Serve over cooked rice or in tortilla shells.

Yield: 4 servings

Childlike Faith

And he said: "Truly I tell you, unless you change and become like little children, you will never enter the kingdom of heaven."
MATTHEW 18:3 NIV

"Jesus loves the little children." I'm sure you have sung that song since you were a little child. God requires an open heart and a childlike faith in order for us to truly follow Him through the gates of heaven. There is one word in that scripture that bears emphasis: the word *change*. Jesus did not expect those to whom He was speaking to have already reached that point in their walks with Him. Instead, He is giving them the chance to change, to move closer to the faith He wishes them to have.

Family Dinnertime Tip

Remove the odor of onion from your hands by rubbing them with a paste of salt and vinegar.

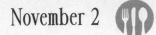

Slow-Cooker Western Omelet

1 (32 ounce) bag hash browns, frozen
1 pound sausage, cooked and drained well
1 small onion, diced
1 medium green bell pepper, chopped

1½ cups shredded cheddar cheese
12 eggs
1 cup milk
1 teaspoon salt
1 teaspoon black pepper

Lightly spray the inside of slow cooker with oil. Cover bottom of slow cooker with layer of frozen hash browns, followed by layers of sausage, onion, green pepper, and cheese. Repeat layering process two or three times, ending with layer of cheese. Beat together eggs, milk, salt, and pepper. Pour egg mixture over top layer of cheese. Cover and cook on low heat for 10 to 12 hours.

Yield: 6 to 8 servings

Hidden Faults

But who can discern their own errors? Forgive my hidden faults.
PSALM 19:12 NIV

Part of the process of purchasing a home is having an inspection done of the property. Purchasing a used car requires a similar process, at least if the buyer is smart. In neither case would you want to find out later that hidden faults are causing major issues. We humans have hidden faults, too. Sometimes it is us who keep them hidden, and other times we miss seeing them completely. Ask God to show you your hidden faults and to show you how to remedy them before major issues occur.

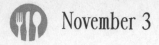

Popcorn Cake

4 quarts popped corn
1 pound gumdrops
½ (12 ounce) package
   candy-coated chocolate
   pieces

½ pound salted peanuts
½ cup butter
1 pound marshmallows
½ cup vegetable oil

Mix popcorn, gumdrops, chocolate pieces, and peanuts in large bowl. Place butter, marshmallows, and oil in saucepan over low heat. Stir until marshmallows are melted. Pour over popcorn mixture and stir. Immediately place in greased 9x13-inch pan and press firmly. Cool before cutting into squares.

Yield: 16 servings

Hope in Mortals

Hopes placed in mortals die with them;
all the promise of their power comes to nothing.
PROVERBS 11:7 NIV

Are you a family who enjoys keeping up with current events? Perhaps you like having discussions about issues of the day or even actively participate in supporting causes that are important to you. Maybe you have even strongly supported political candidates, even to the point of believing that if your candidate is elected then all will be well, but if that person loses then God cannot help us any longer. God encourages us to be active members of society. However, never come to believe that a person's promise is more important than God's promise. Long after this generation is gone, God will still be standing. What a reassuring promise that is!

Dirt Cake

¼ cup butter, softened
1 (8 ounce) package cream
   cheese, softened
1 cup powdered sugar
2 (4 serving size) packages
   instant vanilla pudding mix

3½ cups milk
12 ounces whipped topping
20 ounces chocolate sandwich
   cookies, crushed

Line 10-inch unused flowerpot with foil. In bowl, cream butter, cream cheese, and sugar. In separate bowl, prepare pudding with milk. Combine pudding and cheese mixtures. Fold in whipped topping. In flowerpot, layer cookie crumbs and pudding several times, ending with crumbs on top. If desired, stick gummy worms and silk flower on top and serve with brand-new garden spade.

Yield: 8 servings

To Speak or to Remain Silent?

A time to be silent and a time to speak.
ECCLESIASTES 3:7 NIV

Do you have a hard time keeping your mouth shut? Are words begging to come out that you can barely keep from saying? Maybe you say things that you later regret. God says there are times to speak. Indeed, He encourages us to speak up when He has given us the words to say. Other times, however, He wishes for us to remain silent.
Which is harder for you, to speak or to remain silent? Why?

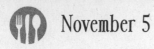

Carrot Cake

1¾ cups flour
½ teaspoon nutmeg
½ teaspoon baking soda
1 teaspoon cinnamon
¼ teaspoon salt

1½ cups sugar
3 eggs
1 cup vegetable oil
1 cup carrots, grated
1 cup pecans, finely chopped

Sift all dry ingredients. Add eggs and oil; mix well. Add carrots and pecans; stir until well mixed. Bake at 350 degrees for 55 minutes. Best topped with cream cheese frosting.

Yield: 16 servings

Speaking Up

"But what about you?" [Jesus] asked. "Who do you say I am?"
MATTHEW 16:15 NIV

Jesus poses an interesting question to His disciples. They already know who He is, and He knows that they know. Jesus could have easily discerned each man's thoughts without having to ask them anything. So why does He ask them to respond? Because He wanted those men who had followed Him to publicly declare Him! In the same way, He wants us to speak to others of who He is and what He has done. Can you speak up? Will you?

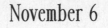

Mexican Chicken Soup

2 to 3 boneless, skinless
   chicken breasts, cooked
   and cut into chunks
2 (14 ounce) cans chicken broth
1 tablespoon cumin

1 teaspoon chicken bouillon
   powder
1 (15 ounce) jar white northern
   beans
1 (24 ounce) jar salsa
2 cups shredded cheddar cheese

In large stockpot, combine all ingredients and heat through. Serve with tortilla or corn chips, additional shredded cheese, and sour cream.

Yield: 4 to 6 servings

What Do Your Eyes Say?

My son, give me your heart and let your eyes delight in my ways.
PROVERBS 23:26 NIV

The eyes tell so much. When two people are in love, they often have eyes only for each other. When you're not happy with someone, your eyes convey a completely different emotion, don't they? What do your eyes tell God when He looks at you? Do you adore Him and only have eyes for Him, or are you unhappy with Him right now? What do your eyes say?

Beef and Vegetable Soup

Small beef roast or 1 pound
   beef stew meat
2 cups water
1 quart diced tomatoes with juice
Vegetables (your choice of
   potatoes, onion, carrots, peas,
   celery, green beans, corn, baby
   lima beans, okra, small
   turnips, or shredded cabbage)

2 teaspoons salt
½ teaspoon pepper
1 teaspoon chili powder
1 teaspoon fresh garlic
½ teaspoon cumin

Brown meat in large stockpot; add water and cook meat until nearly tender. Chop and add vegetables as desired. Add seasonings. Let soup simmer at least 1 hour, adding more water if needed.

Yield: 4 to 6 servings

When Two or Three Come Together

*"For where two or three gather in my name,
there am I with them."*
MATTHEW 18:20 NIV

There is something deeply stirring about worshiping the Lord with others in a congregation on Sunday morning. When voices unite in song or people sit together and listen to a pastor's sermon, the presence of the Lord is often quite strong. Did you realize, though, that God does not wait until a large group is assembled? When even two or three are together, He is there! When you and your family said grace over your meal, He was there. What an amazing God we serve!

Cinnamon Apple Crisp

6 apples, sliced
1 cup water
1 box white cake mix
1 cup brown sugar, packed

½ cup margarine, melted
1 teaspoon cinnamon
Vanilla ice cream

Arrange apples in bottom of ungreased 9x13-inch pan; top with water. In separate bowl, combine cake mix, brown sugar, margarine, and cinnamon; stir until blended (mixture will be crumbly). Sprinkle crumb mixture over apple slices. Bake at 350 degrees for 50 minutes or until lightly browned and bubbly. Serve warm with vanilla ice cream.

Yield: 16 servings

What Are You Asking For?

Then Hannah prayed and said: "My heart rejoices in the LORD."
1 SAMUEL 2:1 NIV

Every year Hannah went to the temple and prayed for a child only to be continually disappointed. A chance encounter with a man of God changed her path and caused her to stop praying for a child for herself and to begin praying for a child she could give to God. When her prayers changed, so did her situation. Consider this: Have you been praying the wrong prayers? Do you need to reconsider what you are asking for?

Fresh Peach Cobbler

Base:
1 cup flour
1½ teaspoons baking powder
Pinch salt
½ cup butter
½ cup milk

Topping:
2 cups fresh peaches, sliced
1 cup hot water
1 cup sugar
Pinch salt
1 teaspoon vanilla

Mix together dry base ingredients. Melt butter and add milk; beat together with dry mixture and pour into lightly buttered 7x11-inch baking dish. Combine topping ingredients and pour over batter. Bake at 350 degrees for 1 hour.

Yield: 8 to 10 servings

Rebuilding the Wall

"What are those feeble Jews doing? Will they restore their wall?.... Can they bring the stones back to life from those heaps of rubble—burned as they are?"
NEHEMIAH 4:2 NIV

We can assume that those watching had little hope that the wall around their city would be rebuilt. While observers saw the impossible, the Jews saw something that was only possible with God. Are you tasked with something that seems impossible to others? Ignore them and listen to the Lord. Not only did He rebuild that wall, He also silenced the critics.

Wacky Cake

3 cups flour
2 cups sugar
½ cup cocoa
2 teaspoons baking soda
1 teaspoon salt

⅔ cup oil
2 teaspoons vanilla
2 tablespoons vinegar
2 cups warm water

Sift flour, sugar, cocoa, baking soda, and salt into large mixing bowl. Make three wells in dry mix. Pour oil and vanilla in one well, vinegar in another, and water in the third. Mix well. Pour into greased 9x13-inch pan dusted with cocoa. Bake at 350 degrees for 35 minutes.

Yield: 16 servings

What Would You Do?

"Shall we accept good from God, and not trouble?"
JOB 2:10 NIV

If you know the story of Job, you know that he was a man who had led a blameless life. He was prosperous and happy with a wife and a family. Most importantly, Job loved the Lord. However, life took a turn for Job and soon he lost everything including his family and his health. Even then, he refused to sin and deny God. Don't you love that kind of faith? What would you do under those circumstances?

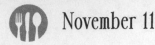

Roman Apple Cake

4 cups apples, chopped
2 cups sugar
½ cup oil
2 teaspoons vanilla
2 eggs

2 cups flour
2 teaspoons cinnamon
2 teaspoons baking soda
1 teaspoon salt
1 cup nuts, chopped

Blend all ingredients until well moistened. Place in 9x13-inch pan and bake at 350 degrees for 40 minutes.

Yield: 16 servings

A New World

The wolf will live with the lamb, the leopard will lie down with the goat. . .and a little child will lead them.
ISAIAH 11:6 NIV

Have you ever been to a zoo? A zookeeper would never place a lamb in a cage with a wolf or a leopard with a goat. The result would not be pleasant, either for the zoo-goers or the goat and lamb. But God says someday the world will be different. Everyone and everything, including the animals, will live in peace. Can you imagine such a world? What a great place it will be!

Chocolate Chip Cheesecake

3 (8 ounce) packages cream
   cheese
3 eggs
¾ cup sugar

1 teaspoon vanilla
3 tubes refrigerated chocolate
   chip cookie dough

Beat together cream cheese, eggs, sugar, and vanilla; set aside. Slice cookie dough into ⅓-inch slices. Arrange half of cookie dough slices on bottom of greased 9x13-inch glass baking dish. Press slices together so no holes remain. Spoon cream cheese mixture evenly over top. Cover with remaining cookie dough. Bake at 350 degrees for 45 to 50 minutes. Remove from oven and allow to cool. Refrigerate. Do not cut until well chilled.

Yield: 16 servings

Bearing Our Burdens Daily

Praise be to the Lord, to God our Savior,
who daily bears our burdens.
PSALM 68:19 NIV

Do you have any chores you do daily? Perhaps you sweep floors or take out the trash each day. Likely you cook meals and shower, perhaps read the newspaper or go off to the office. You do these things every day, so they are second nature to you. In the same way, God bears our burdens each day. It is second nature to Him. Isn't that comforting?

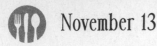

Zucchini Brownies

2 cups flour
½ cup cocoa
1½ teaspoons baking soda
1 teaspoon salt
2 cups grated zucchini

½ cup vegetable oil
½ cup water
2 teaspoons vanilla
1¼ cups sugar
½ cup nuts, chopped (optional)

Blend flour, cocoa, baking soda, and salt; set aside. In large bowl, combine zucchini, oil, water, and vanilla. Stir in sugar, then add dry mix. Stir in nuts if desired, then spread in greased 9x13-inch pan. Bake at 350 degrees for 25 to 30 minutes. Top cooled brownies with chocolate frosting of your choice.

Yield: 16 servings

Shelter in the Storm

*See, the storm of the LORD will burst out in wrath,
a driving wind swirling down on the heads of the wicked.*
JEREMIAH 30:23 NIV

Have you ever been caught out in a nasty storm? When the wind blows, the rain pelts down like needles, and the heavens rumble with thunder and flash with lightning. When you're in the middle of such a storm, all you want is to find shelter, don't you? God is your shelter in the storms of life. Aren't you glad?

Family Dinnertime Tip

Create some time for daily spiritual renewal. Encourage your family members to relax in their favorite spot with tea or another beverage, their Bible, a devotional, and a simple treat. Enjoy!

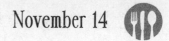
Sloppy Potatoes

3 medium potatoes, sliced
1 medium onion, sliced
1 tablespoon butter

½ teaspoon salt
1½ to 2 cups water

In medium saucepan, bring all ingredients to boil. Reduce heat to low and cook for 15 minutes, stirring occasionally.

Yield: 4 servings

Let Go!

"Those who cling to worthless idols turn away from God's love for them."
JONAH 2:8 NIV

Are you someone who loves to go antiquing? Perhaps you like nothing better than to poke around on dusty shelves and look for treasures. What great fun it is to find just the right item, bring it home, and polish it to perfection only to find your bargain has great value. God says those aren't bad things, but He wants better things for you. Do not cling to things that are worthless. Cling to Him. He is the greatest treasure of all.

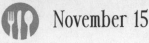

Cream of Broccoli Soup

1 (10 ounce) package frozen
   chopped broccoli
Onion or onion powder to taste
1 (14 ounce) can chicken broth
1 (10¾ ounce) can condensed
   cream of celery soup

1 (10¾ ounce) can condensed
   cream of mushroom soup
1 to 1½ cups shredded cheddar
   cheese

Cook broccoli and onion in chicken broth. Combine soups and stir into broccoli mixture. Bring to gentle boil, stirring constantly. Add cheese, stirring until melted. Serve hot.

Yield: 6 servings

The Less Fortunate

*"'For I was hungry and you gave me something to eat,
I was thirsty and you gave me something to drink,
I was a stranger and you invited me in.'"*
MATTHEW 25:35 NIV

Jesus is clear when He says that He wants us to take care of His people. What are you doing to make that happen in your community? Do you volunteer at a soup kitchen or sort clothes for a clothing ministry? Perhaps you bring snacks in your car to hand out to the homeless begging along the roadside. God says to be purposeful in your care of the less fortunate. What can you do today to achieve this?

Low-Sugar, Low-Fat Strawberry Pie

1 package sugar-free vanilla
   pudding mix
2 cups cold water
1 (3 ounce) package sugar-free
   strawberry gelatin

4 cups strawberries, sliced
1 (9 inch) graham cracker crumb
   piecrust
1 (8 ounce) container light
   whipped topping

In saucepan, mix pudding mix into water. Bring to boil, stirring constantly. Add gelatin, stirring until dissolved. Remove from heat and cool for 10 minutes. Add strawberries, then pour into piecrust. Refrigerate until set. Top with whipped topping.

Yield: 8 servings

Complete Faith

"But say the word, and my servant will be healed."
LUKE 7:7 NIV

A centurion sent elders and friends to find Jesus in the crowd to ask for healing of his servant. The man knew of the power of Jesus and believed that this power could be used in any way Jesus wanted it to be used. His belief was strong enough to depend solely on Jesus for the healing of His servant. Do you have that kind of faith? Can you believe that Jesus is capable of anything?

Old-Fashioned Potato Soup

8 medium potatoes, peeled
   and cubed
1 quart milk
2 teaspoons salt
⅓ teaspoon pepper

1 tablespoon butter
½ cup flour
1 egg, beaten
2 to 3 tablespoons milk

In large saucepan, boil potatoes in salted water until tender; drain. Add 1 quart milk to potatoes and warm over medium heat, then add salt and pepper; stir. Cut butter into flour; mix in egg and just enough milk to make mixture thin enough to drop into hot soup. Drop large spoonfuls of flour mixture into soup; cover and cook over low heat for 10 minutes, stirring occasionally to prevent scorching.

Yield: 8 servings

Don't Stop!

*"And will not God bring about justice for his chosen ones,
who cry out to him day and night? Will he keep putting them off?"*
LUKE 18:7 NIV

Jesus often taught in parables. He told stories with meanings that could be understood by His listeners. In this parable, Jesus tells us of the woman who was relentless in pursuing her cause before the judge. Finally the judge granted her request because he knew she would continue to come to him until he did. God tells us to continue coming to Him with our requests, to keep on praying until we see an answer. Do you have that kind of faith?

Squash Medley

½ medium green zucchini,
    sliced or chunked
½ medium golden zucchini,
    sliced or chunked
2 to 4 pods okra, sliced
½ small onion, chopped
¼ large green pepper, chopped

1 pint canned tomatoes or 3 fresh
    tomatoes, chopped
1 chicken bouillon cube
½ teaspoon garlic, minced
1 teaspoon sugar
½ teaspoon salt

Place all ingredients in saucepan. Add enough water to cover vegetables. Bring to boil; lower heat. Let simmer until vegetables are tender.

Yield: 4 to 6 servings

Wait on God

*I say to myself, "The LORD is my portion;
therefore I will wait for him."*
LAMENTATIONS 3:24 NIV

In this world of instant gratification, how good are you and your family at waiting? When you really want something, you want it right then, don't you? God says there are things worth waiting for. With the Lord as your portion, how can you fail to wait and see what He will do? What are you waiting for? How will you manage the wait?

Low-Fat Pistachio-Nut Cake

Cake:
1 box yellow cake mix
1 (1 ounce) box sugar-free instant
   pistachio pudding mix
1 cup fat-free sour cream
½ cup applesauce
4 eggs
½ teaspoon almond extract

Filling:
½ cup walnuts, chopped
¼ cup sugar
1 teaspoon cinnamon

Combine cake ingredients; pour half of batter into greased Bundt pan. Combine filling ingredients; sprinkle half over batter in pan. Add remaining batter and top with remaining nut mixture. Bake at 350 degrees for 55 minutes.

Yield: 12 to 14 servings

The Ultimate Inheritance

Giving joyful thanks to the Father, who has qualified you to share in the inheritance of his holy people in the kingdom of light.
COLOSSIANS 1:12 NIV

Don't you love stories where rich relatives leave surprise fortunes to someone, thus saving the day? What a great thing that would be if it happened to you, right? But most of us will never know what it is like to have that sort of surprise fall upon us. We will have to manage without the support of an inheritance of that sort. But God has another inheritance prepared for us that is vastly better. Those of us who are believers will one day share in His kingdom for all eternity. What a great inheritance that will be!

Slow-Cooker Stuffing

2 tablespoons butter or
  margarine
1 cup sliced fresh mushrooms
1 cup chopped celery
1 cup chopped onion
10 cups day-old bread cubes
¼ cup butter

1 tablespoon chicken bouillon
  powder
1½ cups hot water
1 teaspoon dried parsley flakes
2 teaspoons poultry seasoning
1 teaspoon salt
1 teaspoon black pepper

Melt butter in skillet. Sauté mushrooms, celery, and onion in butter. Pour over bread cubes in large bowl. Place butter and bouillon powder in small bowl; pour hot water over mixture and stir to melt butter and dissolve powder. Pour over bread mixture. Add remaining seasonings and toss to coat. Turn into lightly greased slow cooker; cover and cook on low for 6 hours.

Yield: 8 servings

Be Shepherds of God's Flock

*Be shepherds of God's flock that is under your care,
watching over them—not because you must,
but because you are willing, as God wants you to be.*
1 PETER 5:2 NIV

Have you ever stopped to think that God has given you a flock to care for? If you are a parent, you have a flock of children who depend on you. You also have friends and family members whom God has placed in your life for you to see to. Each of these people has been put into your life specifically by God for a purpose, and He is greatly pleased when He sees you take your duties seriously.

Broccoli Noodle Soup

6 cups water
6 chicken bouillon cubes
1 (8 ounce) package fine noodles
2 (10 ounce) packages frozen
   chopped broccoli

1 pound processed cheese, cubed
6 cups milk
Salt and pepper to taste

In large saucepan, bring water to boil. Add bouillon cubes and noodles; cook for 4 minutes. Add broccoli; reduce heat and simmer until broccoli is tender. Reduce heat to low; add cheese, milk, and salt and pepper. Cook, stirring constantly, until cheese is melted.

Yield: 8 to 10 servings

What Do You Hope For?

*I remain confident of this: I will see the goodness
of the Lord in the land of the living.*
PSALM 27:13 NIV

King David had everything and yet he was on the run and fearing for his life. His one hope was to see God's glory while he still lived. What is it you're hoping for? As you go around the table at this meal, ask each person seated there what his or her greatest hope is, and then share yours. Whatever your hopes are, remain confident that God can bring each of them to fruition just as He did with David.

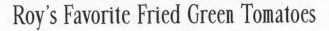

Roy's Favorite Fried Green Tomatoes

Vegetable oil
¾ cup flour
¼ cup cornmeal
¼ teaspoon salt

¼ teaspoon pepper
2 large green tomatoes, sliced
 medium thin
¾ cup milk

Cover bottom of frying pan with oil; heat. Blend flour, cornmeal, salt, and pepper. Dip tomato slices in milk, then coat in dry mix. Fry, turning once, until tomatoes reach desired browned—or charred—look. Serve on bread with butter.

Yield: 2 servings

Something from Nothing

This is what the Lord says: "Heaven is my throne, and the earth is my footstool. Where is the house you will build for me? Where will my resting place be? Has not my hand made all these things, and so they came into being?" declares the Lord.
ISAIAH 66:1–2 NIV

Do you like to work with your hands? Perhaps someone in your family loves making crafts, or even working with wood. Maybe creating, be it wood, scrapbooking, or something else, is an activity that you all like to do together. Consider all the things God has created: from nothing He made the earth and all its contents. Can you imagine?

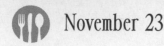

Wonder Fudge

¼ cup margarine
1 (12 ounce) package semisweet
    chocolate chips
¼ cup corn syrup

1 teaspoon vanilla
1½ cups powdered sugar, sifted
2 cups crisp rice cereal

Mix margarine, chocolate chips, corn syrup, and vanilla in large saucepan. Cook over very low heat, stirring constantly until smooth. Remove from heat. Add powdered sugar and crisp rice cereal. Stir until cereal is evenly coated. Press mixture into buttered square cake pan. Refrigerate until firm. Cut into squares.

Yield: 9 to 12 servings

Meaning

*I called upon your name, Lord,
from the depths of the pit. You heard my plea.*
LAMENTATIONS 3:55–56 NIV

Did you know that everyone's name has a meaning? It's true! Some names like Hope, Charity, or Hunter are pretty easy to tell. Maybe your name is like one of those. However, there are guidebooks and websites that can tell you the meaning of your name. For fun, why don't you find out what your name means and then talk about it with your family tomorrow? But what about the name of the Lord? What does His name mean? He has a list of names by which He is known, and each of them has a special meaning that describes a certain part of who He is. But guess what, no matter which of His many names you might use, He always answers when you call. Isn't that great to know?

Family Dinnertime Tip

Give the stresses of your day to God. He wants you to!

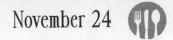

Holiday Slaw

1 (1 pound) package broccoli
   slaw mix
⅔ cup raisins
¾ cup coarsely chopped
   walnuts or pecans

1 large apple, chopped
1 cup prepared poppy seed
   dressing

In large bowl, combine first four ingredients. Pour prepared dressing over mixture and stir gently until evenly coated. Chill for 2 to 3 hours to blend flavors before serving.

Yield: 8 servings

Share the Bounty

Nehemiah said, "Go and enjoy choice food and sweet drinks, and send some to those who have nothing prepared. This day is holy to our Lord. Do not grieve, for the joy of the Lord is your strength."
NEHEMIAH 8:10 NIV

Don't you love a celebration? Sitting down together with family and friends is always a cause for celebrating, don't you think? But what of those who have nothing to celebrate? God calls us to share our bounty with those who have less than we do. Consider inviting a few extras to your celebration this year. You will get as much out of it as they do. More, probably.

Chili

1 pound lean ground beef
  (or ground venison)
1 small onion, chopped
1 small green bell pepper,
  chopped
1 (15 ounce) can dark red kidney
  beans

1 (7 ounce) can tomato sauce
2 cups tomato juice
2 tablespoons chili powder
½ teaspoon garlic
2 teaspoons salt
½ teaspoon pepper
½ teaspoon cumin

In large saucepan, brown meat with onion and green pepper; drain. Add beans, tomato sauce and juice, and seasonings. Let simmer for 30 to 40 minutes on low heat. Stir to keep from sticking. Good served with corn chips or crackers.

Yield: 6 servings

Our Refuge

The Lord is good, a refuge in times of trouble.
He cares for those who trust in him.
NAHUM 1:7 NIV

Where do you turn in times of trouble? If you are a child, you go to a parent. If you're an employee, you go to your boss. But what if your trouble is beyond something that can be handled by a loved one? What if your troubles are such that only God can fix them? Good news! He says in His Word that is exactly what He does. Run to Him in times of trouble. He loves you!

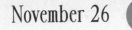

Festive Holiday Punch

8 cups apple juice
8 cups cranberry juice cocktail
2 red apples, sliced

2 cups cranberries
3 liters lemon-lime soda
Ice cubes as needed

Combine apple and cranberry juices in punch bowl. Fifteen minutes before serving, add apple slices, cranberries, soda, and ice cubes. Do not stir.

Yield: 24 servings

A Special Dream

I will praise the LORD, who counsels me;
even at night my heart instructs me.
PSALM 16:7 NIV

Have you ever awakened from a dream knowing that there was something special about that dream? Perhaps it was something that you felt you were meant to learn or maybe it was something that might be to come. God says in His Word that He offers counsel to us not only in our waking hours but while we sleep. Next time you have a dream that you feel might be important, ask God to show you what it means. He will.

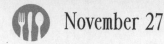

Almond Florentines

1 cup butter (no substitutions)
1 cup sugar
⅓ cup honey
⅓ cup heavy whipping cream

4 cups sliced almonds, blanched
6 ounces semisweet chocolate
chips

Spray five 8-inch aluminum foil pie tins with cooking oil. Melt butter in large saucepan. Add sugar, honey, and whipping cream. Bring to boil over medium heat. Stir frequently. When boil creates wild froth on top, stir constantly and allow to continue to boil at this level for exactly 90 seconds. Remove saucepan from heat. Add almonds. Quickly pour mixture into pie tins. Bake at 350 degrees for 10 to 14 minutes until rich golden brown (most likely will be bubbling). Cool in pan for 20 minutes, then refrigerate in pan for 30 minutes. Turn out onto waxed paper; stack in refrigerator with waxed paper between florentines. Melt chocolate and spread on bottom of florentines. Let cool. Break into bark. Store in refrigerator with plastic wrap between layers.

Yield: 20 to 24 servings

Grandchildren

Children's children are a crown to the aged,
and parents are the pride of their children.
PROVERBS 17:6 NIV

Do you have grandparents or elderly relatives who live nearby? If so, then it's likely that you have seen photographs of yourself and your family proudly displayed in their home. God says children are a blessing. I bet they would agree. But guess what? As much as you and your family might be loved by a grandparent or other elderly relative, you more loved even more—infinitely more—by the Lord!

Cheeseburger Chowder

1 pound ground beef
½ cup onion, diced
½ cup celery, diced
½ cup butter
½ cup flour

½ gallon milk
1½ pounds processed cheese,
 cubed
3 cups frozen hash brown cubes

In large stockpot, brown beef with onion and celery. Rinse in cool water to remove grease. Return to pot; add butter and heat until butter melts. Stir flour into meat mixture to coat. Gradually add milk, cooking over medium heat. When mixture is hot—not boiling—and starting to thicken, add cheese. Stir until melted. Add hash browns. When soup is hot to your taste, it is ready to serve.

Yield: 4 to 6 servings

Setting Sail

On that very day Noah and his sons, Shem, Ham and Japheth, together with his wife and the wives of his three sons, entered the ark.
GENESIS 7:13 NIV

Can you imagine what it was like to step onto the ark on that day? The size of the craft must have been vast in order to hold all the animals. Oh, and the animals! What a noise they must have been making! Noah and his family entered that ark not knowing what God would do or how He would do it. All Noah knew was that he had heard from God and must obey. Could you have done what Noah did?

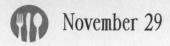

Toffee

1 pound butter
2 cups sugar

1 (6 ounce) package semisweet
chocolate chips, melted

Bring butter and sugar to boil—to 310 degrees on candy thermometer.
Pour mixture out onto greased cookie sheet and place in refrigerator to
cool. Break into pieces and dip in melted chocolate. Place on waxed paper
until chocolate hardens.

Yield: 20 to 24 servings

Are You a Planner?

*Lord, you are my God; I will exalt you and praise your name,
for in perfect faithfulness you have done wonderful
things, things planned long ago.*
Isaiah 25:1 NIV

Are you a planner? Do you have your schedule set for the rest of the
week? The rest of the month? What about the rest of the year? God is a
planner, too. He does things on His schedule and in His own way, but He
has a plan that He set forth before the beginning of time. Nothing will
cause Him to deviate from that plan. Aren't you glad you serve a God who
is unchanging?

Pizza–Meat Loaf Roll

2 eggs
½ cup milk
1 sleeve soda crackers
1 pound ground beef
1 pound pork sausage
1 cup cheddar cheese, shredded
½ cup green pepper, chopped
½ cup onion, chopped

⅛ teaspoon pepper
½ teaspoon salt
½ teaspoon garlic powder
½ teaspoon oregano
1 cup pizza sauce, divided
1 cup mozzarella cheese, shredded
1 cup pepperoni, sliced

In mixing bowl, beat eggs; add milk and crackers. Add meats, cheddar cheese, green pepper, onion, pepper, salt, garlic powder, and oregano. Mix well, using your hands. Place cookie sheet top-down on counter and cover with waxed paper. Spread meat mixture out on pan, shaping it into rectangle about 1 inch thick. Spread ½ cup pizza sauce over meat, sprinkle on mozzarella, and place pepperoni on top. Starting at short end, use waxed paper to help you start rolling up meat jelly roll–style. Cut roll in half. Place into baking dish with seams down. Drizzle ½ cup pizza sauce on top. Bake at 350 degrees for 1 hour.

Yield: 8 servings

The God of the Storm

"He made the earth by his power; he founded the world by his wisdom and stretched out the heavens by his understanding. When he thunders, the waters in the heavens roar; he makes clouds rise from the ends of the earth."
JEREMIAH 51:15–16 NIV

When storms rage outside, we often turn to specialists in meteorology to tell us when the storm will pass and what we can expect while it is over top of us. Their graphs and charts and radar give us valuable information that we can use to keep ourselves safe. In the same way, the one who causes the storms to rage gives us comfort and safety that goes far beyond any specialists in any form of science. The next time the rain falls and the thunder rolls, consider the source!

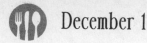

Stewed Tomatoes

1 quart canned tomatoes
1 teaspoon salt
¼ cup sugar
1 tablespoon butter

2 tablespoons flour
½ cup milk
Soda crackers or bread

In medium saucepan, cook tomatoes with salt for 15 minutes. Add sugar and butter. Slowly combine flour and milk until there are no lumps. Add floury milk to tomatoes, stirring over heat until thickened. To serve, break up crackers or bread in serving dish and pour tomatoes over top. Stir and serve.

Yield: 6 servings

Bringing a Savior into the World

This is how the birth of Jesus the Messiah came about: His mother Mary was pledged to be married to Joseph, but before they came together, she was found to be pregnant through the Holy Spirit.
MATTHEW 1:18 NIV

As we begin the Christmas season, let's consider the unique way God decided to bring a Savior into our world. Rather than allow Him a glorious entrance with all the fanfare His position should have demanded, God chose a poor and obscure country girl for the honor of giving life to the Savior. Is this how you would have done it? What changes would you have made to this scenario?

Family Dinnertime Tip

Gather your family together once a week for devotions and dessert. Read through a family-friendly devotional book or study a passage from the Bible. End with prayer and a sweet treat!

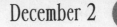

Buckeyes

1 pound butter
2 cups peanut butter
2½ pounds powdered sugar
3 teaspoons vanilla

6 ounces semisweet chocolate chips
¼ pound paraffin wax

Cream butter and peanut butter; add powdered sugar and mix well; add vanilla. Use hands to blend. Consistency should be ready for shaping into balls size of large marbles. Melt chocolate and paraffin in small double boiler. Rest ball of peanut butter mixture between prongs of 2-pronged meat fork and dip into chocolate to coat all but top. Place on waxed paper in refrigerator to solidify.

Yield: 5 dozen

Mary's Risk

"I am the Lord's servant," Mary answered.
"May your word to me be fufilled" Then the angel left her.
LUKE 1:38 NIV

Can you imagine being a young and innocent girl, only recently betrothed, who is then visited by an angel bringing astonishing news? She has been chosen to carry the child of the promise, to become the mother of Jesus. In her culture, a pregnancy outside of marriage was a terrible thing, and she must have understood what would happen to her reputation. Likely her marriage to Joseph would never happen and she might be shunned by her people. And yet look at what Mary says! She's willing to risk all those things to do as God asks. What are you willing to risk?

Stuffed Peppers

3 to 4 pounds ground beef
2 to 3 eggs
1 cup white rice, uncooked
1 cup cheddar cheese, shredded
¼ teaspoon salt

¼ teaspoon pepper
1 small onion, chopped
5 to 6 large green peppers
8 (10 ounce) cans tomato soup
Water

Mix beef, eggs, rice, cheese, salt, pepper, and onion together; stuff into cleaned, hollowed-out green peppers. Place in large soup pan with tomato soup and 3 to 4 soup cans full of water. Cook on stove over medium-high heat, boiling slowly for 3 hours.

Yield: 5 to 6 servings

Jesus' Earthly Father

When Joseph woke up, he did what the angel of the Lord had commanded him and took Mary home as his wife.
MATTHEW 1:24 NIV

In Joseph's culture, he was completely within his rights to have divorced Mary quietly once she delivered the news that she was with child. Marriage and family were serious subjects in those days, and keeping a lineage pure was something that was highly favored. And yet Joseph chose to bring Mary home to be his wife, ultimately causing him to become the earthly father of the Savior of the world. This is a lot for a young husband to consider, and yet Joseph does not hesitate. Can you imagine handling this as well as he did? God chose well, did He not?

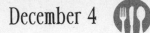
Microwave Peanut Brittle

1 cup sugar
1 cup white corn syrup
1 cup peanuts, roasted and salted

1 teaspoon butter
1 teaspoon vanilla
1 teaspoon baking soda

In 1½-quart microwave-safe casserole dish, combine sugar and corn syrup.
Microwave on high for 4 minutes, stirring every minute. Add nuts and
microwave for 3½ minutes. Add butter and vanilla and microwave for 1½
minutes. Add baking soda and stir gently until foamy. Pour out onto jelly
roll pan to cool. Break into pieces.

Yield: 35 servings

Star of Wonder

When they saw the star, they were overjoyed.
MATTHEW 2:10 NIV

The birth of Jesus was heralded not only by the angels in heaven but by
wise men on earth. God hung a star in the sky that guided wise men to
the place where Jesus was born. It was a sign to these wise men that the
anticipated Messiah had arrived. What a perfect sign for a perfect child!
How would you have announced Jesus' birth?

Baked Spinach and Tomatoes

6 tablespoons butter
1 (20 ounce) can tomatoes
½ teaspoon sugar
1 teaspoon salt
1 bay leaf

1 tablespoon minced onion
4 tablespoons flour
1 (10 ounce) package frozen
   spinach, thawed
½ cup bread crumbs

Combine butter, tomatoes, sugar, salt, bay leaf, and onion. Cook over medium heat until flavors blend, then thicken with flour. In baking dish, put layer of tomato mixture then layer of spinach; alternate layers and top with bread crumbs. Bake at 375 degrees for 30 minutes.

Yield: 4 servings

Mary and Elizabeth, John and Jesus

*When Elizabeth heard Mary's greeting,
the baby leaped in her womb.*
LUKE 1:41 NIV

When Mary first sees her cousin Elizabeth, she is overjoyed at her cousin's reaction. For the baby in Elizabeth's womb has jumped for joy at the close proximity to the as yet unborn Savior. How like God to allow babies not yet born to communicate! He is such a creative God. Do you know who that baby in Elizabeth's womb grew up to be? John the Baptist, closest friend of Jesus, and the man who announced Jesus' impending coming. How wonderful that the Lord allows us a tiny peek at their first meeting.

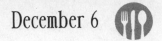

Puppy Chow

1 (12 ounce) package chocolate
   chips
½ cup butter

1 cup peanut butter
1 box crisp corn cereal
1 pound powdered sugar, divided

Melt chocolate chips, butter, and peanut butter together. Stir in cereal and coat well. Put half of mixture in large paper bag with half of powdered sugar. Shake well; repeat with second half. Store in covered container.

Yield: 10 to 12 servings

Glory to God!

Suddenly a great company of the heavenly host appeared with the angel, praising God and saying, "Glory to God in the highest heaven, and on earth peace to those on whom his favor rests."
LUKE 2:13–14 NIV

Don't you love to listen to the choir singing? When all those lovely voices combine, the music they make is just glorious, isn't it? How much more glorious, then, did the angels in heaven sound when they proclaimed the birth of our Savior? Glory to God, indeed!

Wassail

1 gallon apple cider
2 cups orange juice
1 (6 ounce) can frozen lemonade
   concentrate

2 teaspoons cinnamon
1 teaspoon nutmeg
1 teaspoon ground cloves
1 orange, cut into slices

Mix all ingredients except for orange slices in large pan and slowly bring to boil. Simmer for 10 minutes. Float orange slices in hot wassail before serving.

Yield: 18 to 20 servings

Blessed Is She!

"Blessed is she who has believed that the Lord would fulfill his promises to her!"
LUKE 1:45 NIV

By the time Mary had traveled to spend time with her cousin, Elizabeth, she had been married to Joseph a very short time. The child inside her, the future Savior of the world, had become real to her, and she began to allow thoughts of what it might be like to be the mother of a man who was destined to unfathomable greatness. In all, she stayed with Elizabeth, who was also expecting a child, three months. Can you imagine how these two women hated parting company when it was time for Mary to go? And yet both had great destinies to fulfill.

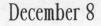

Mexican Casserole

1 pound ground beef
1 small onion, chopped
⅓ bag nacho chips, crushed
1 (15 ounce) can kidney beans
2 cups shredded cheddar cheese, divided

1 (14½ ounce) can stewed tomatoes
1 (10¾ ounce) can condensed cream of chicken soup
2 teaspoons chili powder

Brown beef over medium heat, then add onion; drain. Layer in casserole dish in following order: meat and onion mixture, nacho chips, kidney beans, 1 cup cheese, stewed tomatoes, cream of chicken soup mixed with chili powder, and remaining cheese. Bake at 350 degrees for 30 minutes.

Yield: 4 to 6 servings

Highly Favored

The angel went to her and said, "Greetings, you who are highly favored! The Lord is with you."
LUKE 1:28 NIV

Mary was an ordinary girl living an ordinary life in an ordinary village until the day God changed all of that by sending an angel to tell her of an extraordinary plan. Can you imagine how this girl who was living such an obscure life might have been shocked, even frightened, by all of this? And yet what does Mary do? She takes her plans and dreams and submits them to God, knowing her ordinary life will be over. She understands that living a life surrendered to Him is far preferable to anything she might imagine. And oh how she was right!

Stix and Stones Candy Mix

2 cups mini pretzel sticks
4 cups toasted oats cereal
4 cups crisp corn or rice squares
   cereal
1 cup salted peanuts or mixed
   nuts

1 pound white chocolate coating
   (almond bark), chunked
½ to 1 pound candy-coated
   chocolate pieces

In large bowl, combine pretzels, cereals, and nuts. In large glass bowl, melt coating chunks in microwave, stirring every 30 seconds until smooth. Pour over pretzels, cereal, and nuts and mix well. Fold in coated chocolate pieces last. Spread mixture over 2 to 3 waxed paper–lined baking sheets. Cool and break apart. Store in airtight container.

Yield: 30 servings

Following God

*On coming to the house, they saw the child with his mother Mary,
and they bowed down and worshiped him. Then they opened
their treasures and presented him with gifts
of gold, frankincense and myrrh.*
MATTHEW 2:11 NIV

The magi had come a long way following a star to the place where Jesus lay with His mother, Mary. They knew of the prophecy that a Messiah would come, and they saw the star as proof of that prophecy. When Herod asked them to report back about his supposed Messiah, the men knew immediately that they would not be going back to Herod's court. Instead, they worshiped Jesus and then returned home by a different route. Defying Herod was risky. Would you have been brave enough to ignore the king's demands?

Reuben Casserole

2 (32 ounce) bags sauerkraut,
   drained, divided
1 pint sour cream
1 onion, chopped
2 (15 ounce) cans corned beef,
   crumbled

2 pounds swiss cheese slices
1 loaf rye bread, cubed
1 cup margarine, melted
Thousand Island dressing

In large baking pan, layer as follows: 1 bag sauerkraut, sour cream, onion, second bag sauerkraut, corned beef, swiss cheese slices, and rye bread cubes. Pour melted margarine over top. Cover and bake at 400 degrees for 45 to 50 minutes. Remove cover and bake additional 15 to 20 minutes until bread is browned. Cover again and bake additional 30 minutes. Serve with Thousand Island dressing on side.

Yield: 10 to 12 servings

Do Not Be Afraid

But the angel said to her, "Do not be afraid,
Mary; you have found favor with God."
LUKE 1:30 NIV

Don't you love how the angel reassures Mary? Surely she must have been terrified to see a messenger of God standing in front of her, even before she heard the news he delivered. The angel's presence must have been shocking to a girl of such humble origin, and yet somehow she quickly adjusts not only to his presence but to the news that she has been chosen to give birth to the Messiah. What a memorable visit that turned out to be!

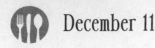

Holiday Punch

1 (3 ounce) package cherry
  gelatin
1 cup boiling water
1 (6 ounce) can frozen lemonade
  concentrate

3 cups cold water
1 quart cranberry juice
Ice cubes
1 (12 ounce) can ginger ale

Dissolve gelatin completely in boiling water. Stir in lemonade concentrate, cold water, and cranberry juice. Chill. Immediately before serving, pour mixture over ice cubes in large punch bowl. Stir in ginger ale.

Yield: 25 to 30 servings

The Census

*In those days Caesar Augustus issued a decree that a
census should be taken of the entire Roman world.*
LUKE 2:1 NIV

When the Roman emperor declared that a census of all the people under his control would be taken, there was no way to claim hardship or explain that travel to the land of Joseph's family was impossible. Instead, Mary, who was greatly pregnant, and Joseph made the long journey to Bethlehem to be counted along with the others from the house of David. While Caesar thought to merely count his subjects, he instead caused yet another prophecy to be fulfilled. The baby Jesus would never have been born in Bethlehem had Mary and Joseph not been required to travel there!

Cottage Cheese Cake

1 (24 ounce) container small-
    curd cottage cheese
4 eggs
1 cup sugar
Cinnamon
Dill

Crust:
2 cups flour
1 teaspoon salt
⅔ cup shortening
5 to 7 tablespoons cold water

Mix together cottage cheese, eggs, and sugar in large mixing bowl. Set aside.

Prepare crust: Mix together flour, salt, and shortening with fork. Add water. Roll out crust to fit cookie sheet. Fill crust with cottage cheese mixture. Sprinkle cinnamon and dill on top. Bake at 375 degrees for 45 minutes. Cool; cut into squares.

Yield: 20 to 24 servings

He Gave Him the Name Jesus

But he did not consummate their marriage until she gave birth
to a son. And he gave him the name Jesus.
MATTHEW 1:25 NIV

Names were taken seriously in Joseph's day. There were certain expectations for names of sons, and surely there had to be people who wondered where the name of Jesus came from. Of course, Joseph knew. God had told him well before his marriage to Mary that the child she carried should be called Jesus. Because Joseph answered to God above anyone else, the name of this child was never in doubt!

Pizza Casserole

1 pound ground beef
1 onion, chopped
1 (28 ounce) can tomato puree
1 (8 ounce) can tomato sauce
1 (8 ounce) can mushroom pieces

Italian seasoning
Garlic salt
1 pound spaghetti, uncooked
2 cups mozzarella cheese
1 stick pepperoni, thinly sliced

Brown beef with onion; drain grease. Add tomato puree, tomato sauce, and mushrooms. Add seasonings to taste and cook for approximately 5 minutes. Cook spaghetti according to package directions; drain. In 9x13-inch casserole dish, place layer of sauce (⅓) on bottom; follow with layer of half of spaghetti; add more sauce with half of cheese and pepperoni; place remaining spaghetti; top with sauce, cheese, and pepperoni. Cover with foil and bake at 400 degrees for 30 minutes.

Yield: 12 to 16 servings

The Magi Follow the Star

*"Where is the one who has been born king of the Jews?
We saw his star when it rose and have come to worship him."*
MATTHEW 2:2 NIV

The magi had been waiting for a sign that the Messiah had come. When they saw the star, they knew the prophecy had been fulfilled. Even Herod, who gave them orders to find the baby and report back, could not keep God's promise from being fulfilled. God orchestrated His plan perfectly so the baby Jesus would be born in Bethlehem to a virgin girl. Nothing is too difficult for God, is it?

Family Dinnertime Tip

When you pray, do you often find you're talking to God entirely about yourself? *I need. . . I want. . . Help me. . .* Remember to ask God to help and bless others. Be courageous. . .and ask Him to use you to impact the life of someone in need.

Chocolate Zucchini Cake

1 cup brown sugar, packed
½ cup sugar
½ cup margarine
½ cup vegetable oil
3 eggs
1 teaspoon vanilla
½ cup buttermilk
2½ cups flour

½ teaspoon allspice
½ teaspoon cinnamon
½ teaspoon salt
2 teaspoons baking soda
¼ cup cocoa
1¾ cups shredded zucchini
1 cup semisweet chocolate chips

Cream sugars, margarine, and oil. Add eggs, vanilla, buttermilk, and flour; stir well. Sift allspice, cinnamon, salt, baking soda, and cocoa together, then sift into wet mixture; beat well. Stir in zucchini and pour into cake pan. Sprinkle chocolate chips on top. Bake at 325 degrees for 45 minutes.

Yield: 20 to 24 servings

A Powerful Ruler with No Power

*When Herod realized that he had been
outwitted by the Magi, he was furious.*
MATTHEW 2:16 NIV

At the time of Christ's birth, Herod was one of the most powerful men in the world. His treasures were vast and his subjects were many. He lived a life of complete control over all who lived in his territories. And yet this man who was so very powerful had no control over a tiny infant, a humble virgin, and a young man named Joseph. Let that sink in a minute. A powerful ruler was outmaneuvered. Only God could make that happen!

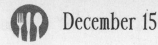

Vicki's Tagalini

1 pound ground beef
1 (14½ ounce) can stewed
   tomatoes
1 onion, chopped
½ cup black olives, sliced
1 green pepper, chopped
2 teaspoons chili powder

8 ounces seashell macaroni,
   cooked according to package
   directions
Salt and pepper to taste
1 (15 ounce) can creamed corn
Provolone cheese, shredded

Brown ground beef; drain. Place in large casserole dish. Add remaining ingredients except provolone. Mix gently. Bake at 350 degrees for 30 minutes. Top with cheese and return to oven until bubbly.

Yield: 12 servings

Son of the Most High

*"He will be great and will be called the Son of the Most High.
The Lord God will give him the throne of his father David."*
LUKE 1:32 NIV

What an amazing prophecy for a baby born to a woman who was neither properly married nor descended from an important family. Mary was a humble girl chosen by God for a mission that she could not have imagined. A girl with no entitlement would be giving life to the Savior. When we think of Christmas, shouldn't we pause to consider the miracle not only of Jesus' birth but also of the way God chose it all to happen?

Chocolate Toffee Bar Cake

1 German chocolate cake mix
1 (14 ounce) can sweetened
   condensed milk
1 (14 ounce) jar caramel ice
   cream topping

1 (8 ounce) tub whipped topping
3 to 6 milk chocolate toffee
   candy bars, crushed

Bake cake according to package directions. While cake is still hot, poke holes in cake about 1 inch apart, using handle of wooden spoon. Combine milk and caramel topping; pour over cake, completely covering it. Refrigerate cake overnight. Before serving, cover cake with whipped topping and sprinkle with candy bar crumbs.

Yield: 20 to 24 servings

The Real Manger Scene

While they were there, the time came for the baby to be born.
LUKE 2:6 NIV

Imagine what it must have been like for Mary and Joseph. Poor Joseph had likely walked all the way to Bethlehem while Mary, huge with child, could not have been comfortable riding on a donkey all those many miles. They must have been exhausted. Then, with no place to stay, imagine how they felt! When you consider the manger scene in your Christmas decorations, stop and think of what the real manger scene must have been like.

Barbecued Spareribs

1 rack ribs
1 large onion, sliced
1 lemon, sliced
1 cup ketchup
⅓ cup Worcestershire sauce

1 teaspoon chili sauce
1 teaspoon salt
2 dashes hot sauce
2 cups water

Place ribs in shallow baking pan, meaty side up. On each individual rib, place 1 slice of onion and 1 slice of lemon. Roast at 450 degrees for 30 minutes. Combine remaining ingredients in medium saucepan and bring to boil; pour over ribs. Continue baking for 45 minutes to 1 hour.

Yield: 3 to 4 servings

A Child Is Born

And she gave birth to her firstborn, a son. She wrapped him in cloths and placed him in a manger, because there was no guest room available for them.
LUKE 2:7 NIV

Think of the last time a baby was born in your family. What an exciting time that was. Likely there were celebrations when news of the mother's pregnancy was announced. Then came baby showers and family gatherings and finally the time for the child to be born. Unlike Mary, the baby in your family was probably not brought into the world in a stable. Why do you think God chose such a humble beginning for Jesus? Surely there were so many other ways He could have allowed this wonderful birth to happen.

Lebkuchen (German Christmas Cookies)

¾ cup honey
¾ cup dark brown sugar, packed
2 tablespoons butter
1 large egg
Grated rind of 1 orange
3½ cups flour
½ teaspoon baking soda
½ teaspoon salt
1 teaspoon cinnamon
1 teaspoon allspice

½ teaspoon nutmeg
½ teaspoon ground ginger
½ cup finely chopped mixed
    candied fruit
¾ cup slivered almonds, finely
    chopped

Glaze:
1 cup powdered sugar
3 tablespoons water

Pour honey into medium saucepan. Add brown sugar and butter and stir over moderate heat until sugar dissolves and butter melts. Do not boil. Remove from heat and cool to room temperature. Stir in egg and orange rind. Sift together flour, baking soda, salt, and spices; fold into honey mixture. Stir in candied fruit and almonds. Chill overnight.

Heat oven to 350 degrees. Divide dough into four sections. Roll each portion on lightly floured surface into 5x6-inch rectangle, ¾ inch thick. Cut dough into 1x2½-inch bars. Place bars on lightly greased cookie sheets. Bake for 10 minutes; transfer bars to wire cooling racks. Cool completely. To make glaze, combine powdered sugar with water; blend well. Add additional water if glaze is too thick. Spread thin coat on each cooled cookie.

Yield: 5 dozen cookies

Lowly Shepherds

*An angel of the Lord appeared to them, and the glory
of the Lord shone around them, and they were terrified.*
LUKE 2:9 NIV

Can you imagine what it must have been like for the shepherds? Generally, herding sheep is a quiet business. And yet they saw and heard from an angel of the Lord! Of course they were terrified. Isn't it interesting that the angel of the Lord was sent to tell the shepherds of Jesus' birth? They were looked down upon by others, so why them?

December 19

Icebox Cake

8 whole graham crackers
2 cups milk

1 (4 serving size) package instant
chocolate pudding mix

Break graham crackers into pieces to line 9x5-inch loaf pan. (You should have enough crackers for 3 layers.) Place one layer of crackers in pan. Set remaining crackers aside. Using milk, prepare pudding according to package instructions. After mixing, work quickly so pudding doesn't set up. Pour about ⅓ of pudding into prepared pan, spreading out evenly. Place layer of graham crackers on pudding. Pour another ⅓ of pudding in, spreading evenly. Place final layer of graham crackers and top with remaining pudding. Cover and chill overnight. To serve, cut into pieces, using spatula to place on dessert dishes.

Yield: 9 servings

A Savior Is Born

But the angel said to them, "Do not be afraid. I bring you good news that will cause great joy for all the people. Today in the town of David a Savior has been born to you; he is the Messiah, the Lord."
LUKE 2:10–11 NIV

The Savior had come; the Messiah was born! Jesus would soon take His place as the one who not only would fish for men but also would go to the cross to save them. But now on this quiet night, He was a newly born baby being cradled by a young woman and being announced to the shepherds. Isn't it interesting how throughout this story God chooses the least likely participants? As you go through the days of this Christmas season, consider God's unique choices, and ask yourself why the humble were exalted while those like Herod, who had great power, were fooled. Perhaps He was making a statement about what—and who—is truly important.

Two-Cheese Spinach

2 (10 ounce) packages frozen chopped spinach
5 tablespoons butter, divided
1 cup ricotta cheese or small-curd cottage cheese
1 egg

3 tablespoons flour
¼ teaspoon salt
⅛ teaspoon pepper
⅛ teaspoon nutmeg
3 tablespoons grated Parmesan cheese

Place spinach in large saucepan and cook according to package instructions. Drain cooked spinach through a colander or sieve, pressing out liquid. Melt 3 tablespoons butter in same pot then remove from heat. Stir in spinach, ricotta, egg, flour, salt, pepper, and nutmeg. Mix thoroughly. Place mixture in greased 8x8-inch baking dish. Dot top with remaining butter and sprinkle with Parmesan cheese. Bake uncovered at 425 degrees for 10 minutes until cheeses are melted.

Yield: 9 to 12 servings

The Best Gift of All

"Look! The virgin will conceive a child! She will give birth to a son, and they will call him Immanuel, which means 'God is with us.'"
MATTHEW 1:23 NLT

God is with us. Have you ever paused to consider what this really means? He loved us so much that He sent Jesus to us. For a time, Jesus walked among the people of the earth just as you and I do. He was a real man, and yet He was God. During the Christmas season, people sing songs and send cards and give gifts to celebrate the birth of Christ. As you go through this holiday season, however, pause to consider how Jesus is still with us. Isn't that the best gift of all?

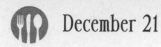

Christmas Tea Mix

1 cup instant tea mix
2 cups powdered orange drink
  mix
3 cups sugar

½ cup red cinnamon candies
½ teaspoon ground cloves
1 envelope lemonade mix

Mix ingredients and store in airtight container. To prepare one serving, add 1 heaping teaspoon to 1 cup hot water.

Yield: 7 cups of tea mix

Go to the Manger

"This will be a sign to you: You will find a baby
wrapped in cloths and lying in a manger."
LUKE 2:12 NIV

In all of your Christmas decorations, do you have a manger sitting out somewhere? Go and look at it now. What do you see? Mary and Joseph, and the baby Jesus, of course. Is there a star overhead to mark the place where Jesus was born? Perhaps your manger scene also has the magi bearing the traditional gifts they brought from afar. And animals and a manger, too, and possibly even an angel standing guard. However, consider to whom God sent His messenger: the shepherds. Those ordinary shepherds were chosen to hear the news before any of the elite and important. Are they in your manger scene? They should be. They were certainly in God's.

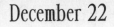

Belgian Christmas Bars

1⅔ cups flour
1½ teaspoons baking powder
½ teaspoon salt
⅔ cup vegetable shortening
1 cup brown sugar, packed
2 large eggs

1 teaspoon almond extract
½ cup chopped blanched
   almonds
½ teaspoon cinnamon
Red and green colored sugar

Combine flour, baking powder, and salt; set aside. In large mixing bowl, cream shortening and brown sugar. Beat in eggs and almond extract. Gradually blend in dry ingredients. Spread evenly in ungreased 9x13-inch baking pan. Scatter almonds and cinnamon over top. Sprinkle with colored sugar. Bake at 375 degrees for 10 to 12 minutes or until lightly browned. Cut into bars while still warm.

Yield: 2 dozen bars

The Angel on Your Tree

Suddenly a great company of the heavenly host appeared
with the angel, praising God.
LUKE 2:13 NIV

At the top of many Christmas trees is the traditional Christmas angel. The angel looks down on the tree below and spreads its wings in majestic glory. Can you even imagine what it must have been like when the heavenly host appeared along with the angel announcing the birth of Christ? It must have been like nothing the shepherds had ever seen. During this Christmas season when you look up at the angel on your tree, consider the angel God sent. What a loving God we serve!

Spanish Chicken and Rice

4 green onions, diced
1 large Spanish yellow onion, chopped
2 cloves garlic, minced
1 cup Spanish green olives with pimientos, drained and chopped
Olive oil

1 teaspoon crushed red pepper
2 teaspoons seasoned salt
1 teaspoon chili powder
6 boneless, skinless chicken thighs, cubed
1 (16 ounce) package Spanish yellow rice
Water

Set electric skillet to 200–250 degrees. Sauté onion, garlic, and olives (in enough olive oil to cover bottom of skillet) until onions are tender. Add seasonings and chicken. Continue to stir and cook until chicken is cooked through. Add rice with seasoning package and just enough water to cover skillet's contents. Remember to thoroughly stir in seasoning. Cover and simmer until rice is desired texture, adding more water if necessary.

Yield: 6 to 8 servings

Never Forgotten

When they had gone, an angel of the Lord appeared to Joseph in a dream. "Get up," he said, "take the child and his mother and escape."
MATTHEW 2:13 NIV

Goodness but that angel has been busy! First he appeared to Mary and then to Joseph and then later to others. At every turn it seems as though God is taking no chances in allowing His people to understand exactly how important this event is. As you prepare to celebrate with your friends and family, do not forget to recall the events that took place more than two thousand years ago, events so important that God took great pains to ensure that they would never be forgotten.

Christmas Crunch Salad

1½ cups broccoli florets
1½ cups cauliflower florets
1 red onion, chopped
2 cups cherry tomatoes, cut in
    half

Dressing:
1 cup mayonnaise
½ cup sour cream
1 tablespoon vinegar
2 tablespoons sugar
Salt and pepper to taste

Combine vegetables in large bowl. Set aside. In small bowl, whisk together dressing ingredients. Pour over vegetables and gently stir to coat. Chill for at least 2 hours before serving.

Yield: 6 servings

The Ultimate Gift

The Word became flesh and made his dwelling among us.
We have seen his glory, the glory of the one and only Son,
who came from the Father, full of grace and truth.
JOHN 1:14 NIV

As we consider the meaning of the Christmas season on this day before we traditionally celebrate Christ's birth, won't you stop to consider what might have happened had the Lord not allowed us a Savior? We would be mired in our own sin with no one and nothing to mediate between us and a holy God. How wonderful, how kind, that our Lord chose to change all of that by allowing His Son to be born of a virgin in Bethlehem. As you thank others for the gifts you will soon be unwrapping, do not forget to thank God for the ultimate gift He gave to humankind.

Holiday Cheese Ring

4 cups shredded sharp cheddar cheese
1 cup finely chopped pecans
1 cup mayonnaise
1 small onion, finely chopped

1 pinch black pepper
1 pinch cayenne pepper
1 dash Worcestershire sauce
1 jar strawberry or raspberry preserves

In mixing bowl, blend together all ingredients except preserves. Spoon mixture into greased gelatin ring mold. Refrigerate for 3 to 4 hours. Transfer cheese ring from mold to serving plate. Spoon preserves into center of ring. Serve with crackers.

Yield: 12 to 15 servings

Merry Christmas!

For to us a child is born, to us a son is given, and the government will be on his shoulders. And he will be called Wonderful Counselor, Mighty God, Everlasting Father, Prince of Peace.
ISAIAH 9:6 NIV

Long before Jesus was born, God was announcing His birth! Look at what He says in the book of Isaiah about the Messiah who is to come. Today on this most holy of days, take a moment away from your celebrations to consider what gift the Creator of the universe has offered us today. Merry Christmas, children of God! Your gift has arrived!

Cheeseburger Soup

½ pound ground beef
¾ cup onion, chopped
¾ cup carrots, shredded
¾ cup celery, diced
1 teaspoon basil
1 teaspoon parsley
4 tablespoons margarine, divided
3 cups chicken broth

4 cups potatoes, diced
¼ cup flour
8 ounces processed cheese, cubed
1½ cups milk
¾ teaspoon salt
½ teaspoon pepper
¼ cup sour cream

Brown ground beef and drain. In large saucepan, sauté onion, carrots, celery, basil, and parsley in 1 tablespoon margarine. Add chicken broth, potatoes, and beef; bring to boil and reduce heat. Cover and simmer for 10 to 12 minutes, until potatoes are done. In small skillet, stir remaining margarine and flour on low to medium heat for 3 to 5 minutes; add to soup. Boil for 2 minutes then reduce heat to low. Add cheese, milk, salt, and pepper. Continue heating until cheese melts. Remove from heat and add sour cream.

Yield: 8 servings

Be Thankful

Thanks be unto God for his unspeakable gift.
2 CORINTHIANS 9:15 KJV

On this day after Christmas, as all the gifts are now opened and the brightly wrapped paper has been bagged and put away, take a moment to reflect on this holiday season. Did you enjoy days with friends and family? Perhaps you shared memorable meals and laughed with those you love. Bask in those memories and tuck them close to your heart. Above all, be sure to thank the Lord for the gift of family and friends, and especially for the gift of His Son.

Mandarin Orange–Pineapple Cake

1 yellow cake mix
¾ cup oil
3 eggs
1 (11 ounce) can mandarin
   oranges with juice

Icing:
16 ounces whipped topping
1 (5.1 ounce) package instant
   vanilla pudding mix
1 (16 ounce) can crushed
   pineapple with juice

Combine cake ingredients. Bake in two 9-inch round pans at 350 degrees for 25 minutes. When cool, cut into 4 layers using dental floss. Fold together icing ingredients. Ice cake layers and stack. This cake tastes best if it sets for 24 hours before serving.

Yield: 10 to 16 servings

The Year to Come

May the God of hope fill you with all joy and peace as you trust
in him, so that you may overflow with hope by
the power of the Holy Spirit.
ROMANS 15:13 NIV

The excitement and hubbub of the Christmas season has wound down and the year is coming to a close. Soon the excitement of turning the calendar over and gaining a fresh start will begin. For now, however, just enjoy this quiet time, this waiting for the change. God tells us to be hopeful, to be at peace, and to have joy. Hang on to those things as you contemplate the year to come.

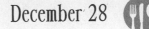
Hearty Chicken Soup

3 pieces chicken, on bone
4 cups water, divided
2 cups canned chicken broth
1 large carrot, sliced
1 stalk celery, chopped
2 tablespoons onion, chopped

1 teaspoon rosemary or rosemary
  herb mix
½ teaspoon curry powder
⅛ teaspoon pepper
1 (24 ounce) bag frozen
  home-style noodles

Boil chicken in 2 cups water for 20 minutes. Remove chicken from pot; cool and debone. Return chicken to pot; add rest of ingredients except noodles. Bring to boil, then add noodles. Simmer for 20 minutes.

Yield: 8 to 10 servings

Packing Away the Tinsel

May all kings bow down to him and all nations serve him.
For he will deliver the needy who cry out,
the afflicted who have no one to help.
PSALM 72:11–12 NIV

Are you packing away the tinsel and bows yet? Perhaps you're sorting through the Christmas cards and saving your favorites for next year. Whatever you're doing today, take a moment to think about who Jesus truly is. Far removed from the manger where He was born, our Savior will someday cause all kings to bow down to Him and all nations to serve Him. He was our Christmas child, and He will be our Deliverer. Just think about that. Can you imagine it?

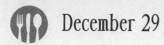

Orange Eggnog Punch

1 quart eggnog
1 (12 ounce) can frozen orange
   juice concentrate, thawed

1 (12 ounce) can ginger ale,
   chilled

In pitcher, mix eggnog and orange juice concentrate until well blended. Gradually pour in ginger ale and stir gently.

Yield: 8 servings

Children of the King

But you are a chosen people, a royal priesthood, a holy nation, God's special possession, that you may declare the praises of him who called you out of darkness into his wonderful light.
1 PETER 2:9 NIV

Do you realize what God thinks of you? Far from any opinion of humans, His is the one that counts. He tells us in His Word that He has chosen us for His own. We are His—isn't that amazing? We ordinary humans have been chosen by God to be His sons and daughters. If you're not feeling so special today, read that verse again. I promise it will show you exactly who you are!

Family Dinnertime Tip

If you're like most busy families these days, you barely have time to yourself between work and things you need to accomplish all in 24 hours' time. When you're feeling stressed, recite the your favorite verse from the Bible and feel the tension melt away!

Maple Nut Drop Cookies

1 cup brown sugar, packed
1 cup butter-flavored shortening
2 large eggs
2½ cups flour
½ teaspoon baking soda

½ teaspoon salt
2½ teaspoons maple flavoring
½ teaspoon vanilla
2 cups walnuts, chopped

Cream brown sugar and shortening. Beat in eggs. Add sifted dry ingredients. Stir in maple flavoring and vanilla; add nuts. Drop by teaspoonfuls onto greased cookie sheet. Bake at 350 degrees for 10 to 12 minutes.

Yield: 2 to 3 dozen cookies

Speaking Aloud

And a voice from heaven said, "This is my Son,
whom I love; with him I am well pleased."
MATTHEW 3:17 NIV

God did not have to speak aloud to communicate with Jesus. Father and Son were so intimately connected that words were not necessary. Instead, He chose to speak out loud so that we could hear and know what He thought of His Son. Well pleased indeed! Oh to have Him say the same about us someday!

New Year's Eve Punch

1 (16 ounce) can fruit cocktail
2 (6 ounce) cans frozen orange juice concentrate
2 (6 ounce) cans frozen lemonade concentrate
2 (6 ounce) cans frozen limeade concentrate
2 (6 ounce) cans frozen pineapple concentrate
1 pint raspberry sherbet

Pour fruit cocktail into ring mold and freeze overnight. Prepare frozen juices according to directions. Pour juices into 10-quart punch bowl and mix well. When ready to serve, float fruit cocktail ring in punch. Scoop sherbet into center of fruit cocktail ring.

Yield: 18 to 24 servings

Happy New Year!

*The light shines in the darkness,
and the darkness has not overcome it.*
JOHN 1:5 NIV

On this last day of the year, take a moment to reflect over what has happened in these last twelve months. Likely there were good times and perhaps a few not so good times. There were spiritual highs and possibly even a low or two. But one thing was a constant throughout the year whether you realize it or not: God was always there. From your first day to your last, He will be the light in your darkness, the guide on your path, and the bright shining star that leads the way. Happy New Year! Follow behind Jesus and know it will be a good year.

Family Dinnertime Tip

Pray together: *Dear heavenly Father, thank You for the gift of friendship. Please help us to remember that although we don't always see eye to eye with our family and friends, they help us to broaden our horizons and see things from a new perspective. Amen.*

Recipe Index

Main Dishes

Salads, Sides, and Vegetables

Family Favorite Recepies